PRAISE FOR
RAISING HUMANS IN A DIGITAL WORLD

"If you need practical, positive advice on how to handle your and your kids' digital lives, look no further. This book tackles the risks and addresses the potential harms, while keeping our eyes on the prize of the remarkable rewards that the online world brings."

—STEPHEN BALKAM,
founder & CEO, Family Online Safety Institute

"*Raising Humans in a Digital World* is not only a timely book, it's *essential* reading for every parent, grandparent, and teacher. Diana Graber empowers you through her educational (proven and practical) curriculum and engages you through anecdotal stories. Brilliantly written—you can be as cyber-savvy as the next generation."

—SUE SCHEFF,
founder of Parents' Universal Resource Experts
and author of *Shame Nation, Google Bomb,* and *Wit's End*

"*Brilliant, compelling,* and *essential* are the first words that came to my mind when reading Diana Graber's *Raising Humans in a Digital World.* Diana not only taps her own exemplary expertise but also assembles a 'who's who' of digital thought leaders to deliver a treasure trove of pragmatic advice via an engaging storytelling style. This is a must-read for parents raising kids in the digital age."

—ALAN KATZMAN,
founder and CEO, Social Assurity LLC

"Every parent has the responsibility to raise responsible digital humans. Technology is likened to the Wild West frontier. Diana Graber not only shows parents how to create safe and responsible relationships in this ever-changing digital world, but she gives them the powerful tools to navigate through the many aspects of what is required to keep kids safe online. The misuse of technology and the cruel behaviors that take place daily by kids and teens can be changed, and Graber shows this in her informative and educational book *Raising Humans in a Digital World.* The book should be every parent's bible as a resource to ensure that their children are responsible and safe."

—ROSS ELLIS,
founder and CEO, STOMP Out Bullying

"This beautifully written book gives you the tools to raise healthy kids in a digital world. The anecdotes underscore the thoughtfulness of today's youth and their hunger for learning how to navigate their world well, instead of just being warned off by fearful adults. It is thoughtfully organized and theoretically sound, and will empower parents to have some of those much-needed conversations with their kids."

—DR. PAMELA RUTLEDGE,
director, Media Psychology Research Center
and faculty member, Fielding Graduate University

RAISING HUMANS
in a
DIGITAL WORLD:

Helping Kids Build a Healthy Relationship with Technology

BY DIANA GRABER

HarperCollins
LEADERSHIP

An Imprint of HarperCollins

For Michael, Elizabeth, and Piper, the humans at the center of my world.

Published by HarperCollins Leadership, an imprint of HarperCollins.

Book design by Catherine Leonardo for Neuwirth & Associates.

Bob Dylan "The Times They Are a Changin'" copyright ©1963, 1964 by Warner Bros. Inc.; renewed 1991, 1992 by Special Rider Music. All rights reserved. International copyright secured. Reprinted by permission.

ISBN 978-0-8144-3980-7 (eBook)

Publisher's Cataloguing-in-Publication data available upon request

ISBN 978-0-8144-3979-1

Printed in the United States of America

18 19 20 21 22 LSC 10 9 8 7 6 5 4 3 2 1

CONTENTS

•

Foreword

●

What kind of kids do you want to raise?

After speaking with more than a million parents on six continents, I've discovered almost all parents want the same thing: They want to raise kids who will grow up to become human beings who are good and kind.

But in a world where screen time is more common than face time, and where digital connections often replace personal connections, this is quite a challenge. Lucky for you, the secret to raising humans in a digital world is in your hands.

While you might find other digital parenting books out there, what's different about this book is its author. I know Diana on both a personal and professional level—we've rubbed elbows at conferences on both coasts, shared stories, and asked each other, *"What do kids need most?"* I can assure you she's a trustworthy authority to answer this essential parenting question in a simple, straightforward manner. Here's why:

- Diana has her pulse on this topic. A digital literacy educator for nearly a decade (rare longevity these days), she's tried and tested everything you are about to read and done so on the best guinea pigs in the world . . . *real* kids.
- Through Cyberwise and Cyber Civics, her two digital literacy sites, she's provided resources to and interacted with hundreds of thousands of parents and their kids over the years.
- She's on the speaking circuit, talking to communities across the United States and listening to their concerns.
- She's done her homework, earning one of the first-ever graduate degrees in a new, and timely, field of study called "media psychology and social change."
- And, most important, she's a parent who cares deeply about kids.

The media knows about Diana, too. NBC's *TODAY* Show visited her classroom at Journey School in Southern California to feature Diana and her students engaging in some of the very activities you'll read about in this book.

I love how she compares raising a human today to building a house, telling you to start with a strong foundation of social skills, like empathy, and to build up from there. She gives you the tools you'll need—and the building plan, too. This book contains a treasure trove of how-tos and simple activities, as well as sage wisdom and insights from interviews with more than forty experts in the field.

My advice? Read this book, keep it by your nightstand, or even pass it on to other parents. But most important, *apply* what you are about to learn. Remember, your kids don't need the latest app or gadget: they need you! Your time and attention, along with what you'll learn in this book, are the secret ingredients to raising humans in our digital world.

Dr. Michele Borba

Internationally Recognized Educator, Speaker, and Bestselling Author of
Unselfie: Why Empathetic Kids Succeed in Our All-About-Me World
Palm Springs, August 6, 2018

Come mothers and fathers
Throughout the land
And don't criticize
What you can't understand
Your sons and your daughters
Are beyond your command
Your old road is rapidly agin'
Please get out of the new one if you can't lend your hand
For the times they are a-changin'

BOB DYLAN, *"The Times They Are a Changin'"*

Introduction

Left to Their Own Devices

●

When left to their own devices people will get up to one of two things: nothing much, and no good.

—LIONEL SHRIVER[1]

One bright September morning I stood at the door of the large auditorium that doubles as my classroom on Mondays and said goodbye to thirty or so seventh graders as they filed out into the bright Southern California sunshine. Wes, a slight boy with big blue eyes who was new to the class that year, stopped abruptly in front of me to ask a question.[2]

"Why are you teaching us this stuff?"

That surprised me. I thought it was obvious. Our class, called "Cyber Civics," met weekly throughout the entirety of their middle-school years—sixth, seventh, and eighth grades—so I could teach students the digital life skills they'd need to use technology safely and wisely. And that's what I told him.

"But isn't that our parents' job?" he asked.

He had me there. Fundamentally, I suppose, this is a parent's job. But in defense of parents everywhere, myself included, we didn't grow up with this stuff. Most of us are still figuring out how to use new technology safely and wisely, and sometimes not doing a very good job at it.

But we grew up in an entirely different world. When we were kids, we could engage in silly, embarrassing—and perhaps even borderline illegal—activities without the worry of our antics being recorded and posted online. Our social networking happened at the mall or on a neighborhood street corner. Peer approval didn't depend on "likes" or friend requests, but rather on an actual smile, nod, laugh, or high five. We learned how to read a map, use a telephone book, and even what "counterclockwise" meant. We owned a camera. If soccer or band practice ended early, we had to wait patiently to be picked up or use a conveniently located pay phone and hope we had a dime in our pocket to call home.

In terms of access to information, the world is almost unrecognizable from a few short decades ago. Consider the task of doing research for a school project. Blessed were those twenty-six volumes of *Encyclopedia Britannica* on the bookshelf! Otherwise it was a trip to the library to navigate a card catalog, then locate and *read* an entire book to find the information needed.

Those days are long gone. Today, kids walk around with information from all the world's libraries accessible via the devices in their pockets, with Google and Siri to lend a hand. And the most amazing part? Young people don't even find this amazing. Why should they? For amazement, they can throw on a virtual-reality (VR) headset and be transported to another world.

So far, this century has been packed with digital innovations that have radically altered childhood. Those of us tasked with raising kids during this period have been caught largely unprepared. New devices and what we can do with them—text, Skype, post, tweet, pin, chat, and so forth—have often distracted us from the job of parenting. Who hasn't mindlessly handed a tablet, smartphone, e-reader, or whatever to a kid to have a moment to check email or post pictures on Facebook? Who can blame parents for not noticing that our children might be growing as addicted to their devices as we are to our own? Or that they might be exposed to inappropriate content, that their personal information could be at risk, or that their digital reputations were being constructed? Brand-new terms have left us scratching our heads, too: sexting, piracy, phishing, trolling, grooming, memes, GIFs, hacking, revenge porn, cyberbullying, predators, finstagrams, digital kidnapping, and more. All of us—kids included—have been left to our own devices trying to make sense of a whole new world.

YOU CAN TEACH YOUR KIDS!

Wes is right. Parents can, and should, be teaching digital life skills to their kids, and this book will show you how. But first, take a deep breath, because the downsides and dangers of this new digital age—many of which I just listed to get your attention—comprise a fraction of what happens online. I promise. Besides, while we worry that digital kids might be connecting with creepy strangers, or posting pictures that will keep them from getting accepted to college, they view their online world through an entirely different lens. A 2017 UNICEF study involving children and young people representing twenty-six countries discovered that these youth are overwhelmingly positive about the role digital technology might play in their lives. They are excited about opportunities for communication, connection, sharing, and yes, *brace yourselves*: even learning.[3] It turns out that when young people gather online, good things can and *are* happening.

GOOD THINGS *ARE* HAPPENING ONLINE

While research over the past two decades has largely zoned in on tech use dangers, which can be serious and important for parents to be aware of, lots of good things are happening online:

- Social media helps young people strengthen existing friendships. More than 90 percent of teens report using social media to connect with people they know in real life.[4] The same is true for those who play online games; 78 percent of gamers say that when they play, it makes them feel more connected to friends they know offline.[5]
- Learning is possible anytime, anywhere. Experts are at our children's fingertips, and many young people are turning to online communities to connect with others who share their interests and hobbies.[6]
- Teens increasingly use social media to keep in touch with family members, strengthening family bonds and feelings of connectedness.[7]
- The internet creates opportunities for at-risk or marginalized youth to seek social support, advocate for themselves, and investigate resources for resilience.[8]
- Social media gives teens a chance to present their best selves, and college recruiters are noticing; 35 percent of college admissions officers say they check social media during the admissions process, and most report that the review benefited the applicant.[9]

- Youth are creating apps that make the world better. For example, sixteen-year-old Natalie Hampton from Sherman Oaks, California, created an app called "Sit With Us" so that no kid would ever have to eat lunch alone.[10]
- Social networking can promote youth civic engagement.[11] This includes a broad range of activities such as volunteering, voting, and raising awareness of issues young people care about.
- Free and low-cost digital tools let young people express their creativity in numerous new ways: They can write blogs, take and share photos, make videos, collaborate on school projects, and more.
- Young people around the world can contribute to significant cultural change. In 2009, a twelve-year-old Pakistani girl named Malala Yousafzai began blogging about girls' rights to education. Her fearless advocacy, even while she lived under the restrictive Taliban regime, captured the world's admiration and earned her the 2014 Nobel Peace Prize.

While all of this is great news, there's a fly in the ointment. Positive online experiences like these don't magically happen when you hand your child a connected device. It takes time and effort to turn a toddler adept at swiping across a tablet into a teenager who uses technology safely, wisely, ethically, and productively. It's on us parents to help youth discover how to minimize the risks and maximize the benefits technology offers.

To date, when teaching kids about tech, education has focused primarily on warning them about negative experiences that *might* happen rather than preparing them for positive ones that can. According to UNICEF, "the discourses available to children currently focus almost exclusively on risk and protection, and this is potentially undermining their capacity to imagine, and articulate, the benefits digital media offers them."[12] It's high time to set our fears aside and get to the task of empowering youth to use technology well.

The good news is that teaching your kids how to maximize technology's benefits is not only possible, but also can be an enjoyable and valuable way to connect with them. In the pages that follow, you'll learn what adults can and must do to help youth have a safe, healthy, and productive relationship with their devices.

RAISING THE DEVICE GENERATION

I couldn't survive without my phone.

—EIGHTH-GRADE STUDENT

Kids growing up today spend more time with screens—smartphones, computers, tablets, etc.—than they do in school, with their families, or sometimes even sleeping. A study conducted by the nonprofit Common Sense Media found that, on any given day, U.S. teens spend about nine hours per day using screens for entertainment. For tweens—kids between eight and twelve years of age—time spent with screens is about six hours per day. This doesn't even include the time kids spend on screens in school or for schoolwork.[13] I asked Kelly Mendoza, Common Sense Media's senior director of education programs, if she found these numbers surprising. "What makes them surprising is the multitasking," she said. "A kid might think, 'Hey, I'm doing my homework,' but actually they're on social media or listening to music. That's what makes the numbers seem immense."[14]

Look up from your own screens for a moment, and you'll see kids everywhere either staring down into phones that now go everywhere they go or busy thumbing yet another text message. Texting is the most common and frequent way teens communicate with one another, with 88 percent texting friends at least occasionally and over half texting them every single day.[15]

It's hard to believe we started texting one another in the United States two short decades ago. I was reminded of this startling fact by Jack McArtney, who was the director of messaging at Verizon where he introduced Short Message Service (SMS), more commonly known as text messaging, to the U.S. market in 1999. He likes to crack, "If you're a parent, I'm sorry. And if you're a kid, you're welcome!"[16]

Teens took to texting like ducks to water. In one month, today's average teen processes 3,700 text messages, and that doesn't even include all the private chatting that happens between kids in apps like Snapchat.[17] I asked McArtney if he had any inkling texting would become so popular with youth. "No," he answered. "And what really shocks me is how much time *everyone* spends with their heads down, looking awkwardly into little screens and not interacting with others, young and old alike. It's not at all what we expected."

But if you stop to consider everything our phones can do today—access the internet, take pictures, deliver music and engaging games, tell time, give directions, order pizza—and most importantly, offer unparalleled social connectivity—it shouldn't be shocking at all. In a short time, these gadgets truly have evolved into "smart" phones.

"All these things came together in ways no one could have predicted," says McArtney. "How can anyone, especially a kid, resist what a smartphone has to offer?"

The answer is, they can't.

THE SMARTPHONE HAS CHANGED CHILDHOOD

Psychologist and author Dr. Jean Twenge, an academic who studies generational trends, has written numerous scientific articles and three books based on her extensive research. Her most recent book, *iGen: Why Today's Super-Connected Kids Are Growing Up Less Rebellious, More Tolerant, Less Happy—and Completely Unprepared for Adulthood*, takes a hard look at the generation she dubs "iGen," kids born between 1995 and 2012, the first kids to enter adolescence with smartphones in their hands.[18] She asserts that these "iGen'ers," a group that includes not only my own two children but also those I teach, are on the brink of the worst mental health crisis in decades. And the cause? You guessed it: their smartphones.

In late 2017, Twenge wrote an article for *The Atlantic* with the provocative title "Have Smartphones Destroyed a Generation?" in which she distills the findings she presents in her book, writing, "the arrival of the smartphone has radically changed every aspect of teenagers' lives, from the nature of their social interactions to their mental health."[19]

When her article hit, I was busy visiting schools and parent groups around the United States, giving talks about kids, technology, and the importance of digital literacy education. Nearly every place I visited, parents had either read or heard about Twenge's findings and were eager to discuss them. While many heartily agreed that the smartphone is to blame for every adolescent problem (depression, anxiety, and sleep deprivation, just for starters), others found Twenge's assertions (e.g., "the twin rise of the smartphone and social media has caused an earthquake of a magnitude we've not seen in a very long time, if ever") overstated and alarmist.[20] But no matter which side of the fence they landed on, parents were united in one concern: *What do we do?*

You see, everyone knows the genie is out of the bottle and not going back in. Kids love their screens too much, and heck, so do we. Besides, it is clear they will need them for school and for work. So, while it's important to be aware of *how* devices are reshaping childhood, we must also prepare youth for an adulthood that will inevitably include devices, or whatever technology comes next.

IS YOUR CHILD READY?

When to give your child today's most coveted gift—her first smartphone (or a "connected" device of any kind)—is one of the biggest decisions a parent will have to make. Remember, a "connected device" is any gadget that connects to the internet. In addition to smartphones, this includes tablets, computers, gaming consoles, e-readers, smartwatches, and even Bluetooth-enabled toys and assistants. All of these have the capability of connecting your kids to all the world's people and information, all the time. Any missteps they make on a connected device may be permanently recorded, for everyone to see. This is a weighty responsibility, and kids are woefully unprepared without guidance.

When parents ask me, "What's the right age to give my children (insert type of connected device here)?" I counter their question with one of my own. Well, seven questions, to be exact. I think every parent should first answer these questions before determining whether his child is ready for a connected device:

- **Have your children developed the social and emotional skills necessary to use their gadgets wisely?** Have they learned how to show empathy, kindness, respect, and civility? These capacities evolve over time. They are in high demand online, and when expressed there, can turn it into the safer, kinder environment adults dream about.
- **Do your children know how to manage their online reputations?** Increasingly, colleges and employers (and others) are looking to the internet to learn about our kids. So, do your children

know that everything they post, and everything others post about them, contributes to an online reputation that speaks volumes about their character?

- **Do your children know how to unplug?** By their own accounts, teens say they feel "addicted" to their devices.[21] Have you equipped your children with strategies (and reasons) to unplug from their virtual worlds and plug into "real" life now and then?
- **Do your children know how to make and maintain safe and healthy relationships?** Can they keep themselves safe from cyber-bullying, predators, sexting, revenge porn, sextortion, and other online dangers? Do they know what to do if they encounter (and they probably will) dangerous or unhealthy relationships online?
- **Do your children know how to protect their privacy and personal information?** In the excitement to sign up for new services and to share with friends, many kids unwittingly give away too much personal information, especially when those too young to know better use social media. (Three-quarters of children between ages ten and twelve have social media accounts, despite being below the minimum age requirement.[22])
- **Do your children know how to think critically about the information they find online?** Are they able to evaluate media messages for their accuracy, authority, currency, and bias? Not knowing how to do so leaves kids vulnerable to misinformation, "fake news," and more.
- **Are your children equipped to be digital leaders?** Do they know how to be upstanders? The internet is in desperate need of kids who can stand up to bullies, create inspiring content, make moving videos, share uplifting stories, and invent new technologies that improve our world. Are your kids equipped to make their digital world better and safer?

If your answer to any of these questions is "no," then your children are not ready for the massive responsibility of owning a connected device. The stakes are too high. However, you can teach them all of these life skills no matter how much, or how little, you personally know about technology. Be forewarned: *These skills can't be taught overnight.* It will take time and patience to teach your kids how to manage, rather than avoid, the digital world's complexities.

It took me a while to figure this out for me and my own children. Frankly, a lot of trial and error was involved (sorry to my girls). Hopefully, by sharing what I've learned along my journey, which began almost two decades ago, yours will go more smoothly.

MY OWN JOURNEY BEGINS

On a cool autumn morning, in September 2000, I held the hand of my nearly five-year-old daughter as we approached the tiny portable structure that would be her kindergarten classroom. Like many mothers delivering children to school for the first time, I was nervous. But my nerves had less to do with day one of kindergarten, and more to do with the "school" we'd elected to send her to. Glancing around at the half dozen dilapidated portables crammed between a church and an adult educational facility, I started to get cold feet.

Our daughter was one of just ninety students to enter the first parent-initiated public charter school in Orange County, California. Named "Journey School," it was the first charter school in Capistrano Unified School District (CUSD), the eighth largest school district in the state and home to forty California Distinguished Schools and eleven National Blue Ribbon Schools. CUSD was, and remains, one of the top-performing districts in California and has a graduation rate of 97.1 percent, much higher than the state's average of 85.1 percent.[23] Every CUSD high school is ranked in the top one thousand U.S. high schools by *U.S. News & World Report*.[24] The schools are clean, safe, and well regarded. The logical decision would have been to send her to one of these perfectly fine schools—after all, charter schools were a relatively unknown and unproven concept at the time. Lawmakers had just passed the 1992 Charter Schools Act, and California was the second state in the country, after Minnesota, to enact charter school legislation. Only 1.7 percent of all U.S. public schools were charters.

On top of being a charter school, Journey School veered off the traditional educational path in another way, too—it was a Waldorf school. The little my husband and I knew about Waldorf schools was gleaned entirely from an article we'd stumbled upon in *The Atlantic*, "Schooling the Imagination." Its author, Todd Oppenheimer, offered a glowing account of schools that encouraged playfulness, imaginative wonderings, and a reverence for childhood. He wrote:

This notion, that imagination is the heart of learning, animates the entire arc of Waldorf teaching. When that concept is coupled with the schools' other fundamental goal, to give youngsters a sense of ethics, the result is a pedagogy that stands even further apart from today's system of education, with its growing emphasis on national performance standards in subjects such as mathematics, science, and reading and its increasing rigor in standardized testing—to say nothing of the campaign to fill classrooms with computers.[25]

Oppenheimer went on to describe how Waldorf schools fill their classrooms with handmade, natural objects and encourage children to interact with those, and each other, before screens. It sounded magical, and we were easily sold. What we didn't know then was how popular Waldorf schools were, and continue to be, with parents who work in the tech industry, specifically because these schools believe "technology can wait."[26]

NO MEDIA AT THIS SCHOOL!

Shortly after dropping off our daughter, we attended the school's parent orientation, where several forms were passed out for parents to read, sign, and hand back to the school principal. One of these was the school's media contract:

MEDIA CONTRACT

As you know, Journey School's philosophy includes the exclusion of media during the week, from Sunday evening through Friday morning. This includes all electronic media: radio, CDs, cassettes, karaoke, electronic toys, videos, and TV. Our interest is in the children being connected to the warmth of a human voice rather than a voice that is electronically transmitted.

My husband and I shot each other a sidewise glance before signing this one. At the time, we were working on a cable television series for the Outdoor Life Channel called *To the Edge*. These were TV shows that profiled professional athletes engaged in various treacherous feats on rock cliffs, big waves, and churning rapids. The show's success, and our livelihood for that matter, depended on people staying home to watch television rather than going outside to engage in these activities themselves. So yes, signing this media contract was a tad hypocritical. But the idea of raising kids without the blare or distraction of the television in the background of our daily lives was appealing. We liked the thought of conversations at the dinner table and time for crafts, games, and baking cookies. We imagined raising kids who could engage in interesting conversations and make eye contact. With this in mind, we signed the dotted line.

THINGS WERE EASIER BACK THEN

Thinking back upon that time, I often wonder if we would have so readily agreed to restrict our media consumption had there been digital media to contend with. But the media environment was entirely different in the year 2000:

- There were only 361 million internet users in the entire world. For perspective, that's barely two-thirds of the size of Facebook today.[27]
- Google was only two years old.
- Neither Friendster nor MySpace (remember those?) had been invented or gone out of business.
- Facebook, LinkedIn, Wikipedia, YouTube, Twitter, Flickr, and Instagram didn't exist.
- Evan Spiegel, Snapchat's founder, was only ten years old.
- There were no iPods, iTunes, or iPhones. And we were a full decade away from the first iPad.

The only media exposure we had to worry about limiting was television. Even that was no big deal. We relegated our one TV to the upstairs office, where it couldn't tempt us, and went about our daily lives.

And then, *everything* changed.

As our daughter, and her sister who followed her by three years, approached middle school, our nondigital world's simplicity started to fade into a distant memory. "Media" became more than just television. It became digital, and social, and mobile. Kids loved it, and parents weren't ready for it. Including me.

MEDIA PSYCHOLOGY TO THE RESCUE

In 2006, while mindlessly scrolling through my email, which had begun to consume too many hours of my day, something caught my eye. An email from my alma mater announced a brand-new field of study: Media Psychology and Social Change. UCLA was offering four pathway courses that would lead to a master's degree through Fielding Graduate University. Figuring this would be a great way to understand media's transformation—and in turn help me help my kids navigate a new digital world—I enrolled, and for the next four years immersed myself in the study of media's effects upon human behavior.

As I worked my way through grad school, technological advancements seemed to occur weekly. The iPhone appeared in 2007, shortly followed by the iPad. In 2010, the Kaiser Family Foundation reported that the amount of time young people were spending with entertainment media had risen dramatically. They discovered that eight- to eighteen-year-olds were devoting an average of seven hours and thirty-eight minutes to using entertainment media across a typical day (more than fifty-three hours a week). And because youth were spending so much of that time "media multitasking" (using more than one device at a time), they were packing a total of ten hours and forty-five minutes worth of media content into those seven hours.[28]

"Holy cow, that's a lot of media," I thought. Kids were spending more time with media than doing almost anything else—going to school, playing sports, engaging with their families, sometimes even sleeping. How, I wondered, were they navigating these new changes?

Not very well, I would soon learn.

DIGITAL DRAMA HITS HOME

New digital technologies were finding their way into the lives of kids at Journey School, too, despite the school's media contract. In 2010, when my oldest daughter was in eighth grade, the school experienced its first social media "incident."

Back then, Facebook was all the rage (remember, this was before Instagram or Snapchat, so young people were using Facebook to post pictures and communicate the daily events in their lives). Young people were using Facebook to post pictures and communicate the daily events in their lives. A new girl, Arial, joined my daughter's class that year and introduced her classmates, including my daughter, to this social media platform. Arial was a prolific Facebooker. She posted pictures of herself and her small group of girlfriends every day, carefully selecting each photo to make sure she looked perfect (hair in place, pretty smile, etc.). Unfortunately, she did not extend the same level of care to her friends. In the same pictures they generally had funny expressions on their faces, hair out of place, or worse. Her friends caught on to this inconsideration pretty fast. I heard about it from my daughter, who found it funny. But another girl, named Reece, found no humor in it whatsoever.

Reece was a vlogger. She kept a video blog of her daily events, sort of a virtual diary that was online and public. In one of these vlogs, she complained about the Facebook posts and the girl who posted them, saying she felt "stabbed in the back." She even made the repeated hand motions of someone being stabbed. Parents caught wind of this video, and even those who didn't see it heard about the stabbing bit and found the thought disturbing. Before long, parents reported this "cyberbullying" incident to the school, and Reece found herself in the principal's office.

Let's pause here for a moment. Parental overreaction aside, what occurred was a minor incident, especially judged by today's standards. It was normal teenage behavior that *seemed* different only because it was playing out in a new environment. Arial, the Facebooker, was dabbling with a new, exciting tool, probably without adult guidance. Plus, she was engaging in a form of "identity construction," when adolescents try to figure out who they are and how to portray themselves to the world. Reece, the vlogger, was also learning to use new tools, recording and posting videos, also without adult guidance. These are wonderful new media skills! She was also expressing strong opinions and ideas, which is normal teenage behavior, too. Nothing these girls did was very bad or even wrong, but it *was* the first time technology use had disrupted our school, and it caught new principal Shaheer Faltas entirely off guard.

"Because this was new terrain," Faltas told me years later, "there was fear at all levels—among the parents, the teachers, and even the students. I'd only been at Journey for a few months and all of a sudden, I had this huge issue on my hands and a lot of questions. What constitutes cyberbullying? Is this the parents' problem or the school's? Why are students even using Facebook? And most importantly: What do we do to keep this, or an even worse incident, from happening again? These were all questions we had yet to answer."[29]

When this transpired, I had just finished my studies. Dr. Pamela Rutledge, a professor at Fielding Graduate University who had been my mentor and later became a dear friend, encouraged me to submit my final capstone for publication to the *Journal of Media Literacy Education*, and I did. My article, "New Media Literacy Education (NMLE): A Developmental Approach,"[30] was published around the same time this digital drama was playing out among my daughter's friends. The paper made a case for teaching kids the moral, ethical, and social guidelines necessary to be good online citizens. It was apparent that such an education was needed at my own daughters' school, and I was excited.

OUT OF LEMONS, LEMONADE

After a week of watching the traffic of crying students, irate parents, and confused teachers flow in and out of Faltas's office as he attempted to navigate Journey School's first cyberincident, I asked if I could teach "digital citizenship" to my youngest daughter's sixth-grade class. This, I assured him (secretly hoping I was right), would keep future problems out of his office. He considered my proposal for about three seconds. "When can you start?" he asked.

"I had no idea what 'digital citizenship' was at the time," said Faltas, "but I knew that doing nothing was not an option. It was clear that issues related to digital media were sure to crop up again, and we needed to be proactive rather than reactive. I knew I needed help."[31]

CYBER CIVICS IS BORN

Faltas allowed me to appropriate the school's weekly civics class and turn it into "Cyber Civics," a course I've been teaching to middle-school students ever since. Today it is a three-year series of weekly activities that cover the entire spectrum of digital literacy—digital citizenship (the safe and responsible use of digital tools), information literacy (how to find, retrieve, analyze, and use online information), and media literacy for positive participation (using critical thinking to analyze media messages, including "fake news"). Faltas encouraged me to place the entire curriculum online, so other schools could use it, too. As of this writing, schools in over forty U.S. states (and four other countries) teach Cyber Civics to their students, and the program continues to grow. With this book, hopefully some of these civics activities will find their way into your homes as well.

CIVICS FOR A DIGITAL AGE

Civics, the study of citizenship, has an entirely new meaning today. We live in an age when we are as much a citizen of the online world as we are of our town, state, or country. In a captivating TED Talk, Eric Lui, founder of Citizen University and the executive director of the Aspen Institute Citizenship and American Identity Program, describes civics as "the art of being a pro-social, problem solving contributor in a self-governing community."[32]

I love this definition and can't think of any communities more "self-governing" than those online. Can you? Consider the social media communities where youth hang out, share information, and spend the bulk of their time—like Snapchat, Instagram, YouTube, and so forth. These communities are largely devoid of parents, internet police, crossing guards, or even rules to keep their users in line or safe. Kids are left to their own devices to figure out how to be a good citizen in places like these.

Lui further explains civics by quoting Microsoft founder Bill Gates's father, Bill Gates Sr., who says civics is "simply showing up for life."[33] I love that descriptor, too, and especially the three things Lui says it encompasses:

- A foundation of values
- An understanding of the systems that make the world go round
- A set of skills that allow you to pursue goals, and have others join in that pursuit

These were three things I was hoping to accomplish through Cyber Civics. By guiding kids through a series of discussions and activities surrounding a range of technology-related topics, I thought that, given time, we could realize these same objectives. This holistic approach to "digital literacy"—possibly the most important skill kids need today, given the time they spend with tech—achieves an important end. It arms kids with the superpowers to keep themselves safe and be super online and off.

Digital Literacy is more than technological know-how. It includes a wide variety of ethical, social, and reflective practices that are embedded in work, learning, leisure, and daily life.[34]

The Experiment Works!

Much to my relief, within a few years of implementing Cyber Civics at Journey School, my assurances to Faltas were validated. He told me that few tech problems ever reached his office, "which is rare for a school in the twenty-first century." On top of that, standardized test scores for his middle-school students were on the rise, in spite of warnings that sacrificing precious academic time for these classes was a risk. A 2015 article in *District Administration Magazine*, based on an interview with Faltas, says, "In the first two years after implementing Cyber Civics, the school's Academic Performance Index score grew from 766 to 878—the highest in the school's history." The article adds, "Only three incidents of poor digital behavior or online bullying have been reported since 2011, and none have occurred in the last two years."[35]

"It's a gamble not to give your kids these lessons," he has said.

EVERY KID NEEDS THESE LESSONS

Teaching kids how to be safe, thoughtful, and ethical users of technology doesn't have to—and can't—happen only in a classroom, and that's the reason for this book. Parents and caregivers can achieve the same ends with their own children at home. It's sort of like building a house. You must first lay a strong foundation before helping your child build a structure that will keep them safe. Then they can enjoy the benefits of interacting with a larger community.

That is how you'll find this book organized:

- **Part One: A Solid Foundation.** Your child's house must be built upon a solid foundation, and part one will show you where to start. The skills you nurture while your children are young will pay off in spades as they grow older.
- **Part Two: A Sturdy Structure.** The next step is to help your children build a sturdy structure, comprised of four strong pillars, that will withstand any storms that may blow their way. It will be as durable and secure as the effort you both put into it.
- **Part Three: A Vibrant Community.** Here's the fun part. With a strong foundation and sturdy structure in place, part three will show you how to help your children connect and engage—critically and confidently—with new communities and opportunities online. The goal is for them to use digital technologies to learn, inspire, be inspired, and share their unique talents with the world.

To help you with this building project, this book is packed with activities that you and your children can do together, called "Cyber Civics Moments." They will help your children, and your family, build a safe, happy, and healthy relationship with technology.

Where to start? At the beginning, as I do.

CYBER CIVICS MOMENTS

Every fall I greet a new crop of sixth graders eager to embark upon our Cyber Civics lessons. After all, they know that in this class they'll get to talk about the thing that already consumes much of their interest and time: technology. The first day I start by asking a simple question: When you think of "technology," what comes to mind? Students respond enthusiastically by naming all the technologies they love—smartphones, tablets, gaming consoles, computers, laptops, smartwatches, etc. Rarely do they mention any technology invented prior to the computer.

But new technologies are as old as humankind, and many of them significantly altered, and worried, the societies they were introduced to. Consider the stylus. When this writing instrument was invented, many feared it would mark the end of oral history. The great philosopher Socrates warned it would "create forgetfulness in the learners' souls, because they will not use their memories."[36]

Centuries later another new technology, the printing press, caused a similar stir. Suddenly, large amounts of information could be shared quickly and cheaply, and some people found this disturbing. Respected Swiss scientist Conrad Gessner even worried that this flood of information would be "confusing and harmful" to the mind.[37]

Eventually, humans became accustomed to both writing and reading, thank goodness, even though the technological innovations that made both possible were met with apprehension, resistance, and fear. Students easily draw the connection to today's technologies when they hear these stories. Their parents, they say, aren't so crazy about smartphones either.

Helping children understand technology's social impact is an important place to start. In a terrific book I recommend to parents, titled *Digital Community, Digital Citizen*, by Jason Ohler, a professor emeritus of educational technology and virtual learning at the University of Alaska, as well as a professor in the media psychology PhD program at Fielding University, Ohler suggests challenging students to become what he calls "de-'tech'-tives" (see activity below). As a student at the University of Toronto, Ohler studied under famed media theorist Marshall McLuhan, who coined the phrase "the medium is the message." He remembers McLuhan explaining how every technology introduced throughout history both connects and disconnects humans from one another. While the connections make new tools exciting (think of the telephone, which finally enabled users to speak with faraway family and friends), disconnections are what we either worry about or fail to recognize at first (the phone also displaced face-to-face communication). I remember my own parents being upset about our telephone-induced disconnections. They didn't like it when my siblings and I talked to friends during dinner or when we were supposed to be helping with chores. Like today's parents, they thought technology was disconnecting their children from important things.

I've conducted Ohler's activity hundreds of times, with both kids and adults. While it's always fun with kids, this lesson is a good one for adults, too—especially the most tech averse. If that's you, and even if it's not, spend a few moments doing the following activity with your children.

Become a De-"Tech"-Tive

You and your children can use the following steps to investigate technology's impact throughout history:

1. Think of three new technologies, or "tools," introduced throughout history—the pencil, bow and arrow, microwave oven, radio, telephone, automobile, or any other technology.
2. With your children, think of ways each of these tools changed society for better or worse. More specifically, talk about how each tool connected people to one another, and how it disconnected them. For example, when I've challenged students with this activity (using the bow and arrow as their "tool"), here's what they came up with: The bow and arrow connected people to one another because they could easily get more food to cook and eat together. (One student told me that when Cupid releases an arrow, it makes a love connection!) On the other hand, the bow and arrow disconnected people because they could hunt alone. They no longer had to be in groups to catch and kill a big animal. Also, if used as a weapon, the bow and arrow becomes a huge disconnection.
3. Finally, discuss how today's technology—specifically, the smartphone—connects and disconnects users. Have an honest discussion on the pros and cons of this new tool.

What Was Life Like Before the Cell Phone?

This might seem like a ridiculous question, but most kids today don't remember a world without cell phones or connected devices, and you do. So encourage them to use their "de-'tech'-tive" skills to discover how you survived without today's seemingly indispensable tool.

When I do this activity with students, they love to share the results of their sleuthing. They are amazed to discover that their parents carried change in their pockets to use a pay phone, or that they played with their friends after school in real life—no social media required. Some students come to class with an old flip phone, or even a brick phone, that a parent found tucked in a drawer at home. Their classmates are so excited to see these relics you'd think they'd dug up a dinosaur bone in the schoolyard.

You Can Also Do This at Home

1. Let your child interview you (or a grandparent or older relative) to discover what your life was like before the cell phone. Be sure to answer these questions:

   - How did you get along without it?
   - Did you have an early version of a cell phone? If so, what was it like?
   - Do you think having a cell phone makes your life better or worse?

2. Talk with your child about all the digital innovations you've witnessed in your lifetime, and how they may have changed your life, for better or worse.

Understanding Citizenship

Every kid today will use technology to connect with others in all kinds of new ways, becoming a "citizen" of online communities you may or may not know about. Understanding how to be a good community member offline is fairly easy—the real world is governed by rules, laws, and norms established over time—but that's not the case online. Many online communities lack rules, laws, and norms, and if there are any, they are sometimes hard for kids to figure out (think of age restrictions buried in the "terms of use" for most games or social media sites). Plus, who cares when online rules are broken?

That's why it's important to introduce young people to the five "themes of citizenship."[38] Tell them that every good citizen—online and offline—should demonstrate the following traits:

- **Honesty.** Be truthful and fair. Good citizens must be honest with others, and with themselves.
- **Compassion.** Show care for people and reverence for living things. Compassion gives citizens an emotional bond with their world.

- **Respect.** Show regard or consideration for others, and even toward inanimate things or ideas. Good citizens should have respect for laws and reverence for all living things.
- **Responsibility.** Be answerable and accountable. Citizens should recognize that their actions have an effect, either positive or negative, upon others.
- **Courage.** Do the right thing even when it's unpopular, difficult, or dangerous. Many people throughout history—including Martin Luther King Jr., Susan B. Anthony, and Mahatma Gandhi—have demonstrated great courage.

It never occurs to many kids that these principles of citizenship should apply online, and that's too bad, because they would help make the internet safer and kinder. Just like playing a soccer game without rules or a referee would be no fun for anyone, an online world devoid of basic rules or principles ends up being a bummer for just about everyone, too.

Many good kids believe they can act entirely different online than they do in real life. Here's an example: If I were at your home and asked your nine-year-old her age, chances are I'd get the truth. That's probably because your child knows it's her responsibility to be honest and respectful. This is how people act in real life; it is what you and other adults model and what most kids have learned.

Consider this same scenario online. Let's say your child wants to open an account on Snapchat. Perhaps "all his friends" have an account, and he just wants one. While Snapchat, like most social media networks, requires users to be at least thirteen years of age, all young children have to do is enter a fake birth date, and *presto*, they have an account. Most don't think twice about ignoring the first theme of citizenship, honesty, online. If I had a dime for every time I've had a young student tell me, "Nobody cares when you lie about your age online," I'd own a Caribbean island. But I care, I tell them, and venture to say you do, too. I don't think honesty (or compassion, respect, responsibility, and courage) are principles that anybody wants to throw out the window.

This activity can help your children discover how to be the same good citizen online as you expect them to be offline. Do the following:

1. Explain the above principles to your children. Tell them that in the offline world these traits are generally expected of good citizens. They are norms that civilizations have established over time.

2. Talk to your children about all the offline communities they belong to: sports teams, classroom, city, state, country, even family. Ask them to tell you how they might demonstrate these citizenship principles in one of these communities. Be sure to discuss what it would be like if these communities *did not* follow these principles.

3. Talk to your children about the online communities they, or you, belong to—a social media network or a gaming community, for example. Ask them how the citizenship principles might be demonstrated in one of these communities. Be sure to ask them to tell you what it would be like if these communities did not (or do not) follow these same principles.

Each year I ask students to write a sentence, or to draw a picture, describing how each citizenship trait is exemplified in an offline community they belong to. Last year, a sixth-grade student, Blake Hirst, bounded into class waving an entire essay he'd written, eager to share it with the class. Here is what he wrote:

> I was told that I had to do a report on how a community I belong to shows citizenship, so I chose to do it on my classroom community. Hope you enjoy!
>
> **HONESTY:** Suppose there are two different math quizzes, and they don't have names on them. Your teacher asks you which one is yours. One has a better grade, and the other one doesn't. The one with the bad grade is yours. So, do you say the one with the good grade is yours, or not? Most likely you would be honest and admit you got the lower grade. This is honesty.
>
> **COMPASSION:** This can mean helping someone when they are in a time of need. Sometimes at my school we have "Compassionate Campus," where we do something like clean or write nice letters to teachers. This is a slight rendering of what compassion is.
>
> **RESPECT:** Respect is a value that everyone *should* have. Respect, for example, is not talking out of turn in class or not saying bad things about a person when they are not around. I think everyone in the world would benefit by showing each other more respect.

RESPONSIBILITY: Let's say you were late to class at school, and it was your fault because you were out playing basketball. That's irresponsible, right? Responsibility would mean you would stop playing basketball and head back to class when the bell rings.

COURAGE: Maybe you are at school, and someone is picking on a friend or someone who is sort of unpopular, and you stick up for them. That's an example of courage. Even if it's you being made fun of, it shows courage not to do it back. Courage is one of the most essential things a citizen should have.

Well that is my report on citizenship, and I hope you learned something from it and had fun reading it.

PART ONE

A Solid Foundation

Chapter 1

A Digital Journey Begins

•

What we may need most is an app that reminds parents that they need to ditch their own screens at home and spend real face time with their kids.

—MARY AIKEN, *THE CYBER EFFECT*[1]

When a precious newborn enters this world, chances are a smartphone will be in the delivery room, to capture that first photo. That image may end up on Facebook or Instagram, or be sent via text to an aunt, uncle, or grandparent, who might share it on their social networks. Thus, that tiny infant has become a citizen of a digital world.

The work of helping that little digital citizen build a solid foundation that will stand up to the uncertain weather and shifting sands of the digital age starts early. Family and friends are constructing children's digital lives, and children have unprecedented access to mobile devices, at increasingly younger ages. In the United States, nearly all kids age eight and under (98 percent) live in a home with some type of mobile device, and close to half (42 percent) have their own tablet. Mobile device usage for children in this age range tripled between 2011 and 2017—from only five minutes per day to forty-eight minutes per day—and one-third of their total screen time is spent using mobile devices.[2] Even more striking is that 44 percent of children under the age of one use mobile devices *every single day*. By the age of two, that jumps to 77 percent.[3]

You see the evidence of this everywhere you look—young children in cars, restaurants, and other public places with tiny heads bent over the glowing screen of a smartphone or tablet. There's even a name for this posture. Chiropractor Dean Fishman coined the term "text neck" in 2008, while examining a young patient who complained of headaches and neck pain.[4] "Text neck" results from bending one's head over a mobile device. The gravitational pull on the head, which can weigh ten to twelve pounds, and the stress it places on the neck, can lead to incremental loss of the curve of the spine.

I see text-necking toddlers all the time. Recently, while riding my bike along the California coast on a dazzling winter morning, I counted five toddlers in strollers, all bent over an electronic device and completely oblivious to seagulls fighting noisily over a piece of trash, surfers surveying the growing swell, the bright red lifeguard truck passing by, and pelicans skimming low over the water's surface. Five kids missed all this and more because their attention was locked on their screens.

WORLD'S BEST BABYSITTER

Mobile tools *are* excellent babysitters. They can soothe a fussy child or keep fidgety ones occupied, so a busy parent can make dinner, check email, or even go on a much-needed run. A 2014 study of children aged six months to four years in an urban, low-income, minority Philadelphia community revealed that almost all had access to devices that their parents used liberally as "babysitters"—when the parents did chores (70 percent), to keep kids calm in public (65 percent), during errands (58 percent), and at bedtime (28 percent).[5] Parenting is relentless work, and for many, childcare is an unaffordable luxury. Besides, with over eighty thousand apps and games classified as "education- and learning-based," it stands to reason that these young kids might be learning something.[6] The preschool/toddler category in Apple's App Store is its most popular, accounting for 72 percent of the top paid apps.[7] What could possibly be the harm?

That's the thing. We don't know. After all, the iPad is not even ten years old; it's a babe in terms of scientific research. Even kids who used them as toddlers are barely young teens today, so definitive data on their impact upon youth is pending.[8]

As a comprehensive literature review published by UNICEF in late 2017 puts it, "research in this area still suffers from theoretical and methodological weaknesses that makes the evidence collected so far unreliable and inconclusive."[9] The long-term impact of the short-term phenomenon of tablets, smartphones, and all the other mobile devices that have popped up in the recent past is unknown. That makes children the guinea pigs of our grand experiment.

I asked Dr. Pamela Hurst-Della Pietra about this. She is the founder and president of Children and Screens: Institute of Digital Media and Child Development, a nonprofit organization working to stimulate dialogue about the impact of digital media on toddlers, children, and adolescents. This national interdisciplinary research organization brings together experts in medicine, social science, neuroscience, education, and other fields to address three vital questions about children and technology:

1. How is technology enhancing or impairing children's ability to live happy, healthy, and productive lives?
2. How are years of electronically mediated interactions shaping children's physical, cognitive, emotional, and social development?
3. What should we do about it?

"Parents need to understand that this is all very new, and we don't have a lot of definitive studies yet," Hurst Della-Pietra told me. "Meanwhile, there has been a sea change in accessibility; now you can take these devices anywhere. While there are some amazing benefits—Skyping with loved ones, for example—there are risks, too, and we don't completely understand them. But we do know there are developmental milestones young children need to hit in order to reach their full potentialities."[10]

HELPING CHILDREN REACH THEIR FULL POTENTIAL IN A SCREEN-FILLED WORLD

Around the world, children and adolescents account for an estimated one in three internet users, yet the technology they use was not designed with their developmental needs in mind.[11] While little is known about the long-term impact of today's devices upon a young child, a lot is known about healthy child development.

Babies require rich, multidimensional experiences in a real, three-dimensional world. They need opportunities for hands-on exploration and human interaction with loving adults.[12] They thrive when they are read to, talked to, played with, and when they play with other children in real life.[13] They benefit from being out in nature.[14] A screen—regardless of whether it's a TV, tablet, smartphone, gaming console, computer, or even an internet-connected toy—can't deliver the same experiences as the real world.

A quick peek under the hood explains *why* infants need these real-world experiences. A newborn has trillions of brain cells, or neurons, waiting to be called into action. Each of these tiny brain cells has about 2,500 synapses—connections that pass signals between these neurons. When electrical signals pass between these neurons, these synapses are stimulated. Like footpaths linking remote villages, every time they get used, or stimulated, they improve, and the remote villages pop into life. Every experience a baby has, from birth on, stimulates these connections, and repeated experiences strengthen them, shaping the child's behavior for years to come.

Just as important as the real-life experiences young children have are the ones they *don't* have, as this influences brain development, too. Neurons that aren't used—or synaptic connections that aren't repeated—get pruned away, while remaining connections are strengthened.[15] Stimulated synapses then get hardwired and form the permanent foundation upon which the child's future cognitive functions are built.

Although children's brains continue this hardwiring or "intricate tapestry of the mind" well into their mid-twenties, much of the critical work happens between birth and age three.[16] This is an extremely sensitive development period, when children need specific experiences from their environment to properly stimulate their developing brains and lay the foundation for all of their future relationships—online and offline.

ALL THEY NEED IS LOVE

One specific type of stimulation babies need is a parent or caregiver's loving gaze. The absence of stimuli delivered through facial expressions and eye contact could lead to disastrous consequences. In *The Cyber Effect*, author and cyberpsychologist Dr. Mary Aiken writes, "Many experiments over the past century have shown the catastrophic effects of sensory and social deprivation during this critical period in early childhood, and the subsequent effects on later development."[17]

What happens to an infant whose parents spend more time gazing lovingly at their smartphones than at them? Aiken suggests that, over time, these babies may be less able to interact face-to-face, less likely to form deep bonds, and less able to feel or give love.

Even though the middle-school students I teach are years removed from being infants, they continue to seem to crave a parent or caregiver's attentive gaze. They often complain how crappy it feels to be playing basketball or to be in the middle of a dance recital, only to look up and see a parent looking down at his or her phone. "It sucks," more than one preteen has told me. While this is sad, the thought of an infant not getting proper attention is even worse. The long-term implications of an entire generation of children not receiving the facetime they need from loving caregivers remains to be seen.

Screens also rob children of time spent talking, playing, interacting with parents and friends, engaging in creative activities, and so forth. Obviously, when they are looking at their phones or computers, parents talk and play less with their children. And if kids are on their own devices, which more seem to be, then they are not talking or engaging with their parents or with other kids.

Dr. Jenny Radesky, a developmental behavioral pediatrician and mother of two small children, wanted to find out how common it was for adults to use mobile devices around children, so she conducted what has since become a widely cited study.[18] She and her researchers surreptitiously watched fifty-five caregivers, usually a parent, with one or more children, in fast-food restaurants around the Boston area. Of the fifty-five adults they watched, forty used a mobile device during the meal. Sixteen used the mobile device throughout the entire meal. The researchers noted that the children, under ten years of age, bid for the phone-using adults' attention in escalating ways; while adults typically ignored the children's bids at first, they eventually responded in scolding tones, seeming insensitive to the children's needs. As of yet, no comprehensive study has measured the long-term impact on children who are ignored by caregivers whose absorption in their devices is so intense.

But consider the "still face experiment" conducted by developmental psychologist Dr. Edward Tronick in 1975, long before mobile devices distracted parents from their children.[19] His experiment was simple: Mothers and their six-month-old infants were asked to engage in normal, animated play that included mirroring each other's facial expressions. Then the mothers were instructed to suddenly make their facial expressions completely "still" or expressionless for three minutes. At first, the babies anxiously tried to reconnect with their mothers, but if the mother remained still, the child showed ever-greater signs of confusion and distress before finally turning away, looking sad and hopeless.

This commonly replicated finding in developmental psychology demonstrated that infants find the lack of face-to-face contact more disturbing than other violations of normal social interactions. Even adults who get "still faced" by partners who turn to their phones instead of toward their bids for emotional connection find this distressing. Michele Weiner-Davis, of an organization called *Divorce Busting*, writes, "Every time you turn away from your spouse or he/she turns away from you, whether you show it or not, your response is not dissimilar to the baby."[20]

In short, young children—and, as it turns out, married people—crave authentic human interaction. So if you or your young children are spending more time looking at gadgets than each other, critical neural pathways likely are not being properly stimulated, thus putting the development of important relationship-building human qualities at risk. As Aiken puts it:

> A baby's needs are not high-tech . . . technology has proven to be less than beneficial for [babies'] healthy development. So far, no electronic device or app can replace cuddling, talking, laughing, playing a silly game, holding hands, or reading a book with your child. I have no doubt that someday tech developers and designers will create apps that can truly enhance learning for infants and toddlers, and then the educational value of screens will change. Until then, what we need most is an app that reminds parents that they need to ditch their own screens at home and spend real facetime with their kids.[21]

BUT SCREENS ARE EXCITING!

While handing a screen to a crying child might have immediate calming effects, for both you and the child, the long-term impact may be the opposite of what you bargained for.

Dr. Pamela Hurst Della-Pietra worries about mobile devices being used as "digital pacifiers," as she calls them. "When parents do this," she says, "babies and toddlers are not learning how to soothe themselves, and that is really, really important." She suggests giving children "activities that promote discovery and wonder. Traditional toys, such as blocks, have been time-tested, and we know have multiple benefits for young children. Giving children a chance to be bored isn't such a bad thing either."[22]

Letting children experience boredom is becoming increasingly difficult in a digital world that competes mightily for their attention. After all, much of what children see and do on screens is exciting! Rapid scene changes and fantastical stories make real life appear dull and boring in comparison. The downside of capitulating to your children's requests for digital entertainment is that their ability to pay attention and focus may be adversely affected by overstimulation during important developmental windows, especially in early childhood.[23]

In 2015, I attended one of Hurst-Della Pietra's gatherings of researchers and scientists at UC Irvine. During a compelling presentation about his research on technology's impact upon young children, Dr. Dimitri Christakis, director of the Center for Child Health, Behavior, and Development at Seattle Children's Hospital, shared this: The more TV a child watched between the ages of one and three, the greater likelihood that child would develop attention problems by age seven. For every hour of television watched per day, risk of attention problems increased by almost 10 percent. Conversely, the more cognitive stimulation a child received before the age of three (e.g., being read to or talked to by a caregiver), the less likely they were to have attention problems.[24]

Sensitive young brains show immediate effects from overstimulation by television, too. Researchers from the University of Virginia discovered that preschoolers who watched just nine minutes of a fast-paced cartoon performed significantly worse on tasks that required attention than kids who spent twenty minutes drawing.[25]

While both of these studies involved television and not today's interactive technologies, TV and video studies remain the best we have to go on when trying to figure out what new screens may be doing to young minds.

WHAT *IS* KNOWN ABOUT TV, VIDEO, AND YOUNG CHILDREN

For children ages two and under, the effects of screens have been mostly negative, particularly regarding two important components of healthy development: language development and executive function.[26]

Let's look at language development first. Numerous studies have demonstrated that videos and television are ineffective at helping children under age two gain these skills. One study of children between twelve and eighteen months set out to determine if they could learn twenty-five new words more effectively via a screen or interaction with a live human. One group watched DVDs containing the new words several times a week for four weeks; another group was introduced to the words by parents who used them in their everyday interactions. The result? The children who learned the most words were those who learned them from their parents.[27] This study, and many others like it, demonstrate that the best way for a baby to learn to talk is through live interaction with human beings.

It's not just language that young children have trouble learning from a screen. In another study, a group of children from twelve to eighteen months were shown a multistep sequence of movements on a screen, while a second group of young children was taught the same movements by a human. The human-instructed children learned the routine better. This phenomenon has since become known as the "transfer deficit."[28] Scientists believe that the root of the transfer deficit is that children under two years of age do not have the symbolic thinking skills necessary to understand that what's on a screen is a symbol for the real thing.[29]

But an emerging body of research on new, interactive technologies suggests that their impact upon young children may be different from TV and video. Researchers recently discovered that children aged between twelve and twenty-five months who participated in a daily video chat (think Skype) with the same partner over the course of a week not only learned new words via these interactive exchanges, but also created and maintained social bonds.[30] Even though this study did not include a live interaction group for comparison, it's important to keep in mind that, for many families, live interactions with faraway grandparents or other relatives is impossible. It is wonderful to have evidence that using screens to connect loved ones has positive benefits, even for very young children.

PREPARING CHILDREN FOR SCHOOL

Of all the possible effects screens may have on young minds, I think the one that begs for closer scrutiny is any impact they may have on executive function.

In case you are unfamiliar with the term, executive function is commonly thought of as the CEO of the brain. It's in charge of making sure we can focus on, retain, and work with information in our minds, filter distractions, and switch gears.[31] When children have executive function problems, any task that requires planning, memory, organization, or time management becomes a challenge. Executive function becomes increasingly important as children make their way through school and have to pay attention in class, keep track of their work, complete homework assignments, and apply previously learned material to their current studies.

Executive function is an essential capacity for children to develop. According to a Harvard University report, "Acquiring the early building blocks of these skills is one of the most important and challenging tasks of the early childhood years. [Executive function] strength is critical to healthy development throughout childhood, adolescence, and early adulthood."[32]

While there is considerable concern that screen exposure may negatively influence the development of executive function, research on this issue has produced mixed results.[33] But we do know this: Attention-Deficit/Hyperactivity Disorder (ADHD)—which some researchers believe is a deficit in executive function—is on the rise.[34] According to the Centers for Disease Control and Prevention, in the U.S. alone:

- One in ten children between four and seventeen years of age have been diagnosed with ADHD.
- The number of young children (ages two to five) with ADHD increased by more than 50 percent between 2007 and 2012.
- The percentage of children with an ADHD diagnosis continued to increase, from 7.8 percent in 2003 to 9.5 percent in 2007 and to 11.0 percent in 2011–2012.[35]

There is no consensus on what is causing this alarming rise of ADHD. More awareness of ADHD? Earlier diagnosis? Increased screen time? Many lay the blame on screen time, pointing to studies that show a correlation (though not necessarily causation). Lesley Alderman, who reported on this issue in *Everyday Health*, wrote, "A recent study assessed the viewing habits of 1,323 children in third, fourth, and fifth grades over thirteen months and found that children who spent more than two hours a day in front of a screen, either playing video games or watching TV, were 1.6 to 2.1 times more likely to have attention problems."[36]

As debate rages on as to whether too much screen time is causing inattention in school or elsewhere, Dr. Nicholas Kardaras, one of the country's foremost addiction experts, writes in *Glow Kids: How Screen Addiction Is Hijacking Our Kids—And How to Break the Trance* that he would "offer several arguments to push the dial toward causation rather than correlation—meaning that screens are indeed causing disorders of attention."[37]

DO SCREENS MAKE IT HARDER
FOR KIDS TO FOCUS IN SCHOOL?

I've made it a habit to ask educators if they think technology contributes to inattention in the classroom. Shelley Glaze-Kelley, the educational director at Journey School, is one of them. For the past two decades, she's been either a teacher or an administrator and thus has spent a lot of time in various classrooms. Glaze-Kelley and I have taught Cyber Civics together, so I've had the opportunity to see how kids light up when she enters a room; they know she's about to entertain them with a funny story or an impromptu dance party. It is hard to imagine that she ever struggles to hold the attention of a classroom full of kids, yet she tells me, "The biggest difference I've seen in students is the lack of focus and the amount of time a student can stay focused. Ten years ago, when I was a fourth-grade teacher, I typically held class meetings that lasted for forty-five minutes. But today when I work with fourth graders, I find they can only pay attention for, say, fifteen to twenty minutes before needing to transition into a game, side conversation, or some other activity. Their attention spans just aren't the same."[38]

She believes this is the biggest challenge in education today. "We're dealing with children who are so stimulated and so used to seeing something for five minutes, and then something else for five minutes, and then 'oh, if I don't like that, I can swipe and get something else.' Educators can't match those same experiences. So students are uninterested mostly because of their attention spans, which is extremely unfortunate and hard for a teacher to fix. It's become a major challenge in today's classrooms."[39]

I find it challenging, too. Today, a small latte from Peet's Coffee no longer sustains me through the four back-to-back classes I teach at Journey School on Mondays. It takes a large espresso with an extra shot, and sometimes that's not even enough caffeine to catapult my energy level into the same stratosphere as my students. What's got them so amped? Judging from their chatter, it's the video games they're playing, the coding they're learning, the YouTube videos they're watching, the pictures they're taking and posting, and the group texting they're participating in. While adults worry that kids can't focus in class, these same kids seem pretty darn capable of focusing their attention on the things they do online.

It's the same at every school I visit—large and small, private and public, those with the strictest media policies and those that have a laissez-faire attitude toward tech use. Kids everywhere are excited about technology and eager to talk about it. Even families who do their best to keep their young kids tech-free are raising them in a world where technology dominates our spaces and conversations, and that's not going to change. But Glaze-Kelley is right: This cultural shift *is* making it harder for everyone to get through the school day. Somehow, we have to help kids gain the skills they need to be successful both offline and online.

This work must start when you have young ones at home and can exert a modicum of control over their day. Be mindful of the potential impact of screens upon their social skills, language development, and attentional capacities. This is the foundational work you must do while you have the chance. It will pay off in spades as they get older and their enthusiasm for all-things-tech kicks in.

As Dr. Pamela Hurst-Della Pietra puts it, "I'm not saying there is no place for technology. It can be hugely beneficial, but it also poses huge risks. It's up to us to understand what those risks are and to mitigate them."[40]

MAXIMIZING BENEFIT, MITIGATING RISK

Unless you plan to raise your kids with paper bags securely fastened over their young heads, it is inevitable they will encounter screens—probably interactive ones—as they grow. And as determined as you may be to shield your youngest children from them, this is an impossible task today.

"I'm a pragmatist in these things," says David Kleeman. "Families do what they have to do to make their lives work."[41] Kleeman, who describes himself as an itinerant children's media expert, is the senior vice president of global trends for Dubit, a strategy and research consultancy and digital studio based in the UK. He has led the children's media industry in developing sustainable, kid-friendly practices for over three decades, and thus has watched families grapple with this issue for a long time.

"Between ages zero and two, there is no need for a child to be on devices; they are just not going to get anything from them that's going to be critical in later life." However, Kleeman told me it concerns him when parents are made to feel guilty about exposing their young children to screens.

As we spoke I recalled delivering a presentation at a school that was staunchly tech free. A young mother raised her hand to ask if I thought it was okay to let her toddler watch a kids' show on her iPad while she made dinner. "I'm with my child all day, and by five o'clock, I'm exhausted. Sometimes I just need a few minutes to get something done." Though I was there to support the school's no-screens-for-young-eyes policy, in this case I couldn't do it. I flashed on all the times I'd been utterly exhausted, too, with a husband out of town, and two small children begging to be entertained while I tried to pull dinner together. Thank goodness for Steve Burns, the engaging host of the children's show *Blue's Clues*. Without his help, my young children most certainly would have starved, and that's what I told the young mother. We do the best we can do.

"I don't say ban it; I don't say it's all fine. I say let's empower families with the knowledge they need to make their lives work," says Kleeman.[42] If early societies could figure out how to live with their new tools, certainly we can figure out how to live successfully with ours as well.

INTRODUCING TECHNOLOGY IN DEVELOPMENTALLY APPROPRIATE WAYS

In 2012, the National Association for the Education of Young Children (NAEYC) and the Fred Rogers Center (FRC) crafted a joint position statement to help early childhood educators understand how to use technology in developmentally appropriate ways with their students.[43] Although published in 2012, eons ago in technology years, according to Dr. Chip Donohue, director of the Technology in Early Childhood (TEC) Center at the Erikson Institute and one of the authors of the statement, it "has stood the test of time."[44] Their recommendations are relevant today, for both educators and parents:

- When used intentionally and appropriately, technology and interactive media are effective tools to support learning and development.
- Intentional use requires early childhood educators to have information and resources regarding the nature of these tools and the implications of their use.
- Limitations on the use of technology and media are important.
- Special considerations must be given to the use of technology with infants and toddlers.[45]

Current screen time recommendations for infants and toddlers are as follows:

- For children younger than eighteen months, avoid use of screen media other than video chatting.
- Parents of children eighteen to twenty-four months of age who want to introduce digital media should choose high-quality programming and watch it with their children.
- For children ages two to five years, limit screen use to one hour per day of high-quality programs.[46]

"We're seeing great promise when technology is used intentionally and appropriately and in the context of relationships," says Donohue. "We've gone from worrying about technology to having deeper conversations about its appropriate and intentional use and more."[47]

USING TECHNOLOGY WITH INTENTIONALITY

It seems fitting that the Fred Rogers Center is still providing guidance on how to use technology with intentionality. Most adults fondly remember the *Mister Rogers' Neighborhood* television series from their own childhoods. I know I do. Even though my parents hated it when my four siblings and I plopped ourselves in front of the TV, as they were sure it was rotting our brains, they never complained about Mister Rogers. I can hear his soft, melodious voice coming from the TV in my family's living room as he sang his theme song, "Won't You Be My Neighbor?" while changing into his sneakers and trademark cardigan sweater. Who can forget being transported to his "Neighborhood of Make-Believe" to visit King Friday, Lady Aberlin, and Henrietta Pussycat, before returning to the quiet comfort of Mister Rogers's house via the castle's adorable trolley? Rogers skillfully employed the technology of his day—television—to thoughtfully and purposefully introduce children to positive character traits. My siblings and I remember the lessons we learned from this kind and gentle role model. Even today, Mister Rogers provides a powerful example of how technology—whether it's TV, a tablet, or a smartphone—might be used to deliver positive content to children in developmentally appropriate ways.

Face it—we aren't going to win the battle against screens in the daily lives of our young ones. My parents couldn't do it with TV, and it's even more difficult now that the screens go everywhere we go. But we *can* and *must* be intentional about their use, especially with young children. This includes choosing Mister Rogers–like content (like the PBS series *Daniel Tiger's Neighborhood*, the animated program built upon Rogers's social-emotional understandings), limiting screen time, co-viewing, explaining, and basically being present. Sorry, folks, but you have to put down your own devices to do all of the above.

As parents, caregivers, and educators grapple with the daily, continued encroachment of tablets, smartphones, voice-activated home speakers (like the Amazon Echo), interactive toys, and other devices, Fred Rogers reminds us that we can find a sensible path forward.

In a follow-up report to the original position paper, authors Dr. Katie Paciga and Donohue continue to draw upon Rogers's approach to whole-child development. They write, "Like Rogers emphasized, too, we argue that the child's interactions with other people remain incredibly important—the screen cannot ever replace the impact and influence of a caring adult."[48]

"Screen media and technology tools should always be used in the context of (or with the potential for) social interaction," says Donohue. He advises parents to "understand how technology can be a tool to encourage interactions and strengthen relationships, not just disrupt or prevent them."[49] In the words of Rogers himself, "Nothing will ever take the place of one person actually being with another person. There can be lots of fancy things like TV and radio and telephones and the internet, but nothing can take the place of people interacting face to face."[50]

TIPS FOR RAISING YOUNG
CHILDREN IN A WORLD OF SCREENS

While you can't change that screens are here to stay, you can change how you raise your little ones in a screen-filled world. Be mindful of what young children need most—face-to-face interaction with loving human beings. This is how children gain social skills, emotional self-control, creativity, resilience, and most of all, the ability to get along with other people and to see things from other perspectives.[51] These are also the seeds of digital literacy. Screens keep these seeds from taking root and growing.

The work you do today will set the foundation for all of your child's interactions tomorrow, with people and with screens. It will be well worth your effort. Enact these four guidelines from "Children and Screens":

- **Set boundaries.** Limit exposure for the very youngest children, turn off devices during mealtimes or one to two hours before bedtime, and make children's bedrooms media free.
- **Monitor use, behavior, and content.** Block inappropriate content, watch and play the video games your children are playing, keep electronic media in public places, and talk to the parents of your children's friends about what your children do at their homes.
- **Be clear about what is acceptable.** Establish and enforce house rules about screen time, and don't let media interfere with family relationships.
- **Engage and lead by example.** Obey your own house rules, and remember your children are watching.[52]

If you do decide to use interactive technologies with your young children (please heed the advice from the American Academy of Pediatrics and avoid screen use before eighteen months of age), consider the "Top Ten Tips for Using Technology and Interactive Media with Young Children," which Donohue recently shared with *Imagine Magazine*:

1. **Remember that relationships matter most.** Using technology with young children begins with low-tech, high-touch opportunities for interactions, shared experiences, discoveries, and joint-engagement with media.
2. **Integrate technology use into social and emotional learning.** Technology should be used in ways that support positive social interactions, mindfulness, creativity, and a sense of initiative.

3. **Use technology as a tool.** Technology is an additional important tool for exploring, learning, and creating that you can put in children's hands. It is not more or less important than other tools children use to learn in the early years.

4. **Trust your instincts.** Focus less on how many minutes a child engages with screen media and more on the quality of the content, the context for using media, and the engagement level. Pay more attention to what the child is doing, not simply on how many minutes.

5. **Empower children to use technology as a tool for twenty-first-century learning.** Select technology that encourages inquiry, exploration, discovery, documentation, and demonstration of what they know.

6. **Provide beneficial technology experiences.** Offer media experiences that are engaging and interactive; include positive interactions with others; give the child control; emphasize interactions, language use, and relationships; and invite co-viewing and joint engagement with media.

7. **Make media use a language-rich experience.** Narrate your own technology use, and when children are using screen media, talk about what they're doing, ask questions, make comments, and offer suggestions about what they can do after the screen is turned off.

8. **Help children progress from just consuming media to creating it.** Simple tools like a digital camera are powerful media-creation tools when paired with a child's curiosity and creativity.

9. **Pay attention to your own technology use in front of children.** Children learn media habits and how and when to use technology by observing the important adults in their lives.

10. **Be a media mentor.** Young children need trusted adults who are active and intentional media mentors and role models to guide them safely in the digital age.[53]

CYBER CIVICS MOMENTS
Skype with Loved Ones

My dear friend Patti Connolly is a school development specialist who has consulted and worked with schools, primarily Waldorf, for nearly thirty years. Today she advises them on how to slowly introduce technology in developmentally appropriate ways. "Just as you would never hand over a kitchen knife to a two-year-old, you shouldn't just hand them a digital device either," Connolly told me. She suggests "satisfying a young child's natural curiosity by showing them what these screens are all about and then how to use them in intentional ways."[54] There's that word again. Intentional. I asked Connolly to give me an example of intentional and developmentally appropriate technology use with young children.

Connolly's work has taken her and her husband, Tim, also a longtime Waldorf teacher and administrator, to far-flung locations around the globe to work with various schools. They are also devoted grandparents to twin grandsons and use Skype regularly to stay in touch. "The boys don't just want to chat," Connolly told me. "They want you to move around and show them things, so that's what we do. This is a great way to demonstrate some of the positive benefits of new technologies to young children. It shows them that it can be used for communication and connecting. People feel like screens close us off from one another, and this demonstrates the exact opposite. Screens can connect us with those we love."[55]

Here's what you can do:

1. Do you have distant relatives and friends? Show your young ones how you use screens to keep in touch. If you don't already have one, sign up for a Skype account (or one of the many other free communication tools available on the internet, like Google Hangouts or Apple FaceTime). If you have never used Skype, or other videoconferencing software, turn to Google or YouTube and type "how to use Skype" (or whatever tool you use). Dozens of instructional texts and videos will pop up to guide you through the process of installation and use. Let your young children see you using technology to figure out this new software.

2. When you use Skype (or another videoconferencing tool) to connect with your loved ones, ask them to use their screens to show you and your children where they are, who they are with, or what they may be doing. You and your children can do the same. Explain to your young children that, although your loved ones appear on the screen, they live in another house far away. Your children's developmental stage will determine how much of this information they will or will not comprehend.

Explain, Explain, Explain

Satisfy your young children's natural curiosity by *explaining* technology to them every time you use it. Remember, children are mimics. They watch and note every move of the adults around them to learn how to become humans themselves. Think about what they see: adults compulsively grabbing their phones to check text messages, email, the weather, recipes on Pinterest, and who knows what else. Is it any wonder many small children grow into teenagers who can't put down their own phones?

Breaking this cycle begins with two steps:

1. Be mindful of how many times you use your phone in front of your young child.
2. When you must use your phone or other connected device, *explain* what you are doing and invite the child to do it with you. You can say:

- Grandma is calling, and I'm going to answer the phone to see how she is doing. Would you like to talk to her, too?
- I'm not sure what to make for dinner tonight, so let's look for a yummy recipe together.
- We are going to the zoo tomorrow, so I'm going to look at the map to find out how to get there. Do you want to look with me?
- The zoo is so much fun! Can I take a picture of you, so we can look at it later to remember what a good time we had together?

This exercise serves an ulterior motive. Explaining technology to your children every time you use it reminds you that you may be using it more than you need to. For example, try explaining this to your child: "Mama is checking her work email for the fifth time in a half hour." Unless you are expecting to find something urgent, doesn't that sound a bit ridiculous?

Explore Interests

When young children observe adults binge-watching dozens of episodes of a TV show, the message they get is that digital tools are entertainment-only devices. Chances are your little imitators will do the same—binge-watch mindless programming—when and if they are left alone with technology. So make time, especially when your children are young, to demonstrate how to use technology to learn and explore interests.

1. Do you have a young child with a fixation on trucks, insects, or cooking? Use your screens to explore these topics together. YouTube Kids can be extremely helpful with this. But be forewarned: Whatever you are planning to watch with your child, be sure to watch it by yourself first. In 2015, Google-owned YouTube launched YouTube Kids with the best of intentions. The idea was to offer a kid-friendly version of their platform, which would be full of child-appropriate videos, many supplied by Disney and Nickelodeon. The site was supposed to automatically filter inappropriate content. But in late 2017, the *New York Times* reported that not-so-child-friendly videos were slipping past YouTube's filters, and young children were being exposed to inappropriate or even disturbing imagery. One such video showed a claymation Spider-Man urinating on Elsa from *Frozen*.[56] Not the type of thing you want your four-year-old to see. Although YouTube claims it has since remedied this problem, play it safe and pre-screen whatever you plan to watch with your children.

2. Limit your viewing to a maximum of fifteen-minute increments, and keep screen time limitations in mind. Remember that the American Academy of Pediatrics recommends *no* screen time for children under eighteen months of age (other than videoconferencing with loved ones), supervised screen time between eighteen and twenty-four months, and no more than one hour maximum for children up to age five. Never leave your young child unsupervised, and be sure to co-view and explain what you are watching. Remember, young children cannot draw connections between what they see on the screen and real life. It's your job to do that for them!

Chapter 2

Learning to Be Human

●

A computer can help you learn to spell *hug*, but it can never help you know
the risk or the joy of actually giving or receiving one.

—FRED ROGERS[1]

When your children head off to school and spend less time under
your watchful eye, helping them build a strong foundation will
become increasingly difficult. As their friends start getting their
own mobile devices, you'll start hearing about it. "But *everyone* has one" is
likely to become a recurrent refrain aimed at breaking you down. Their
school may require that they use technology for various purposes, and as
they begin to explore the world beyond your home and their school, they
will find it filled with exciting new technologies—ever-new gaming devices,
wireless headphones, smartwatches, humanoid robotic toys, virtual-reality
playgrounds, augmented-reality apps, and other gadgets. Helping your children develop a healthy relationship with technology will feel like a 24/7
endeavor, so stay strong, my friends! The foundational work you do now will
bear its fruit in just a few short years.

SCHOOL IS DIFFERENT TODAY

Our oldest daughter spent most of her kindergarten career outside. Thanks
to the idyllic climate of coastal Southern California, the great outdoors
offered her teacher a preferable alternative to their "classroom"—a crappy
portable structure with cracked acoustic ceiling tiles and buzzing fluores-
cent lights. Not uncommon digs for charter schools that usually rent whatever space their sponsoring district has available. After a short "circle time"
of singing, followed by dramatic storytelling in softly lit, silk-draped

surroundings that camouflaged the portable's starkness, they'd head outside. Following a bike trail, they'd wander about a mile and a half through historic San Juan Capistrano—thirty children skipping merrily along, stopping to gather small sticks, observing a frog in the riverbed, marveling at a yellow and green monarch caterpillar, or tossing stones into San Juan Creek. Upon reaching their final destination, a grassy, tree-filled park, they'd play to their hearts' content before making the final trek back to school, arriving just in time for 12:30 p.m. pickup.

Carefree kindergarten mornings like these are a novelty today. Kindergartners are more commonly found indoors, hard at work learning to read and write or solving math problems. According to Common Core State Standards (CCSS) for kindergarten, students should be writing words, sentences, and paragraphs, and begin constructing mathematical equations. The CCSS for public school students, used in over forty U.S. states, list over ninety standards for kindergartners, and many schools introduce technology early to make sure their students don't get left behind.

NO PRESCHOOLER LEFT BEHIND

A couple of summers ago, I attended an educational technology conference in Los Angeles, where I found myself sharing lunch with three preschool teachers. Surprised to find them at the event, I asked how learning about technology in the classroom was relevant to their three- and four-year-old students.

"We use interactive whiteboards and iPads," they told me. "Our students have to be tech ready."

With great enthusiasm, they explained how they use technology to show videos and teach basic language and math skills. "We were even able to get rid of our manipulatives," one of the teachers told me.

I was pretty sure "manipulatives" was teacher-code for toys. I would have asked, but I was too busy picking my jaw up from the floor. Then lunch ended, and we went our separate ways.

By the Monday morning following the conference, I had sufficiently recovered my wits but was curious about the use of iPads in a preschool classroom. So I turned to Google to see how commonplace this practice might be. Dozens of websites and articles popped up, from "iPads Work

Well for Little Kids in Preschools," to "15 Must-Have iPad Apps for Pre-school Teachers," and even, "Technology Lesson Plans for Preschool."

Across the United States, school district leaders, principals, and teachers have come under increased pressure to ensure that all students, even the very youngest, are "tech ready." By the end of 2016, over half of United States K–12 students had access to a school-issued personal computing device. Globally, the market for devices in K–12 has heated up as well. Futuresource Consulting Ltd., a UK-based research firm that tracks tech trends in forty-six countries, reports that most nations are increasingly investing in school technology to improve the skills of their workforces.[2] In the U.S., many school districts are buying into "one-to-one" initiatives. This means they supply one device— usually a Chromebook or iPad—to every student.

Bloomington School District in Bloomington, Minnesota, is in the pro-cess of making all its schools one-to-one. In a television interview, Minne-sota Department of Education's Doug Paulson explained that it's important to supply every child with a device because "computers are the present and the future."[3] When asked how this was improving educational outcomes, he answered, "Oftentimes we think about technology as our answer, but we haven't really thought about our question first."[4]

But maybe we *should* think about our question first. So here's one: What do children need to learn today to become happy, healthy, and successful tomorrow—online and offline?

WHAT SKILLS WILL THEY NEED?

When my husband and I decided to send our daughters to a tech-free school, many well-meaning colleagues, family members, and friends thought we were crazy. They'd ask how our kids would be prepared to succeed in a dig-ital world.

Before we had a chance to come up with a well-informed answer to this question, the media provided one for us. In a widely circulated *New York Times* article titled "A Silicon Valley School That Doesn't Compute," jour-nalist Matt Richtel reported that eBay's chief technology officer sent his children to a Waldorf school in California's Bay Area, as did employees of Google, Apple, Yahoo!, and Hewlett-Packard.[5] The school profiled in the story—the Waldorf School of the Peninsula in Los Altos, California (a school that now teaches Cyber Civics)—claimed that three-quarters of its student population had parents with strong high-tech connections, yet wanted their own children shielded from technology for as long as possible. According to a parent who had worked for Intel and Microsoft, "Engagement is about human contact, the contact with the teacher, the contact with their peers." Another parent, who worked at Google, was asked if he was worried about his kids' lack of technology skills. "No," he answered. "It's super easy. It's like learning to use toothpaste. At Google and all these places, we make technology as brain-dead easy to use as possible. There's no reason why kids can't figure it out when they get older."

That's what my husband and I came to realize as well. Watching our twelve-year-old daughter intuitively navigate my iPhone or block the pop-ups on my computer confirmed our suspicions. One day I was struggling to learn how to use a new presentation software program called Prezi. As is common for most internet users of my generation, I resorted to reading Prezi's expansive user manual. Meanwhile, my daughter was on her own computer next to mine. She opened Prezi and in about two minutes created a short presentation. "How in the world did you figure out how to use Prezi so fast?" I asked her. "How in the world did you not?" she responded.

So, while technical skills didn't seem to be what our daughter would be lacking, I did wonder what skills she would need in a newly digital world. I discovered the answer to my question while pursuing my graduate studies in media psychology, in a paper titled "Confronting the Challenges of Participatory Culture: Media Education for the 21st Century" by Henry Jenkins, who was the director of the comparative media studies program at the Massachusetts Institute of Technology. Jenkins and his team of researchers wrote of the urgency to help youth "develop the cultural competencies and social skills needed for full involvement" in the emerging media environment.[6] That caught my attention. "Cultural competencies" and "social skills" didn't sound very techy, and they aren't. They can be acquired, I learned, by engaging with real, live people, and even without using technology at all.

Jenkins calls these competencies "new media literacies" because collectively they constitute a new literacy—the ability to "read" and "write" in an environment that lets kids not only consume media, but also make it, by shooting and posting videos, taking and sharing photos, responding to social media posts, and other activities.[7] To successfully participate in this environment, young people need these "new" literacies: play, performance, simulation, appropriation, multitasking, distributed cognition, collective intelligence, judgment, transmedia navigation, networking, and negotiation. All of these capacities are technology neutral, meaning that they are as applicable to today's smartphone as they will be to any gadget invented tomorrow. Together they answer the question: What skills do kids need in this new digital world?

THE NEW MEDIA LITERACIES

- **Play:** the capacity to experiment with one's surroundings as a form of problem-solving
- **Performance:** the ability to adopt alternative identities for improvisation and discovery
- **Simulation:** the ability to interpret and construct dynamic models of real-world processes
- **Appropriation:** the ability to meaningfully sample and remix media content
- **Multitasking:** the ability to scan one's environment and shift focus, as needed, to salient details
- **Distributed cognition:** the ability to interact meaningfully with tools that expand mental capacities
- **Collective intelligence:** the ability to pool knowledge and compare notes with others to work toward a common goal
- **Judgment:** the ability to evaluate the reliability and credibility of different information sources
- **Transmedia navigation:** the ability to follow the flow of stories and information across multiple modalities
- **Networking:** the ability to search for, synthesize, and disseminate information
- **Negotiation:** the ability to travel across diverse communities, discerning and respecting multiple perspectives, and grasping and following alternative norms

As I studied Jenkins's list, I thought of my own young daughters, who were probably at that moment engaged in some sort of creative, playful, and collaborative activity that to many wouldn't look like "learning" at all. In fact, I remember exactly what my youngest daughter was doing at the time.

In elementary school, she was learning math by building a wooden bench, using hand tools. This is how her class, as is common in Waldorf schools, learned measurement and the rudiments of geometry. It dawned on me that she was also learning new media literacy skills. Her benchmaking partner was Billy, a boy as strong-willed and sure of himself as was my daughter. So these two engaged in a great deal of negotiation. Their task also required visualization (having a mental picture of a finished project), judgment (deciding when to measure and when to cut), collective intelligence (checking and comparing their progress with their teacher and peers), and distributed cognition (using hand tools like hammers, augers, saws, and nails).

I walk by that well-made bench every time I arrive to teach at Journey School today, and it gives me immeasurable pleasure to be reminded how my daughter learned many of the cultural competencies and social skills she uses today as a college student—whether she's online or offline.

LEARNING "DIGITAL LITERACY" WITHOUT THE "DIGITAL"

Erin Reilly, former research director for Project New Media Literacies, oversaw the resources Jenkins's group created, including guides to help educators incorporate the new media literacies into their practice. Today, as the CEO and cofounder of ReillyWorks, she sits at the intersection of academia and industry and helps others, like me, understand emergent technologies. Reilly is the person you call when you want to know what kids need to be prepared for next. That's why I asked her if she thought the skills the MIT team identified over a decade ago are relevant.

"Absolutely," she told me. "I think still they are even more relevant today because children are getting more involved and connected to new media. It's part of their daily practice, just as much as learning, reading, and writing." She explained that when we fail to help children learn these social skills, they don't know how to become active participants online. "And that is when they run into problems."[8]

Reilly reiterated that kids don't have to be in front of a computer to learn new media literacy skills. In a follow-up report, "Shall We Play?" she provides examples of how each of the literacies can be taught in every type of school, high-tech to no-tech. She also suggests that a hyperfocus on technology alone, especially at the expense of "human" skills, might be counterproductive:

A mere technology-based solution will simply result in an arms race where each school spends more and more of its budget on tools while stripping bare the human resources (e.g., teachers, librarians) who might help students learn how to use those tools in ethical, safe, and creative ways. . . . In practice, many of the core skills needed to join a networked society can be taught now, even if schools have grossly uneven access to technologies. In fact, for practicing certain skills, low-tech or no-tech contexts often prove just as effective, if not more effective, than high-tech counterparts.[9]

While this information often surprises the many parents I have shared it with, it's no surprise to those who know the most about technology. In the years since Richtel wrote his story about tech insiders sending their off-spring to tech-free schools, or raising them in tech-free homes, this practice has become almost a trend among techies.

In late 2017, Paul Lewis wrote in *The Guardian*, "It is revealing that many of these younger technologists are weaning themselves off their own products, sending their children to elite Silicon Valley schools where iPhones, iPads, and even laptops are banned. They appear to be abiding by a Biggie Smalls lyric from their own youth about the perils of dealing crack cocaine: Never get high on your own supply."[10]

Similarly, author and programmer Jarod Lanier, who many consider the father of virtual reality, told *Business Insider*, "The more a parent is involved in the technology industry, the more cautious they seem to be about their kids' interactions with it. A lot of parents in Silicon Valley purposefully seek out anti-tech environments for their kids, like Waldorf schools."[11]

Suddenly the decision to send our own kids to a public Waldorf school didn't seem so wacky, especially when two bestselling books reported on this trend. In the opening pages of *Irresistible: The Rise of Addictive Technology and the Business of Keeping Us Hooked*, author Adam Alter asks, "Why are the world's greatest public technocrats also its greatest private technophobes? Can you imagine the outcry if religious leaders refused to let their children practice religion?"[12] And in the new preface of the paperback edition of his book, Dr. Nicholas Kardaras interviews Debra Lambrecht, former administrator for the Alliance for Public Waldorf Education, who now runs a tech-free school in San Rafael, California. She tells him, "The argument for technology in the early grades is often rooted in the fear of children falling behind." She believes it's more important "to ensure children can effectively use technology as a tool and will bring all of their best thinking, creativity, and innovation to bear."[13]

That's what Shaheer Faltas told me as well. Journey School's former administrator now leads the Greenwood School in Mill Valley, California. His school is "no-tech" from kindergarten through fifth grade and "has a purposeful approach to technology" in middle school. By his estimate, approximately one-third of his students' parents work in the tech industry. "These parents understand that their kids need abundant time away from screens in order to become the caring, creative, socially adept, out-of-the-box thinkers our world needs today. They feel that tech introduced too early stands in the way of that," he says.[14]

As Kardaras writes, "There is not one credible research study that shows that a child exposed to more technology earlier in life has better educational outcomes than a tech-free kid." Kardaras, who in addition to being an addiction expert is an Ivy League-educated psychologist and former clinical professor at Stony Brook Medicine, advises, "If you really want a child to thrive and blossom, lose the screens for the first few years of their lives. During those key developmental periods, let them engage in creative play."[15]

TO BE OR NOT TO BE TECH-FREE

Keeping my kids tech-free when they were young should have been easy. After all, this was *before* we had to contend with smartphones and tablets. But radio, CDs, cassettes, and even karaoke were harder to give up than you'd think, and it didn't take long before we were guilty of minor transgressions. More than once (okay, every day, if you must know) music blared from the cassette and then the CD player when I drove the carpool to school, all of us singing along with whatever movie soundtrack was popular at the time—*The Lion King, Moulin Rouge, Evita, The Jungle Book*, you name it. We were indiscriminate movie soundtrack junkies. We also listened to the *Harry Potter* audiobooks. All of them. Twice. Through the years, every passenger in my car, from the eighth grader down to the kindergartner, knew the rules: When we arrive at the front of the carpool line, not a window was to be rolled down or door cracked open until the music was turned off. We didn't want to get caught breaking that media contract. (My apologies to anyone who was ever part of my carpool if this is the first you are hearing about this.)

Aside from finally realizing that treating media use like a crack-cocaine habit—hiding it from others for fear of being judged—is terrible role-modeling, this experience taught me three important lessons:

- Setting strict time limits on media use sets everyone up for failure.
- Not all media are created equal, so why throw out the baby with the bathwater?
- There's a better way to equip kids for success in a media-filled world.

A BETTER WAY

Erin Reilly doesn't believe in saying "no" to technology, in setting strict limits on its use, or in what she calls "walled gardens," platforms that restrict a child's access to other parts of the web. "I would rather have my child feel comfortable sitting next to me and having conversations about what he is doing online and actually asking me questions," Reilly told me. "I think shutting down access or letting kids figure it out on their own is a mistake, because every kid is going to try to figure it out on his own eventually, and in that case, he or she might not have the mentorship needed to really reflect on technology properly."[16]

Reilly's instincts lie right in line with the work of technology writer and researcher Alexandra Samuel. Samuel spent two years conducting surveys on how families manage technology, gathering data from over ten thousand North American parents. Her research revealed that parents who play an active role in guiding their kids onto the internet—"digital mentors," as she calls them—end up with kids who have the healthiest and most balanced relationships with technology. On the other hand, she discovered that parents who focus on minimizing their children's use of technology, whom she calls "digital limiters," tend to raise offspring who engage in problematic behaviors online. As Samuel explains, "They're twice as likely as the children of mentors to access porn, or to post rude or hostile comments online; they're also three times as likely to go online and impersonate a classmate, peer, or adult."[17]

Samuel compares shielding children from technology to abstinence-only sex education, saying that neither strategy is effective. While she admits that the limiters *are* successfully fostering their children's capacities for face-to-face connection, she believes these kids will need help linking those skills with online life.

LINKING OFFLINE SKILLS WITH ONLINE LIFE

Over the years, I've visited dozens of tech-free schools that deliver Cyber Civics lessons to their students, beginning in sixth grade, specifically to help them link face-to-face capacities with life online. I believe kids like these, who've had a chance to hone their social skills and cultural competencies offline and *then* learn how to wield these capacities online, will be well equipped to withstand the digital world's inevitable pressures—an unkind text, a post that doesn't get many "likes," an unsolicited advance from a stranger, a request for a sexy image, a humiliating photo shared online, or a barrage of f-bombs, which my students tell me is the normalized language of multiplayer games. I'd bet my last dollar that the online problems adults fear most, like cyberbullying and sexting, would simply disappear if more kids had a chance to develop "human" capacities that could guide them online. Alas, today, even very young kids are spending more time with screens than with people. Those who don't use devices in school still have access to them at home, or at their friends' homes, or at their grandparents' house. Some even hide in public bathrooms, where they know they can secretly gather around their friend's phone and access Wi-Fi (true story!). Even the most well-intentioned, tech-free family or school exists in a plugged-in world.

So, while limiting tech when kids are young so they can develop social skills and cultural capacities might be the ideal, we have to adapt to a non-ideal world. Children must be introduced to technology, hopefully by their parents, in developmentally appropriate ways. If parents don't do this "tech mentoring," kids will be left trying to figure out vast digital spaces without the adult role models or guides they need. Or, even worse, when they do find access to technology, they may binge on the forbidden fruit they were shielded from. I've seen this happen too many times. However, there's a better way.

DIGITAL ON-RAMPS

Longtime Waldorf educator and mentor Patti Connolly also thinks there's a better way to introduce children to technology. "Children see parents on screens, and of course they want to use them, too," says Connolly. "There are too many positive uses of screens today not to look for healthy ways to introduce their use to young children. So why not put our attention on the positives and help them learn how to use them in this way?"[18]

A few years ago, Connolly and I began discussing the impracticality of saying no to tech and, instead, how to introduce it slowly and developmentally appropriately by using "digital on-ramps." Just as a freeway on-ramp provides a safe way for a vehicle to accelerate to the speed of fast-moving traffic, a digital on-ramp offers the same approach to the information superhighway.

Today we both visit schools to talk about this slow-tech approach. We've found that parents like concrete ideas on what, when, and how to introduce their kids to technology. Instead of shutting down their children's natural curiosity, they can on-ramp them at appropriate ages and stages. Also, a focus on the positive uses of tech—using it to connect with loved ones, to learn new things, to be creative—breeds positive online habits that will, hopefully, last a lifetime.

Here are some "digital on-ramps" that might work for your family:

AGES 0–2	* Videoconference with loved ones, with child on lap and parent providing explanation.
AGES 3–6	* Co-view educational content, with parent explaining. * Write emails together to friends and family. * Send texts and photos together to relatives and friends.
AGES 7–9	* Play child-friendly video games together. * Find and use creative apps together, like a drawing app. * Keep online notes, recipes, homework reminders, and more. * If you go on a family trip, keep a digital journal, and post the photos/videos you take.
AGES 10–12	* Do school research together. * Help your children pursue their out-of-school interests online. * Find homework help or tutorial videos online to assist with schoolwork. * Show them (or ask them to show you!) how to download and read ebooks and music.

These digital on-ramps serve another purpose. By becoming involved in your children's online lives from day one, you've planted yourself as a "guide on the side," who will be there if and when things get confusing or uncomfortable online.

Feel free to adapt these suggestions for your own family, keeping in mind that some children will express more interest in tech than others, and some families will want their kids to have more or less exposure. The point is that saying no is not only next to impossible, but also sets kids up to lie, hide, or be unprepared for a digital world that is here to stay.

PEOPLE FIRST

No matter how or when you choose to introduce technology to your children, please remember one thing: Don't ever let tech get in the way of a chance for your children to develop the social skills and cultural competencies the online world demands from its users. The easiest way to remember this is to follow a simple rule I learned from Erin Reilly: "When my son was in the zero to five range, the rule that we gave our family was this: *People before technology*. Three simple words any child at this age can understand. He knew if anyone in the family said, 'People before technology,' it was screens down, heads up. It was 'pay attention to me, I'm talking to you, and you're ignoring the people around you because you're putting technology first.'"[19]

Today, at fourteen years of age, Reilly's son remembers and knows this rule. It helped him grow up with tech yet develop the life skills he needs to be a well-rounded human being.

TWO E-SSENTIAL ELEMENTS FOR YOUR FOUNDATION

Thus far you know how important "human" skills will be to your children's future endeavors as a digital citizen. Before moving on to building the actual structure that will help keep your children safe and protected online, you must know about two final foundational elements: *ethical thinking* and *empathy*. Both are e-ssential to raising kids who will have a healthy relationship with technology.

Ethical Thinking

Installing ethical behavior—the ability to figure out the right thing to do
and how to get it done—ought to be our number-one concern.

—MARC PRENSKY, *TEACHING DIGITAL NATIVES*[20]

Nearly everything your children will ever do online will involve ethical
thinking. Just *think* about it:

- Your young daughter is at a sleepover, and she is wondering
  whether to post a picture on a social media site, even though girls
  not invited to the gathering will see it.
- Your son is working on a report for his history class and finds a
  passage online, which he wants to cut and paste into his paper.
- Your ten-year-old is engaged in a multiplayer game where other
  players use foul language, and she sees no harm in joining in.
- There's a movie your kids really want to see, and they find it on a
  "free" video site.
- To open a Snapchat account, your nine-year-old has to lie about his
  age.
- Your young teen is in her first relationship, and her new boyfriend
  wants her to send him a revealing photo.

Until they reach about twelve or thirteen years of age, most kids aren't
equipped with the working hardware upstairs to puzzle through the consequences—on themselves or others—of these all-too-real-scenarios. That's
why many young kids make mistakes online that they often later regret.

How Ethical Thinking Happens

Ethical thinking is "taking the perspective of others, awareness of one's
roles and responsibilities in the communities in which one participates, and
reflection about the more global harms or benefits of one's actions to communities at large."[21] What is known about ethical thinking today is due

largely to the work of two prominent figures who studied cognitive and moral development, Jean Piaget and Lawrence Kohlberg.

While Kohlberg focused primarily on moral development, he based his theories on the cognitive development understandings of Piaget, who forged what is considered the most comprehensive and compelling theory of children's intellectual development.[22] Piaget studied how children played games to learn how they developed a sense of right vs. wrong. He observed that they developed cognitively and morally in four distinct stages:

- **Sensorimotor.** From birth to two years, children experience the outside world through their immediate actions, senses, and feelings. Unstructured play, manipulation of physical objects, and interaction with loving caregivers are the essential ingredients for healthy cognitive and motor development at this stage.
- **Preoperational.** From ages two to seven, children can solve one-step logic problems, and they begin to think using symbols and internal images. However, they have huge limitations in their abilities to reason, think long term, or anticipate the consequences of their actions. They engage largely in self-centered thinking.
- **Concrete.** From ages seven to eleven, or middle childhood, children begin to develop the capacity to think systematically, but only when they can refer to concrete objects and activities. While they are beginning to become aware that other people have their own unique perspectives, they cannot yet guess exactly how or what the other person is experiencing.
- **Formal.** From age twelve on, children finally develop the capacity for logical and abstract thinking, which is necessary to engage in ethical thinking. While a child in the *concrete stage* may understand his actions have consequences (having been told so), a child in the *formal stage* will realize that her decisions pertaining to moral and ethical issues also have consequences.

It is critical for parents to learn about these stages *before* turning over a connected device to a child. Though the average age for children getting their first smartphones is ten, children between age seven and eleven are in the *concrete stage* of thinking, making it unlikely they'll fully appreciate the impact an unkind text or an unflattering photo can have on another person.[23] It's not kids' fault when they do something thoughtless online. They start life with a completely egocentric view of the world and can't understand how someone else's viewpoint or feelings might differ from their own. Thankfully, children slowly decenter from this mindset as they move through the developmental stages, but this sense of egocentrism lingers even into the *formal stage*, or the teen years.[24]

Kohlberg furthered Piaget's work by developing a theory of moral development consisting of three levels: *preconventional, conventional,* and *postconventional*. He believed that during the *preconventional level*, which often lasts until age nine, children are only able to reason as isolated individuals, not as members of a larger society.[25] Between the ages of ten to fifteen, when children enter the *conventional level*, they begin to believe people should live up to the expectations of their communities and behave in "good" ways.[26] At the completion of this level, youth *finally* have the cognitive ability to perceive themselves as citizens of a larger society. Kohlberg's last level of moral development, *postconventional*, encompasses the upper domain of abstract thinking. He believed that while this stage could be entered into as early as age twelve, some individuals never attain this pinnacle of moral thinking. (If you need proof of this, take a quick scroll through Twitter.)

Understanding how ethical thinking slowly unfolds sheds light upon the difficulty many young children have reasoning their way through ethical scenarios like the ones listed above. These situations are, to put it simply, beyond children's cognitive abilities. Which begs the question: Why are so many young kids online?

I had the opportunity to hear Joseph Chilton Pearce, the prolific author of numerous books on human and child development, address this topic years ago, shortly before he died. Here is his summation:

> We must encourage children to develop the ability to think first, and then give them the computer. After that the sky's the limit. But if you introduce the computer before the child's thought processes are worked out, then you have disaster in the making. This is because, as Piaget pointed out, the first twelve years of life are spent putting into place the structures of knowledge that enable young people to grasp abstract, metaphoric, symbolic types of information. The capacity for abstract thinking developed as a result of the natural concrete processes that have been going on for millions of years.[27]

Age Matters

While technology *has* altered the world, it hasn't altered the time it takes a child's brain to develop the ability to use technology well. That's why social media age restrictions matter. Nearly every network—from Instagram to Snapchat, Facebook, and more—requires users to be at least thirteen years of age to open an account. Although I'd love to report that social media networks require this because they want to give children a chance to mature into their ethical thinking capabilities, that's not why. Social media networks must abide by a law known as the Children's Online Privacy Protection Act (COPPA).

Passed in 1998, COPPA protects every child under the age of thirteen. The act requires website and online service operators to provide notice and obtain permission from a child's parents before collecting the child's personal information, such as name, address, phone number, and screen name. Companies also cannot collect geolocation data that could identify the child's street address, or store any files containing the child's image or voice. Anything that can identify what the child is using, like cookies, IP addresses, or the unique device identifier (UDID) for mobile devices, is restricted by COPPA.

When social network accounts are created for children under thirteen, or when children make up false birth dates, this federal law cannot protect their personal information from being collected and shared with third parties. Yet 60 percent of parents with children aged ten to fifteen say they would allow their children to pretend they are older to bypass these age restrictions.[28]

Empathy

It's more important than ever to teach empathy from the very beginning, because our kids are going to need it.

—MELINDA GATES[29]

Years after the initial cyberincident that was the catalyst for Cyber Civics at Journey School, another minor social media transgression occurred. This time, a boy in seventh grade shot and posted a video on YouTube that made fun of a girl who had made fun of another boy IRL ("in real life"). Follow that? This contradictory mix of insensitivity (toward the girl) and empathy (for the boy who was made fun of) is typical of the confusing and complex nature of middle-school social life. Classmates who saw the video immediately brought it to the faculty's attention and wanted to talk about in class. They hoped to keep it from escalating to an allegation of cyberbullying "that parents would freak out about."

When we discussed this incident in our Cyber Civics class the next day, students impressed me with their abundance of empathy—not only for the boy who had been made fun of in class *and* for the girl who was made fun of in the video, but also for the "bully" who posted the video. "We've all been there and made mistakes we've regretted later," a girl in the class said to the boy who posted the video. "We forgive you, so let's just move on." And so they did.

Talking about their online social lives in real life helps kids process human relationships they are still figuring out how to navigate. Not many schools or even families carve out time from a middle schooler's busy day to do this, and that's a shame.

Empathy Needed

Nearly every expert I spoke with while writing this book said if they could equip kids with one digital superpower, it would be empathy. Empathy is the ability to put oneself in another's shoes. It encompasses perspective taking, and it allows you to feel what another is feeling. Educational psychologist Michele Borba, author of an indispensable parent's guide to raising kind kids called *UnSelfie: Why Empathetic Kids Succeed in Our All-About-Me World*, explains that empathy is "the cornerstone for becoming a happy, well-adjusted, successful adult. It makes our children more likable, more employable, more resilient, better leaders, more conscience-driven, and increases their lifespans."[30]

Empathy is on a steep decline. Between 1979 and 2009, American college students' scores on two measures of empathy dropped a whopping 40 percent, with the steepest decline occurring from 2000 onward.[31] During the same time period, narcissism was shown to be on the rise.[32]

I was curious to learn if empathy has continued to decline since 2009, the last year of this study, so I asked Borba. She told me that it has "continued to free-fall and seems to be falling faster in hypercompetitive countries and ones that are more technologically plugged-in as well."[33]

The researchers who conducted the empathy-dip study, Sara Konrath and Edward O'Brien from the University of Michigan Institute for Social Research, also believe technology may contribute to empathy's decline. According to O'Brien, "The ease of having 'friends' online might make people more likely to just tune out when they don't feel like responding to others' problems, a behavior that could carry over offline."[34] The pair also noted that the generation of college students they studied grew up with video games, and a growing body of research is establishing that "exposure to violent media numbs people to the pain of others."[35]

Even so, Borba warned me to be careful about placing empathy's plunge *entirely* on technology's shoulders. "But, that said, technology is definitely playing a role because the gateway to empathy is emotional literacy." Emotional literacy, she explained, is the ability to "read somebody's face or body language and understand that he looks upset or he looks sad. Empathy is feeling with another person, and you can't feel with another person unless you can read or understand that person's emotions."[36]

Like ethical thinking, the capacity for empathy grows as the child grows. When an infant feels attachment to a parent or loving caregiver, the seeds of empathy are sown. Little by little, Borba explains, "as egocentricity fades, and social-centricity comes up, kids become more aware of others and are slowly able to cognitively step into another person's shoes." But children need experiences, nurturing, and deliberate attempts from adults to help these seeds grow, she says. "While children are hardwired for empathy, there are lots of things you can do to cultivate it. Intentionality, particularly in a plugged-in, trophy-driven world, is crucial."[37]

Growing Empathy

Like almost everything related to technology, a direct correlation hasn't been drawn between empathy's decline and technology. But you don't have to be a rocket scientist with a big research budget to figure out that digital interaction has some serious deficits. Lack of eye contact, facial expression, human touch, and voice intonation are a few. Learning how to read and understand these human cues are empathy-building experiences. In the absence of such practice, it stands to reason that kids might end up with an empathy deficit. Don't believe me? Fair enough. Here's a study to prove it.

In 2014, scientists from UCLA studied two groups of sixth graders from a Southern California public school. One group spent five days at a nature camp just outside of Los Angeles, which didn't allow students to use digital devices. The other group of students used their digital devices as usual. After only five days at camp, the non-tech-using kids showed significant improvement in their abilities to read facial expressions and nonverbal cues, as compared to the other group of kids. Which means that those kids—the digital device–using ones—were less adept at reading human emotions.

According to the study's lead author, Yalda Uhls, "If you're not practicing face-to-face communication, you could be losing important social skills."[38]

Raising Empathetic Kids in a Plugged-In World

How do you raise empathetic kids in a plugged-in world? According to Borba, you start early. "Number one, put down your own phone. Relationships are key," she says. "Empathy grows from face-to-face connections with your child." She recommends that parents do the following:

- Set up digitally unplugged family time.
- Teach kids to look into others' eyes. "It helps to teach your children to note the eye color of those they are speaking with," says Borba.
- Talk emotions. Point them out at every age, but particularly when children are young.
- Read books and see movies that are emotionally charged. "A great way to build moral imagination is to step into another person's shoes," she says.
- Take advantage of mealtimes, bedtimes, and carpool to connect emotionally with children.

"Remember," says Borba, "there are no take-backs in parenting." All of these activities will help your child gain face-to-face communication skills in a very plugged-in world.

CYBER CIVICS MOMENTS
Tell Stories

We are our stories.

—DANIEL PINK, *A WHOLE NEW MIND*

One of the most effective ways to build human skills in digital kids is also one of the simplest. Tell stories. Stories are how humans make sense of a confusing world. Stories inspire us, they guide us, they entertain and soothe us. In *A Whole New Mind: Why Right-Brainers Will Rule the Future*, author Daniel Pink argues that the ability to understand and tell stories—those *about* ourselves and those we tell *to* our ourselves—is a skill needed now more than ever.[39] Dr. Pamela Rutledge agrees, writing in *Psychology Today*, "Stories are the pathway to engaging our right brain and triggering our imagination. By engaging our imagination, we become participants in the narrative. We can step out of our own shoes, see differently, and increase our empathy for others. Through imagination, we tap into creativity that is the foundation of innovation, self-discovery, and change."[40]

Even kids understand the power of story. Just look at the features they love most on the apps they use. "Snapchat Stories"—created with pictures and videos taken throughout the day, strung into a compelling narrative that users share with their friends—is a wildly popular feature. Every Snapchat-using kid I know tells a "Snapchat Story" daily. It's such a popular feature that Instagram, Facebook Messenger, WhatsApp, Medium, Google, and others have copied it. A quick spin through YouTube reveals countless videos crafted by budding storytellers. I learned from my young assistant that kids surreptitiously tell stories through their Instagram feeds. By uploading photos in a certain order, or that share a complementary color scheme, images viewed together form a compelling picture or story that relays a larger narrative.

Telling stories to kids, especially young ones, is a delightfully easy digital on-ramp. It's how the teachers at Journey School sow the seeds of early digital literacy in our students. From the moment children enter the warm comfort of a kindergarten classroom, they are immersed in stories that carry moral lessons—from fairy tales and fables in the earliest grades to

Nordic and ethnic myths as they get older. To the outside observer this may not look like "digital literacy," but it is. Rich, imaginative stories with moral lessons help children build the understanding and empathy they'll need as they begin connecting with countless online strangers with differing worldviews, opinions, and expression modes. And, let's be honest: Who doesn't love a good story?

Here's what you can do:

1. Tell stories the old-fashioned way, by reading a book or from memory. Or you can read an ebook on a digital device. Any way you do it, be sure to choose stories with strong characters and moral lessons. You can start with some age-old favorites, like Aesop's fables: "The Tortoise and the Hare" (teaches persistence and humility), "The Ant and the Grasshopper" (teaches personal responsibility), or "The Honest Woodcutter" (teaches that honesty is the best policy).

2. Don't ask your children too many questions about the stories you tell. Don't ask for their analysis or judgment either. Instead, let the moral lessons sink in. Help your children build moral imagery by encouraging them to draw pictures about the stories or, even better, role-play the stories with them. As Journey School's Shelley Glaze-Kelley points out, "Young kids can't ethically reason or abstractedly think yet, so they need to play moral lessons out through someone else. That's why we do a lot of storytelling or reading books where the characters, whether they are human or animals or whatnot, have problems to solve. This is a hundred times more powerful than an adult trying to explain right from wrong. They will draw upon these lessons as they get older, and especially when they go online."[41]

Send Email

One of my most surprising discoveries as a middle-school teacher has been how little students know about email etiquette. Sometimes I ask students to email me their homework, and am aghast at the lack of salutation, the textspeak, and their ridiculous or downright cringeworthy email addresses. How long, I'd wonder, before they would be embarrassed by their own email illiteracy?

As a kid, I remember being taken through the painstaking mechanics of writing an actual letter. Although today's kids may never write or send a physical letter, they will compose thousands of emails or other digital correspondence. Employers, teachers, and business colleagues will expect to see proper composition, correct spelling, and sentences uncluttered with *lols* and emojis. You can teach your children this skill when they are young, as you concurrently demonstrate how to use technology to connect with others in a meaningful way.

One of the safest ways to introduce young kids to email is through a platform designed specifically for them. Brittany Oler is the cofounder of KidsEmail, a company that offers such a service. She explained that while KidsEmail works like a regular email client, such as Gmail, it also offers safety features that parents like. "We keep kids from seeing inappropriate messages or spam," says Oler. "Parents can also be copied on all of their children's communication. But probably the biggest thing parents like is that they can set up a contact list, so their kids can only email, say, Grandma or Grandpa or a few select friends. It's a great way to let kids start using technology to communicate with others, but in a safe environment."[42]

Whether you decide to use KidsEmail or Gmail, you can follow these steps to get started.

1. Open an email account for your child. This is a good time to explain why she should choose an email account name that won't embarrass her in ten years. For instance, marydoe@gmail.com is preferable to marygoesbananasformonkeys@gmail.com.

2. Together with your child, make a contact list. Decide on the friends and family members you are comfortable having him communicate with.

3. Teach your children how to construct an email. Show her how to type her email topic in the subject line. Teach her how to write complete sentences, and tell her she should spell words correctly and use proper grammar. Finally, teach her how to address an adult ("Dear Mr." or "Dear Ms.") and how to sign off ("Sincerely" or "Warmly" work well). Because so many kids today start texting before they ever use email, the abbreviations and slang that pass for appropriate communication on that platform are seeping into email communication. That won't go

over so well when Mary enters high school and has to email her English teacher to explain why her homework is late.

4. Engage your family and friends as email buddies for your children. KidsEmail suggests making this fun: Encourage these buddies to send your children a list of things to find (like a tree, a flower, a red pen). Have your kids take photos of these items and email the pictures to their buddies. This teaches children how to write and send appropriate emails, and how to add attachments, too.

"There's so many fun things to do with email," says Oler, "but most importantly, it's a great way to introduce kids to reading and writing. Those basic skills are needed even on a technological platform."[43]

Engage in Random Acts of Online Kindness

It's never too early to teach your children how to be kind online. Tap into their naturally empathetic natures when they are young, and show them how to demonstrate that kindness online. An easy way to do this is by showing children how *you* express kindness online. Support businesses you like, review good books you've read, or post things that make people smile. Here are some ideas:

1. Has your family recently eaten at a restaurant that served you a great meal or offered excellent service? Did you stay at a hotel that you really liked? Did you visit a local business and find the proprietor super helpful? If so, together with your child, go online and give these establishments or services a good review or rating. Use Google ratings, or a rating app like Yelp or TripAdvisor. Explain to your children that when you give an establishment or service a positive review—a thoughtful, kind act on your part—it helps these businesses get more customers and more business.

2. If you read a book together that you like, rate the book to tell the author how much you liked it. Amazon is a great place to do this. Explain to your children that when others see your positive review, they may decide to buy the book, too.

3. Finally, as your children get older, let them watch you scroll through your Instagram or Facebook feeds and "like" photos from friends or

relatives, or posts that tell positive stories or spread kind messages. Explain to your children that your "like" is the equivalent of a vote— it's telling the online world that you approve of this positive photo or message, and it's spreading those positive vibes far and wide.

PART TWO

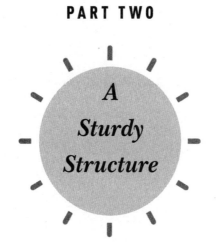

A
Sturdy
Structure

Chapter 3

Reputation

●

The way to gain a good reputation is to endeavor to be what you desire to appear.

—SOCRATES[1]

Harvard is one of the most prestigious colleges in the world and possibly the most difficult one to get into. Imagine the hard work, dedication, and sizable helping of smarts it takes for a student to earn acceptance to this prestigious Ivy League school. An amazing accomplishment to be sure. Now imagine a kid losing this hard-earned acceptance, all because of something he posted online during a moment of adolescent stupidity. Wouldn't that be heartbreaking?

That's what happened in the spring of 2017. Harvard rescinded offers of acceptance to at least ten incoming freshmen because of messages these young people posted in a "private" Facebook group (yep, the same social network former Harvard student Mark Zuckerberg created in his dorm room).

It all started in late 2016, when a get-to-know-you Facebook group called the "Harvard College Class of 2021" was set up for incoming freshmen. Some students broke off from this group, formed a private chat group, and shared memes about popular culture. From there another private group split off, this one calling itself "Harvard Memes for Bourgeois Teens," and then "General Fuckups." To enter this group's discussion, students were required to post the most offensive meme they could come up with.

In case you're wondering what a *meme* (rhymes with *team*) is, it's a captioned photograph or image that is meant to be funny. Often harmless, these visual images poke fun at everyday situations or events and are a popular form of communication on the internet today, especially among youth. Memes are also easily shareable, and the funniest ones tend to quickly go *viral* (i.e., be widely shared). Young people are experts at making and sharing memes. They are less expert, it appears, at understanding there's no such thing as privacy on the platforms where they post these memes. As I tell my young students ad nauseum, *nothing online is private.* I repeat this so many times that by the end of eighth grade, my students are itching to get to high school, just so they never have to hear me say it again! But in my estimation, kids can never hear this enough. Sadly, it seems no one took the time to say it to these oh-so-smart, almost-Harvard students.

According to *The Harvard Crimson*, where the story broke, content shared by the students in this private group included:

- "Memes and other images mocking sexual assault, the Holocaust, and the deaths of children"
- Jokes suggesting that "abusing children was sexually arousing"
- Punch lines "directed at specific ethnic or racial groups"
- A meme referring to "the hypothetical hanging of a Mexican child [as] 'piñata time'"[2]

Appalled by these posts, other prospective students reported the private page to Harvard administrators. One week later, ten students in the private group who had posted these memes had their admissions rescinded.

This, my friends, is our collective failure.

It's the result of neglecting to teach the first generation of students born and raised on digital devices that there can be serious offline consequences for their online actions.

COLLEGES ARE LOOKING

Increasingly, what kids post online and what others post about them (i.e., their "digital reputations") influences their future. According to a recent annual Kaplan Test Prep survey, more than two-thirds of colleges (68 percent) say it's "fair game" to visit an applicant's social media profile to help them decide who gets in. Nearly one in ten of the colleges surveyed said they had revoked an incoming student's offer based on something they found online.[3]

Conversely, according to an earlier Kaplan survey, of those admissions officers who do check a prospective student's social media sites, 47 percent report finding information that gave them a positive impression of prospective students—up from 37 percent the previous year.[4] Some of the things they found that positively impacted applicants' admissions chances included the following:

- A Twitter account that described an LGBTQ panel a student had facilitated for her school. Admissions officers said this made them "more interested in her overall" and it helped them "imagine how she would help out the community."
- Another student who had won an award included a picture of her receiving it, with her principal, on her personal page. An admissions officer said, "It was nice to see."
- One young lady had started a company with her mom, and admissions officers said, "It was cool to visit their website."[5]

Even if it is not a college's official practice to check social media during the admissions process, individual readers for a college might. Beth Wiser, executive director of admissions for the University of Vermont, told CNN that, as a matter of policy, her school does not review a prospective student's social media. But, she added, "if a student includes a link to a digital destination, a YouTube account, or possibly a social media platform, the reader of the application may check out that link."[6] Wiser shared an example of a student who was interested in organic gardening and wanted to major in food systems at the university. Online, she showcased work she had done in this area and then shared the link in her application. Wiser told CNN's Kelly Wallace, who reported this story, "It did show a level of engagement that she's really thought out well what her future plans are and how the university's academic course of study really fit nicely with . . . things she's already doing."[7]

More and more, colleges, employers, landlords, pet adoption agencies, and just about everyone else are turning to social media to learn more about the people they want to accept, hire, rent to, entrust with a living thing, or get to know better. So it's important for young people to make wise decisions when building and maintaining their digital reputations, starting the moment they first venture online.

CRAFTING A POSITIVE DIGITAL REPUTATION

Helping young people craft positive social media profiles is the work and passion of Alan Katzman, an attorney living in New York City, who spent much of his early career serving as in-house legal counsel to several technology firms. One of the companies he worked with owned an investigative arm that employed ex-FBI, ex–Secret Service, and ex-NYPD detectives who were adept at finding out anything about anyone. Katzman observed how they utilized social media whenever they wanted to learn more about people they were investigating. They didn't need search warrants, special investigative tools, or proprietary access to get the information they needed. It was all available online for free.

"This was all so new to me," Katzman told me. "If someone was claiming they were too broke to pay off a judgment yet posted a photo of their new Porsche on Facebook, the investigators had all the information they needed to pursue collection. I was intrigued."[8]

Katzman figured others must be using social media to vet people, too. He was right. He discovered that colleges and employers were going online to learn more about their applicants. "The prevailing expert advice at the time was that it was best for students to remove social media from the equation altogether. Under the guidance of 'don't let your social media damage your future,' experts were largely telling students to shut down, delete, adopt an alias, or simply 'clean' social media before applying to college or seeking a job," said Katzman. "I found this advice to be shortsighted and assumptively negative. If colleges and employers were looking to learn more about their applicants, then it stood to reason that applicants should be taught to post informative content that tells their story."[9]

Although Katzman saw a potential business opportunity in the making, he wasn't quite ready to abandon his day job to pursue his hunch, until one rainy Sunday when he persuaded one of his daughters, then a high school sophomore, to help him clean their basement. During this task, she discovered a crate of vinyl record albums from Katzman's youth.

"Once I convinced her that the black discs actually played music, she insisted I set up my old stereo system, so she could take a listen. I obliged, and she couldn't believe how good analog music sounded to her digitally trained ears," he told me. A few days later, she asked her father if she could start a blog. "This was the first time I ever heard the word 'blog,'" said

Katzman. "Once she convinced me it was a safe thing to do, and I gave my permission, she shared her idea with me."[10]

Her idea was to research each album—to discover when it was released and what was going on in the world at the time—and then write a blog post about her discoveries. She ended up blogging about a half-dozen albums during that sophomore year, and then eight more the year after. Even with the distractions of her senior year, she produced a few more blog entries.

Fast-forward five years. While a junior at the University of Wisconsin–Madison, Katzman's daughter received an unsolicited email from someone working at a subsidiary of Sony Music. The sender was looking to hire a student to do advance work for bands under contract to Sony, who would be playing in the Madison area. He'd found Katzman's daughter on LinkedIn and had followed the link in her profile to her music blog. After reading it, he knew she was the person for the job.

"That's when I knew that I needed to execute my idea for what would become 'Social Assurity,'" Katzman told me. "I realized students needed to learn that social media was a great way to make a positive first impression upon people who were making important decisions about their future. I also knew from my daughter's experience that authentic and intelligent digital content could open doors of opportunity."[11]

Katzman's plan was to show high school and college students how to use social media to showcase their skills, interests, talents, accomplishments, and volunteerism to colleges, graduate schools, scholarship committees, and employers. This is the service Katzman offers through Social Assurity today, and it keeps him plenty busy.

IS IT WORTH THE WORK?

While Katzman's idea of helping kids use social media to showcase their hobbies and talents sounds great, it also seems like a lot of work. When I asked Katzman about this, he replied, "It still strikes me as odd that so many parents cling to the thinking that grades, test scores, a heartfelt five-hundred-word essay, and an abundance of after-school activities and AP classes will get their kids into the best schools, while these schools are valuing character, service, and commitment. Stories of genuine family and community service, proactive engagement with an activity or a cause, commitment, citizenship, and resilience enable a student to stand apart from other qualified applicants. Social media is the perfect platform to deliver these stories directly to an admissions officer's desktop."[12]

Then he told me about Jack, a high-school student with a solid GPA. "But these days that's not enough to ensure acceptance into the most selective colleges and universities," said Katzman.

But Jack had a story. He'd begun playing the viola at eight years of age and had kept at it throughout middle and high school, playing with both school and community orchestras. Jack knew he couldn't miss a practice or rehearsal because it would be unfair to the other orchestra members. He had to develop time management skills to keep his grades up, while also pursuing his love of music. Katzman advised Jack to create a social media profile, where he could showcase his love and appreciation for music and also write about the important life lessons he was learning.

"In its supplement to the Common Application," Katzman explained, "Harvard typically asks whether there is any information the applicant would like to share that hasn't already been disclosed." When Jack got to this part of the application, he shared a link to his LinkedIn profile and suggested that admissions officers visit it to learn more about his extracurricular activities. A few weeks later, Jack called Katzman to report he'd received an alert from LinkedIn. Someone from Harvard's admissions office had looked at his profile, Jack reported excitedly. "A few weeks after that," said Katzman, "he received an offer of acceptance."[13]

While it's impossible to know if the LinkedIn profile tipped the scale in Jack's favor, Katzman's second story convinced me that the time and effort reputation management takes *is* worth it.

Reggie, an average high school student with modest SAT scores, had to help support his family, both financially and emotionally, throughout his high school years. When it was time to apply for college, he used the social media training he'd received from Social Assurity to share the many responsibilities he had to juggle. He applied to several colleges in and around the Atlanta area, knowing he couldn't attend any of them unless he received substantial financial aid. Surprisingly, Reggie not only got accepted into one of his dream colleges, but he also received a generous scholarship offer. The only way to explain both, said his high school counselor, was his social media presence and what it revealed about his character and dedication to his family.

"Learning how to build a reflective digital presence and developing effective social media networking techniques are essential life skills," said Katzman.[14] As they make their future plans, students must understand the important role this presence will play, in both college and job application processes. Like colleges, businesses often turn to social media to learn about prospective employees.

EMPLOYERS ARE LOOKING, TOO

According to a 2017 CareerBuilder survey, 70 percent of employers used social media to screen candidates before hiring them, a significant increase from 60 percent in 2016.[15] Additionally, three in ten employers said they had hired someone dedicated solely to surveying applicants' online presence.

What are employers looking for? Among other things:

- Sixty-one percent are seeking information that supports applicants' job qualifications.
- Thirty-seven percent want to know what other people are posting about the candidate.
- Twenty-four percent are looking for any reason not to hire the candidate.

Over 44 percent of employers found content on a social networking site that made them *want* to hire the candidate. But more than half found content that caused them *not* to hire a candidate. Strikingly, nearly 60 percent of employers reported being less likely to call someone in for an interview if they *can't* find the person online.[16]

CLEAN YOUR DIGITAL ROOM

In the digital utopia I dream about, kids post only positive things online because they've had time and opportunity to learn how to use technology safely, wisely, and kindly. Then I wake up and remember how much work lies ahead to turn this dream into reality.

But we *are* getting there, albeit slowly. Many kids realize that what they post online matters. That it stays online forever, and will possibly be seen by anyone and everyone, whenever and wherever. It may even come back to haunt them when they least expect it. Likewise, parents are learning they must help their children understand all this. Even so, kids will be kids. They will make mistakes, and many will go online before the hardware upstairs is ready to help them make the good decisions the online world requires.

It's imperative to talk to kids about their digital reputations, often and early. Many schools address this by inviting online safety experts to their campus. But often these "experts" either lecture kids or rely on scare tactics that either don't work or backfire completely. Kids take to adults talking *at* them about their digital world like birds would take to dogs telling them how to fly. A better way to help kids understand the importance of maintaining a positive digital reputation is by letting them experience it from a different perspective.

Years ago, I stumbled upon a lesson in one of those curricular guides Erin Reilly worked on when she was the research director of Henry Jenkins's Project New Media Literacies at USC Annenberg. Their team had just partnered with Howard Gardner's GoodPlay group at Harvard University to design a new curriculum called "Our Space: Being a Responsible Citizen of the Digital World." One of their lessons, Trillion-Dollar Footprint, challenged students to choose a contestant for a fictional television show based on the person's digital footprint. That lesson subsequently ended up in Common Sense Media's K–12 digital citizenship curriculum for schools (an excellent resource), where it was adapted for middle school. Taking inspiration from it, I changed it again, deciding to ask my students to pretend they are college admissions officers. I even let them decide what college they want to represent. Since we are in California, the ones that come to their minds include Stanford, UCLA, and Cal, some of the hardest in the state, and country, to get into. Next, the students peruse online content I have gathered (all made up, of course) about two fictional applicants and use that information to decide which candidate is most worthy of receiving the full scholarship they are awarding.

They start by reading each student's (fake) application letter. The candidates—one male and one female—describe themselves and tell of their high GPAs, excellent test scores, and numerous extracurricular activities. Both claim to be outstanding athletes. Since it's impossible to decide which one is more deserving based solely upon this self-reporting, students turn to each applicant's (fake) "digital billboard" to learn more.

Before this activity, students have already learned that a digital billboard is a collection of a person's online activities—their digital reputation. While often referred to as a digital footprint, we call it a billboard for a couple of reasons. First, as students have pointed out to me, footprints are easily washed away. To them, a billboard seems more permanent. Second, anyone and everyone on the "information superhighway" can see a billboard. It advertises what kind of person you are.

My students quickly discover that the content of each applicant's digital billboard isn't so stellar. The male applicant, Dave, a talented soccer player, posted a picture of himself toilet-papering a neighbor's house and also posted a YouTube video of the escapade. Ouch. Plus, a newspaper article said he'd allegedly been caught hacking into his school's computer to access a biology test. Furthermore, a club he said he belonged to posted on its Facebook page that he had been dropped for missing too many meetings.

When the students turn their attention to the female applicant, Kate, a prospective English major in the school's honor society, they discover her food blog is full of grammatical errors and misspelled words. On her Instagram feed, someone had accused her of using a photo that belonged to someone else. She appears scantily dressed in another social media post, and her name does not appear in the list of honor society members on the school's website.

My young students, most of whom are just starting to use social media themselves, judge these applicants harshly. Neither, they decide, is worthy of a scholarship.

But there's more to this lesson. After students make their decision, they must go back to take another look at each candidate's digital trail. Upon closer inspection, they notice that the "Dave" who was accused of hacking was a different person from the "David" who had applied for the scholarship. It is not uncommon for two students at a large school to share a last name, I explain. Besides, had they studied the information I gave them more carefully, they would have noticed that the "Dave" in the article plays lacrosse, not soccer. Plus, I point out, the Facebook post that said he was being dropped from the club's roster was several months old. Something else they had overlooked.

Students realize they missed some important details about Kate as well. Her school's website had not been updated in nearly a year, which explains why she did not appear in its honor society list.

Oftentimes, this closer inspection leaves my students feeling deflated. "It's not fair," they say. "It's so easy for mistakes to happen online, even mistakes that aren't your fault. Plus, sometimes other people post stuff about you that's not true." They also say, "Kids joke around online a lot," and they wonder if adults can tell when kids post things in jest, or when they are being sarcastic. "Do adults take all of this into consideration?" they want to know. My answer? Maybe, but don't count on it.

PEOPLE ARE JUDGING YOU BY WHAT THEY SEE ONLINE

Just as my students made snap judgments about the two fictional applicants, based on a cursory review of each one's digital billboard, people in real life do this all the time. Bradley Shear, a D.C.-based lawyer specializing in social media law, thinks this is a big problem. In an interview with the *New York Times*, Shear says, "Colleges might erroneously identify the account of a person with the same name . . . or even mistake an impostor's account—as belonging to the applicant, potentially leading to unfair treatment. 'Often . . . false and misleading content online is taken as fact.'"[17]

As founder and general counsel of a company called Digital Armour, Shear advises students, professionals, and corporate clients about the legal, privacy, reputation, and security issues inherent in the digital age. "Kids are going to make mistakes," says Shear. "Why should these mistakes be tied to them for the rest of their lives?"[18]

Shear told me about a client of his who had been admitted into one of the most prestigious universities in the world. This applicant had his offer and a $250,000 scholarship revoked because of an alleged inappropriate Facebook like and an emoji about the 2016 presidential election.

"This was a kid with the highest privacy settings," Shear said. Despite this, one of the applicant's "Facebook friends" had taken a screenshot of the alleged inappropriate "like" and emoji, saved it for months, and then sent it anonymously to the admissions office of the school Shear's client had been accepted to. The school contacted the applicant, who verified the long-deleted "like" and emoji. Subsequently, the applicant's offer and scholarship were rescinded.

Shear's story is eerily similar to one I heard from an admissions officer who works for a California university. She told me she'd received a manila envelope in the mail, no return address, filled with screenshots allegedly from the "fake" social media accounts of a female applicant. A note that accompanied the images claimed they were being sent by another prospective student. It read, "You need to know what this girl is really like; she's not as squeaky-clean as you think."

"The envelope was filled with half-naked selfies, posts strewn with foul language," the admissions officer told me. "Not only could I not believe what I was seeing, I also couldn't believe that another student would go to such lengths to bring this to my attention. I thought to myself, 'Is this really what we've come to?'"

According to Shear, "Colleges, graduate schools, and employers do not revoke offers because applicants lack a robust digital life; however, they have and will continue to reject applicants if they find something online that raises a question about an applicant's character, integrity, or judgment."[19]

Please tell your kids that anything they say or do online, or that others say or do about them, speaks volumes about their character. And that character still matters.

GEE, THANKS, MOM AND DAD!

Remember the infant in the delivery room, whose digital reputation was born the moment that first photo was posted on Facebook or Instagram? She's not alone. Many of her peers' digital reputations debuted with their sonograms! Today, children's digital reputations are largely constructed, without their knowledge or consent, by the people who love them the most. It starts out innocently enough—expectant mothers eager to share the results from an ultrasound, fathers proud to share pictures shortly after birth, and grandparents happy to post pictures from parties, holidays, family gatherings, and on and on. All of this adds up and, before you know it, a child's digital billboard is packed with information.

Consider this:

- Ninety-two percent of two-year-old children already have an online profile, with photos and information having been posted within weeks of their birth.[20]

- Thirty-two percent of parents say they upload, on average, eleven to twenty new photos of their child per month.[21]
- Parents post an average of 1,500 images of children on social media before their fifth birthday.[22]
- Twenty-eight percent of parents said they never thought to ask their child if they minded their parents uploading images of them online.[23]

When teaching students about their digital reputations, I hear an earful about their parents' posting habits. I'm sorry to report that *kids are not at all happy* about the photos, videos, posts, and more that the well-meaning adults in their lives have shared on their behalf for years. Sometimes they even ask me to intercede on their behalf. Even if I had the guts to do so (I don't) my interventions would be a decade or more too late. In their parents' defense, I tell my students that much of what their parents have posted about them is positive stuff and will go far in helping them make a good online impression upon others. Yet that's not how my students see it. They feel their digital reputations are theirs to create and that they have been robbed of this opportunity.

OVERSHARENTING

There's a digital-age name for this: *sharenting*, or in extreme cases, *over-sharenting*. This term describes when parents share the details of their children's lives online. Sue Scheff, author of *Shame Nation: Choosing Kindness and Compassion in an Age of Cruelty and Trolling*, and I have discussed this phenomenon at length. She's one the best people to turn to for advice on this topic, because dramatic events in her own life have made her one of the world's foremost experts on digital reputation building and management. In 2003, she became the unsuspecting target of a spiteful client who attacked her maliciously online—spreading rumors, accusations, and lies that ended up wreaking havoc on Scheff's digital reputation. Scheff fought back in court and, in the end, won a landmark $11.3 million judgment for defamation and invasion of privacy, which she wrote about in her second book, *Google Bomb*. Despite her court victory, Scheff's digital reputation had taken a beating, and it took many years of concentrated effort to rebuild it. Today she works

tirelessly to help others avoid a similar fate and, more importantly, advises
adults and youth on how to maintain a positive online presence.

"I think parents need to be more mindful of what they are sharing online
altogether," says Scheff. "What they need to remember is with today's technology, you are never exactly sure who is going to see what you post because
it becomes instantly global." One of her top recommendations to parents
who want to post images of their children is to take advantage of Facebook's
"list" feature. "When you create a list on Facebook, you can easily narrow
down who your posts are seen by. So, if you want to share photos and videos
of your kids, you can make sure they are seen by a select list of just family
and friends, for example," says Scheff. "Remember, kids are sensitive about
what you post."[24]

It's not just parents who post embarrassing things about their kids
online. Often, kids post embarrassing things about *themselves* that they will
regret later. I learned this one day when my eighteen-year-old daughter
burst into my office to ask, "Why in the world did you let me open an
account on Facebook when I was in eighth grade? What were you thinking?" This caught me by surprise. I thought I'd done a good job putting off
her request for social media until her thirteenth birthday, the minimum age
to open a Facebook account. Plus, I checked her posts back then, and they
seemed fine to me, even if they were a bit dorky and childish. "What's the
problem?" I asked, curious.

She was in the process of finding potential roommates at the college
she'd been accepted to and discovered that kids were checking each other
out by viewing their social media accounts. She was mortified by embarrassing photos and posts from years earlier that were still visible and impossible to hide. Even if she deleted items she had posted, friends had tagged
her, and now these embarrassing images showed up on feeds she had no
control over. "You need to warn your students about this," she told me. "No
kid that young should ever be allowed to use social media!"

WHEN YOUNG KIDS USE SOCIAL MEDIA

She's probably right. The thirteen-year-old brain may not be ready for social
media. Even though most kids can start thinking logically, and then ethically, around age twelve or thirteen, recent advances in brain imaging reveal

that certain parts of the brain are not fully functional until about age twenty-five. One of the last areas of the brain to fully mature is the prefrontal cortex, which is largely responsible for rational thought and good judgment, two capacities that come in handy when using social media. Without a fully developed prefrontal cortex, teens process information with their amygdala, or their emotions, and that makes them more likely to:

- Act on impulse
- Misread or misinterpret social and emotional cues
- Engage in dangerous or risky behavior[25]

Although a teenager might *understand* the possible consequences of posting a stupid selfie online, the part of his brain that should be warning, "Hey, hold on a minute—better not post this one," isn't fully operational yet. So guess what happens? The unfortunate image gets posted, shared, and might come back to haunt him later.

But try explaining this to a thirteen-year-old itching to use Instagram (assuming you've been able to hold your kid off that long). Instead of arguing with irrational teens about their irrationality, you might have better luck imparting this simple advice I learned from Scheff. The moment your children open their first social media accounts, tell them to practice what she calls "The Three Cs":

- **Conduct.** Be mindful of how you act online. Remember, a person is on the other side of the screen.
- **Content.** Think about what you share. Ask yourself: Will it embarrass or humiliate me or someone else?
- **Caring.** Be thoughtful, kind, and caring. Remember to post with empathy for others.

HUMBLEBRAGGING

In an effort not to be viewed as conceited in their social media posts, some users resort to a strategy known as "humblebragging." A humblebrag is a "self-deprecating yet self-promoting" post.[26] It's a specific type of bragging that tries to hide itself behind a complaint or even a feeble attempt at humility.

In a study that explores this phenomenon, researchers cite the following "humblebrag" examples:

- I have no idea how I got accepted to all the top schools.
- People keep telling me how cute I am. Awkward.
- I am so exhausted from getting elected to leadership positions all the time.[27]

It turns out these seemingly self-effacing statements meant to impress seldom have that effect upon the reader. People find them insincere and view those who humblebrag as less likable than those who outright brag or sincerely complain.

If you want to brag on social media, current research suggests you should go ahead and do so!

CREATING A MINDSET THAT DIGITAL ACTIONS ARE PUBLIC AND PERMANENT®

One of the hardest-working people I know is Richard Guerry, founder and executive director of The Institute for Responsible Online and Cellphone Communication (IROC2). Guerry zigzags across the country delivering high-energy, information-packed workshops to students and offering on-demand videos to the schools he doesn't have time to visit. During the academic year, he is on the road nearly every day "trying to help a generation of kids use their technology to enhance their lives, not hurt themselves."[28] In 2017, he was in twenty-three states visiting 225 schools. The calendar on his website leaves you feeling utterly exhausted.

Guerry's workshops are centered on his tagline, "Public and Permanent,"® the foundation of what he calls owning a "digital consciousness." He believes it's vital to equip the next generation of technology-wielding adults with a mindset that will help them handle whatever new technology comes their way. That boils down to getting them to remember two things:

- Online actions are public.
- Online actions are permanent.

"We want our kids to be able to go to a party or a wedding or a beach, go to college, join a sorority or fraternity—basically do the same things their parents did," Guerry told me. "They should be able to let loose and be human and not have to worry about someone else taking a picture or filming them and then posting that somewhere. That means we have to help all kids understand that technology is basically the twenty-first-century flame. It can be used for good, or it can burn."

Guerry says kids must have empathy for others when they use technology, because they have power over their *own* reputations as well as their friends' reputations. "That understanding and change has to start somewhere," Guerry says. "I figure it starts with every kid I talk to."

Despite a rigorous schedule, Guerry remains invigorated by his work, "especially when kids tell me it matters." This happened recently while Guerry was visiting a public school in Baltimore. A boy who'd been a student at a private all-boys school told him, "Over the summer between my junior and senior years, I went into a 'quote, unquote' private Facebook group. I thought it was just me and my friends, but it wasn't. The school saw some of the stuff we posted, and I got thrown out, and now I'm in public school. How am I going to explain to colleges why I got kicked out of the school I attended my whole life and ended up in public school during my senior year?" With tears in his eyes, this boy told Guerry, "I wish I had heard you speak before last summer."

"When you're looking at a kid in the eyes as he's telling you this," says Guerry, "as tired as you are, those are the stories that stay in your head and keep you putting one foot in front of the other."[29]

DIGITAL REPUTATION EDUCATION WORKS

Just like Alan Katzman, Sue Scheff, Bradley Shear, and Richard Guerry, I'm passionate about helping kids understand the impact of their digital reputations. I'm lucky in that I get access to my students for a full three years, and we revisit this topic again and again. Even so, I often wonder if lessons "stick" when they go home and find themselves alone with their phones. Kids will be kids, and I've learned to expect mistakes, or as I like to call them, "teachable moments."

Yet kids are full of surprises, too. Billy, my daughter's bench-making partner you met in Chapter 2, gave me one of my more pleasant surprises a few years ago. He and my daughter were in my first group of Cyber Civics students. I fondly remember those students for teaching me more about what they needed to learn than what I thought I needed to teach them about digital literacy. One morning Billy showed up late for class, burst into the room, and marched up to the desk of a pretty girl named April. April had joined the eighth-grade class that year and thus had missed all our previous digital reputation lessons. She had an Instagram account that most of the kids in the class followed, and the night prior she had posted a selfie. In the photo, taken at the beach, she was wearing a tiny bikini and had struck an extremely provocative pose. It was a photo you'd expect the average, red-blooded, eighth-grade boy to love! But that's what surprised me. Instead of snickering about the photo behind her back, Billy strode up to April to give her a good scolding. "You should delete that stupid picture you posted," he said. "It's gonna ruin your digital reputation." She sat there for a moment, trying to figure out what the heck Billy was talking about, before dashing out of the classroom in tears. Although I felt sorry for April, and thought Billy's delivery a bit harsh, it struck me that he'd done what I'd been hoping my students would do: look out for one another in an environment where there are no adults looking out for them. In his crude and somewhat insensitive manner, Billy had done just that. April went home that day and deleted the post.

CYBER CIVICS MOMENTS
Have a Google Party

Have you ever Googled yourself? Your spouse? Your children? Your relatives or friends? If not, take a moment and do this together with your children, or better yet, as a family. A word of warning, though: You may want to Google yourself and your spouse privately first. This advice was shared with me by a teacher who delivers Cyber Civics lessons at her own school. She had followed my advice to Google herself, but had done it with her entire class watching. Unfortunately, she was caught off-guard by some content that popped up. You just never know.

Once you've done this groundwork, follow these steps:

1. Together with your children, Google yourself to see what comes up. Review your results, and ask your children: What was positive? What, if anything, was negative? How could you possibly improve your digital reputation?
2. Next, Google your spouse/relatives/your children/their friends. Try using different search engines, and remember to search any nicknames they may use on social media accounts. Then, ask the same questions as above. Also ask: How might others judge your spouse/relatives/ your children/their friends based on what you found online?
3. Talk about preventative steps your children might take to balance their digital reputations in favor of positive content.
4. Finally, consider setting up a "Google Alert" to receive regular updates on your children's web mentions. This is easily done by signing into a Gmail account, if you have one, and entering the search terms (i.e., your children's names) that you want Google Alert to track. That way you'll be notified if something is posted that might impact their digital reputations.

Tell Social Media Stories

As unexpected as it may seem, many kids—even those already using social media—are unfamiliar with the terminology of the digital activities they are so adept at engaging in. Even if they aren't unfamiliar, you may be, and that's why it's important to review social media terminology together, so you can all be on the same page. Then you can get to the fun part of this activity, telling social media stories.

1. Review the following common terms with your children, to make sure you both understand social media's full impact:

- **Social media site:** Any website or application where users create and share content, including comments. Video sites like YouTube and online games that allow contact between players are social media sites.

- **Tag** or **Tagging:** When you "tag" people (or things), you create a link to their profile. If you or a "friend" tags someone in your post, the post could be visible to the audience you select *plus* friends of the tagged person. This will impact your digital reputation as well as the digital reputation of the tagged person.
- **Screenshot:** A screenshot (sometimes called a screen capture) is an image of a computer or mobile phone screen that can be saved by the person taking the screenshot. Various programs can be used to take screenshots, but it is also easy to do without any special program at all. This is how images and information posted on social media apps that claim content "disappears" (e.g., Snapchat) are saved and can potentially be shared elsewhere.
- **Upload:** When you upload something to the internet, you are moving or copying a file from one computer or device to another (or many others!).
- **Post:** This is a piece of writing, an image, or another item of content published online, typically on a blog or social media website. When used as a verb—as in "to post something online"—it means you are publishing something to an online forum.

2. Now that you and your children know the general terminology, share some stories! It's easy to find stories about social media mishaps in the news. You might even ask your children to share stories they have seen or heard or share your own. If you need a good social media story, you are welcome to use the one that follows. It is one of the true stories we discuss in our Cyber Civics classes.

Teasing Mark

Mark, a sixth grader, tries out to be a junior lifeguard in his hometown and is the only boy in his class to make it. He is excited and proud of this accomplishment, and so are his parents. His mom **uploads** his picture to her own **social media site**, **tags** him, and writes, "So proud of Mark for making the junior lifeguard squad today." Some of Mark's friends see the **post** and think he looks funny in the picture, so they **screenshot** it, post it on their own **social media accounts**, and write sarcastic comments. Someone even teases him by **posting** this falsehood: "Dude, I saw you cheating on the first-aid test!" Other kids see this **post** and share it with their friends and followers.

3. Discuss your stories. If you use the story above, the following questions can serve as discussion starters:

- Who is at fault for spreading the misinformation that Mark "cheated" on his first-aid test?
- Do you think people who don't know Mark well will know his friends were teasing?
- List some of the long-term consequences these posts could have on Mark.
- How could this situation have been handled differently?

Design Your Digital Billboard

This is one of my favorite in-classroom activities, as the artwork it yields decorates our walls. You can do this activity at home as well.

1. Tell your children to think of their digital reputation as a giant billboard on the "information superhighway" that anyone driving by might see. This billboard will display an accumulation of everything they post online, or that others post about them, essentially advertising them to the world.
2. Let your children think about what they want their billboard to say. Will it tell the world they've done well in school? Spent time volunteering? Excelled in sports? Or will it share things they may not want the world to see?
3. On a large piece of white paper, draw a blank billboard (a rectangle with a post holding it up). Tell your kids to customize their billboards by filling it with images and information they would like to see displayed about themselves in ten years. Such information might include a Facebook post about an award they've won, a YouTube video of them performing with their popular band, or an online news article about their work feeding the homeless. Encourage them to be imaginative and creative. Remember, the sky is the limit!

Chapter 4

Screen Time

●

I have come up with my own take on food writer Michael Pollan's famous maxim: "Enjoy screens. Not too much. Mostly with others."

—ANYA KAMENETZ, *THE ART OF SCREEN TIME*[1]

The first time I noticed how screens can interfere with a truly incredible real-life experience was in 1990. I didn't have children of my own yet, nor did I teach other people's kids. Back then I was the director of marketing and television for Surfer Publications (the job was as awesome as it sounds), and one August afternoon found myself on a plane with my soon-to-be husband and four professional snowboarders, headed to the ski slopes of New Zealand's South Island to shoot an episode of *Snowboarder TV*, a series we produced for ESPN.

During our flight from Auckland to Queenstown, we flew over New Zealand's magnificent Southern Alps. It was a gorgeous winter's day with not a cloud in sight, highly unusual for this mountain range. With my face pressed against the cold window, I marveled at the icy spires and vast glaciers that appeared close enough to touch. Suddenly, the massive 12,349-foot Mt. Cook appeared in view, its icy flanks piercing the cobalt-blue sky. It was incredible and undoubtedly one of the most spectacular sights I've ever witnessed.

Appreciating the rarity of the day, the pilot of our small aircraft opened the door leading to the cockpit, so the dozen or so passengers could enjoy more of this breathtaking view. But the snowboarders, all young men in their late teens and early twenties, missed the whole damn thing. Instead of taking in this once-in-a-lifetime spectacle, each one of them was bent over the popular handheld device of the time, the Nintendo Game Boy, busy at play and oblivious to the world beyond their screens.

"How strange," I remember thinking.

If someone had alerted me back then that this would become entirely normal and commonplace teen behavior when I had my own kids, I never would have believed it.

FAST-FORWARD TO TODAY

Given all the digital distractions available today, kids miss the wonders of the physical world all the time. Getting them to realize this is no easy feat, as I was reminded last year when an angry seventh grader named Nick leaped out of his chair during one of our Cyber Civics lessons to announce to his classmates, "What Ms. Graber just asked us to do is illegal!"

You see, I'd just asked Nick and his classmates to abstain from using all digital media for twenty-four hours, over the weekend, and to write one paragraph about the experience. This was the same homework I'd been doling out to seventh graders every September for the past seven years. When I first assigned this task to my own daughter's class, back in 2011, the students accepted the challenge without complaint. They were even excited about it. But every year since, this homework has been met with declining enthusiasm.

Actually, calling my students' reaction "unenthusiastic" is the understatement of the century. They were livid. They spent most of our hour together trying to help me understand why it was impossible for them to give up screens for twenty-four hours:

"But I *have* to get my text messages."

"I *can't* be out of touch with my soccer team."

"How in the *world* will I take and post photos?"

"What about my *Snapstreaks*?"

"My online gaming friends will think I *died*."

"This is child abuse!"

One earnest young girl, tears welling up in her big brown eyes, told me, "It's the *only* thing I look forward to on the weekend."

Although I was prepared for some resistance, this class's response caught me and Shelley Glaze-Kelley, who was co-teaching with me that day, entirely off-guard. You'd think we'd just asked each kid to chop off a hand. But considering that those appendages are usually clutching a phone, I guess that's what this assignment felt like to them.

When one girl volunteered that she had a friend whose teacher had challenged her students to give up using money for twenty-four hours, I finally
felt like I had an ally in the class. "That must have been much more difficult,"
I offered.

"No way," she said. "Giving up my phone would be way, way harder." I
asked her classmates if they agreed. They did. Unanimously. "Wow," I wondered. "How in the world did we get here?"

WE HAVE SMARTPHONES TO THANK

Smartphone ownership has become nearly synonymous with adolescence. In a few short years, the number of teens with smartphones has
skyrocketed. A 2018 report from Pew Research Center finds that 95 percent of teens either have or have access to a smartphone. This represents
a 22-percentage-point increase from the 73 percent of teens who reported
having smartphones in 2014–2015.[2] Even before teens had their own
phones, most cut their teeth using tablets or their parents' smartphones
and computers.

According to the same Pew report, 45 percent of teens say they use the
internet "almost constantly." That figure has nearly doubled from the 24
percent who said the same in Pew's 2014–2015 survey. Another 44 percent
of teens report going online several times a day. In all, roughly nine-in-ten
teens say they go online multiple times per day.[3]

If you think this is unique to the U.S., think again. Internet usage via the
mobile phone is *two times higher* in Asia and Africa. Many countries in these
regions simply skipped using desktops, then laptops, and went straight to
internet-connected phones, as they are cheaper and easier to acquire and
use. Today, studies indicate that anywhere from 1.6 percent to 11.3 percent
of adolescents in China, Taiwan, and South Korea are considered internet
"addicted," and China was the first country to declare internet addiction a
clinical disorder.[4]

The scene I found so odd years ago—teens with heads bent over a screen,
missing everything happening around them—doesn't even raise eyebrows
today. And the time teens spend gazing at screens seems to increase expo-
nentially every year. I observe this with the kids I teach, and the data I collect from them confirms it.

Every year, I ask incoming seventh and eighth graders to write down everything they do from the moment they wake up to the time they go to sleep on a typical summer's day. This is important because, frequently, screen use goes unnoticed. Screens are in supermarkets, restaurants, and gas stations. Kids use screens not only to text, but also to check the weather, find directions to a friend's house, and to Google anything they are curious about. Daily living and screens are increasingly and inextricably entwined, and have been since these kids were babies. So, unless they log their activities, they have no idea how much time they spend using screens.

This is an activity I've conducted annually over the past seven years, and every year the number of screen hours students self-report matches national averages, not only at our school, but also at many others that teach Cyber Civics. Last year, however, the data I collected floored me. In one class alone the average time spent using screens per day was a whopping 11.5 hours per kid.

Students are equally shocked when they discover how much time they spend staring at screens. When I challenge them to ponder what screen time might have supplanted in their offline lives, many wistfully admit they wish they'd "spent more time at the beach" or "with friends" or "playing guitar." That's why I wasn't at all surprised that a 2016 Common Sense Media report found that 50 percent of teens say they "feel addicted" to mobile devices.[5]

COLLEGE STUDENTS SPEND A LOT OF TIME ONLINE, TOO

Joni Siani is a vivacious media and communications professor at Mount Ida College, outside of Boston, Massachusetts. A few years ago, she noticed a marked decline in her students' interpersonal skills, which she attributed to the increasing amount of time they were spending on their phones.

"I started noticing that they were developing a very different relationship with what we once thought of as just a very cool piece of technology," Siani told me. "In one short decade, it seems like they totally changed in the way they interact with one another. They are the most technologically adept generation, yet the most socially awkward one, too."[6]

Siani, who holds an MEd in psychology from Cambridge College in Massachusetts, was interested in exploring the psychological attachment between her students and their phones, so she asked them how their phones made them *feel*.

"If someone took my phone away, it would feel awful," Taylor, a young woman with brightly dyed red hair, told her. "I even take my phone to the shower."

Another student, a young man named Mike, said, "I have to know what everyone is doing. I wouldn't be able to stand the anxiety of not having my phone for this reason alone."

Siani decided to design a social experiment she thought might help her students develop better interpersonal communication skills "not mediated by devices." What she learned in a few short years was so eye-opening that her students urged her to write a book about it. So she did. Then her students told her, "But our generation doesn't read, so you need to make a film!" She did that, too. Her book and award-winning documentary are both called *Celling Your Soul.*[7]

I ran into Siani recently and probed her about the project. Since her students are about a half-generation older than the kids I teach, what I really wanted to find out was what lies in store for my students, who were already exhibiting such a disturbing attachment to their devices.

She told me that after working with her students on their interpersonal skills—like nonjudgmental and empathetic listening—she challenged them to take a break from technology. But, unlike the short twenty-four-hour challenge I assigned to my students, her "Digital Cleanse," as she called it, lasted a full week. Cold turkey. No phones. No internet. Nothing.

According to a student in her class, named Steve, "When Ms. Siani told us that for our final project we have to give up our phones and all internet for a week, my immediate reaction was, 'How can I get out of this and still pass this class?'"

Like my students, most of Siani's were angry about the assignment, and they told her.

"Screw that. It's crap. You can't make us do it."

"Who does she think she is? Being older, she already knows how to be social with people in her life. How will I know what's going on with my friends?"

"The message this generation is getting," says Siani, "is that they can't connect with each other without that thing in their hands to connect with. They all feel 'addicted.'"[8]

IS "INTERNET ADDICTION" REALLY A THING?

Yes.

That's what everyone thinks, anyway. One of the icebreaker questions I toss out when visiting schools and community groups is this: When you think about kids and technology, what's the first word that pops in your head? The most commonly called-out word is *addicted*.

Yet "internet addiction" is not an official clinical diagnosis. It is not included in the most recent *Diagnostic and Statistical Manual of Mental Disorders*, or DSM-5, the authoritative guide to the diagnosis of mental disorders, which is used by healthcare professionals in the U.S. and much of the world.[9] The only behavioral, nonsubstance-related addiction listed in the DSM-5 is "gambling disorder." Nevertheless, the word "addiction" is tossed around casually and often regarding technology. Especially when the discussion surrounds kids.

Dr. David Greenfield, founder of the Center for Internet and Technology Addiction and assistant clinical professor of psychiatry at the University of Connecticut School of Medicine, is one of the world's leading authorities on internet, computer, and digital media compulsive and addictive use. I met him in 2015 at the inaugural Digital Citizenship Summit in Hartford, Connecticut, where he was presenting the event's only session on tech overuse. He explained that, while internet addiction is not an official diagnosis, a majority of people, including kids, show signs of compulsive behavior or are overusing their phones. When this behavior interferes with a major sphere of living—social relationships, academic performance, or family relationships—then it's a problem.

A couple of years later, I spoke to Greenfield again because I was curious whether this problem was getting better or worse. He said that with parents providing phones to increasingly younger kids, he was seeing some as young as twelve and thirteen exhibiting addictive tendencies. These kids, which he calls members of "Generation D" (*D* for Digital), have grown up with tech. Today, it's ingrained into their peer culture at a time when they are particularly vulnerable.[10]

WHAT MAKES KIDS SO VULNERABLE TO TECH?

Greenfield calls the smartphone "the smallest slot machine in the world"[11] and says the internet is the biggest one. Like a slot machine, both run on a variable-ratio reinforcement schedule, which is a fancy way of saying that, whenever we go online, we never quite know what's going to happen next, and that unpredictability is what keeps us going back for more. Think about that ping that announces a new text message, a social media comment, or a news update. Those notifications reward our brains with a small hit of dopamine, a chemical that leads to increased pleasure, and when we go online to see what the ping is announcing, we're rewarded a second hit of this feel-good chemical. The *anticipation* of what that ping might deliver elevates dopamine *even more* than the actual reward of receiving a text, a "like," or a breaking news update.

The dopamine reward center that notifications and rewards activate is the same area of the brain that experiences pleasure from eating, sex, drugs, alcohol, and gambling. This is big news, because for a long time the scientific community believed that the pleasure derived from playing *World of War craft*, for example, could never rise to the same level of addictive pleasure achieved with physical substances. It turns out they were wrong. The patterns of neurons firing across the brain in all these instances are almost identical. Today, PET scans and functional MRIs reveal an increase in glucose uptake in the areas of the brain that are pleasure-oriented, and the neurotransmitter associated with that process is dopamine.

Dr. Nicholas Kardaras addresses this phenomenon in "It's 'Digital Heroin': How Screens Turn Kids into Psychotic Junkies": "We now know that those iPads, smartphones, and Xboxes are a form of digital drug. Recent brain imaging research is showing that they affect the brain's frontal cortex—which controls executive functioning, including impulse control—the same way that cocaine does. Technology is so hyperarousing that it raises dopamine levels—the feel-good neurotransmitter most involved in the addiction dynamic—as much as sex."[12]

It's tough enough resisting technology when one has a fully functional frontal cortex, which, presumably, most adults do. But teens don't have this biological advantage. And if that wasn't enough of a handicap, a trifecta of other factors converge during the teenage years that makes this age group particularly vulnerable to technology's charms.

First, beginning in early adolescence and peaking midway through, teens experience an increase in the activity of the neural circuits that use dopamine. This is why teens gravitate toward substances and experiences that yield rewards, such as social media "likes" and text message pings. During an experiment conducted at UCLA's Ahmanson-Lovelace Brain

Mapping Center, researchers showed thirty-two teenagers' photographs on a computer screen for twelve minutes and analyzed their brain activity, using functional magnetic resonance imaging, or fMRI.[13] Each photo displayed the number of "likes" it had supposedly received from other teenage participants (in reality, the researchers assigned these "likes"). When the teens saw their own photos with a high number of "likes," researchers observed increased activity in their brain's reward circuitry, a region that researchers say is particularly sensitive during adolescence.

Second, in addition to experiencing pleasure from internet activities, teens are more easily addicted to that pleasure than adults. In her book *The Teenage Brain*, Dr. Frances Jensen explains that teens learn behaviors more quickly than adults, and addiction is a form of learning.[14] This efficiency for learning a behavior that could later become an addiction has been observed in adolescents who smoke cigarettes. Teens who smoke cigarettes show higher rates of tobacco addiction than adults who smoke the same amount.[15]

Finally, compulsive or addictive behavior can hijack the brain's ability to access the judgment center in the frontal cortex. That's the part of the brain that should be asking, "How important is this text?" or "Do I need to check Snapchat every five minutes?" Since a person's judgment center is not fully operational until the age of twenty-five, youth are already disadvantaged when making sound decisions. Most car rental car companies know this, which is why twenty-five is the minimum age to rent a car.[16]

So, let's add this up. First, kids receive a dopamine hit every time their phones announce and deliver rewards, which is often. Second, kids are more easily addicted to pleasurable experiences, like those delivered by phones, than adults. And third, kids lack the judgment to know when to put down or ignore their phones.

One can understand why they seem "addicted."

HIJACKING KIDS' ATTENTION

Technology is designed to capture and hold our attention, and an entire science underlies this fact. Dr. B. J. Fogg, founder of the Persuasive Tech Lab at Stanford University, was the first to articulate the discipline, coining the term "captology" in 1996. Captology is the study of computers as persuasive technologies. According to the Stanford Persuasive Tech Lab website, captology includes "the design, research, ethics, and analysis of interactive computing products (computers, mobile phones, websites, wireless technologies, mobile applications, video games, etc.) created for the purpose of changing people's attitudes or behaviors."[17]

Fogg is perhaps best known for his signature "Behavior Model," a system that explains how humans are driven to act a certain way when three forces converge: *motivation, trigger,* and *ability.* When they occur simultaneously, these three elements are the secret to eliciting a desired behavioral response from an unsuspecting device user. Using Fogg's model, technology designers can even identify precisely what stops a user from performing the action they seek. As someone who has spent a good portion of her academic career studying media psychology, I find this utterly fascinating. As a mother, and educator, it deeply concerns me.

Reportedly, in 2007, seventy-five students filled a Stanford classroom to study this model under Fogg: "Ten weeks later, the students—who included future product designers for Facebook, Google, and Uber—had built apps that had amassed 16 million users, made $1 million in advertising revenue, and had cracked the code for creating apps we just can't leave alone."[18]

In his 2003 book, *Persuasive Technology: Using Computers to Change What We Think and Do,* Fogg revealed what makes his model work. He, somewhat apocalyptically, wrote, "No human can be as persistent as a machine. Computers don't get tired, discouraged, or frustrated. They don't need to eat or sleep. They can work around the clock in active efforts to persuade or watch and wait for the right moment to intervene . . . when it comes to persuasion, this higher level of persistence can pay off."[19]

It's impossible for me to read these words and not think about my seventh-grade students and their horrified reactions to being asked to put down their phones for one day. They don't stand a chance against the combined forces of biology and technology. And the tactics used to hijack their attention improve each year.

Here's an example: When kids get "tagged" in a photo, they often receive an immediate notification, unless they've disabled this feature. When they're texting or using Snapchat to message a friend, they instantly see when that friend begins typing a response (unless they also change that in their settings). YouTube, one of the sites kids use most, holds their attention by autoplaying a new video immediately after the one they are watching ends. Netflix and others use this strategy, too, cuing up the next episode or a similar show immediately upon the heels of the one being viewed. These design features are meant to keep kids (and adults) from leaving the conversation, site, or app—and these strategies work.

Snapchat (or "Snap"), one of the most popular social networks among teens, has designed spectacularly effective strategies to hold their attention, including the "Snapstreak." When friends have "snapped" each other within twenty-four hours for more than three consecutive days, a Snapstreak begins. Snap rewards this behavior by displaying a flame emoji and how many days in a row friends have snapped each other, as an incentive to keep it up. Users even see an hourglass emoji next to their name if their Snapstreak is about to expire.

Driven to keep Snapstreaks going, some teens will give friends their login information and beg them to snap on their behalf if, God forbid, they have to be away from their phones (perhaps due to a pesky homework assignment like the no-media one I assigned).

"It's *so* stressful keeping up a streak," one young girl told me. "But I feel like if I'm the one ending it, I'm also ending the friendship, and I don't want to be the one doing that."

Resisting the urge to respond immediately to a text message or maintain a Snapstreak can cause anxiety to spike in teens. Even being in the same room as an unanswered phone or an ignored streak causes adrenals and cortisol (stress hormone) levels to become and stay elevated. This spike in cortisol can increase blood pressure, heart rate, and anxiety, and can cause a dip in mental performance. The easiest way to self-medicate this discomfort is to pick up the phone and attend to whatever is happening on it. Succumb to this urge, and *wham,* you're rewarded with a comforting dose of dopamine.

I think about this while watching my own teenage daughter try to do her homework. She seems to get interrupted every minute with a question or comment from a friend (although most interruptions are related to her homework). Even with her ringer off, that damn phone buzzes like an angry rattlesnake. We've talked about this endlessly, and though she is pretty good at "unplugging" (interestingly, it's usually when I need to get in touch with her), that's not realistic when she needs her device to do homework.

So why don't companies who invent the products kids use take their vulnerabilities (and homework) into consideration when designing these devices? Don't they have a social responsibility to do so? I asked Ouri

Azoulay this question. Based in Tel Aviv, Israel, Azoulay is the former CEO of PureSight, one of the world's original parental monitoring software companies. Today, PureSight's software is used all over the world, and one of its most popular features lets parents control how much time their kids spend online.

"It's just as easy to design an algorithm that *keeps* kids from using phones excessively, as it is to create one that encourages them to use phones excessively," says Azoulay. "But remember, when consumers spend more time online—whether that consumer is seven or seventy—that means more money, more advertising revenues, and more in-app purchases. Bottom line, it's a business."[20]

That's what Gabe Zichermann told me, too. One of the world's foremost experts on gamification, user engagement, and behavioral change, Zichermann is an entrepreneur, behavioral designer, public speaker, author of multiple books, and self-described "bon vivant." Despite his obvious enthusiasm for technology, he finds the issue of addictive technology "really insidious and deeply concerning."[21] His newest venture, an app called "Onward," uses the latest science and artificial intelligence to help users *curb* addictive behaviors.

"The most important headline here," explains Zichermann, "is tech companies can't charge for the products by and large, and as a result they have resorted to coming up with ways to get and keep people addicted to their products, meaning, we will not shame Facebook or the games industry into making their products less good. That's not going to happen." Zichermann says this problem "cuts across every socioeconomic status, every category of product and service—it's everywhere. Although Facebook and Instagram are two of today's biggest offenders, they're only two of many companies. There's no possible way to pressure everyone."[22]

IS CHANGE ON THE HORIZON?

Tristan Harris, a former Google design ethicist (and a graduate of B. J. Fogg's Stanford lab), left Google and founded a nonprofit called Time Well Spent. His mission is to persuade technology companies and designers to make products that don't "hijack our minds." As he explained to National Public Radio (NPR), "most companies aren't really thinking about how their products might affect kids, because most designers aren't much more than kids themselves."[23]

"Age really matters," explained Harris, "because if you don't have anybody in the company with kids, for example, how sensitive would you be to what this is doing to that generation?" Harris calls this "a huge blind spot, especially at a young company like Snapchat."[24] Snapchat, whose founders were in college when they designed the app in 2011, is used daily by 54 percent of U.S. teens, 47 percent of whom claim it as their most important social network.[25]

Many leading technologists and tech investors have recently jumped on to Harris's bandwagon. Two of Apple's biggest investors asked the company to study the health effects of its products and to make it easier to limit children's use of iPhones and iPads.[26] Apple's chief executive officer, Tim Cook, told *The Guardian* there should be limits to technology in school and that, personally, "he does not want his nephew to use a social network."[27] In a highly publicized interview, Sean Parker, of Napster fame and the founding president of Facebook, told Axios that the company knew it was creating something addictive and said, "God only knows what it's doing to our children's brains."[28] Dozens of pediatric and mental health experts have called on Facebook to abandon "Messenger Kids," a social media messaging service for children as young as six, saying it "preys on a vulnerable group developmentally unprepared to be on the social network."[29] Meanwhile, a growing movement called "Wait Until 8th" encourages parents to take a pledge not to give their children smartphones until eighth grade.[30]

Today, Harris has a new venture, the Center for Humane Technology, which is supported by an impressive group of concerned technologists. Its website announces their bold vision: "Reversing the digital attention crisis and realigning technology with humanity's best interests."[31] A webpage titled "The Way Forward" claims, "Humane design is the solution," and that the center will be "creating humane design standards, policy, and business models that more deeply align with our humanity and how we want to live."[32]

Zichermann told me of his concern with this vision, which he says he's raised directly with Harris, and it's this: "Companies and organizations, when they feel put upon, by government or by pressure groups, end up agreeing to self-regulate. And in the process of doing so, it ends up being mostly just lip service." He urged me to recall the pressure that was once exerted upon the alcohol industry. What we ended up with was a tagline:

Please Drink Responsibly. "This was literally the maximum that alcoholic beverage companies had to do to address the question of the addictiveness of their product. So that's where this ends up," says Zichermann, *"unless* we empower people with tools to set their own limits."[33]

EMPOWERING KIDS TO SET THEIR OWN LIMITS

While empowering your kids with tools to set their own limits with technology sounds oxymoronic, it's the most effective strategy I can offer you (short of waiting for government or industrywide regulation or reform to happen). The following steps will help you achieve a happy and healthy balance between online and offline life, for your entire family.

Step 1: Educate Yourself About Screen Time Guidelines

In the spring of 2015, I accepted an invitation from the American Academy of Pediatrics (AAP) to attend "Growing Up Digital: A Media Research Symposium" in Rosemont, Illinois. The purpose of this event—which brought together leading social scientists, neuroscientists, media researchers, educators, pediatricians, and others—was to give the AAP a chance to explore the current evidence-based research on the impact of increasing media exposure upon a child's physical, cognitive, social, and emotional health.

For many years the AAP, a respected source of information for parents and pediatricians, stood by a policy statement they issued in 1999 and, even as media changed, their policy did not: *Children ages two and under should avoid all screens, and for children older than two, parents should allow a maximum of two hours per day of high-quality material.*

If, as you read this, you find yourself muttering, "Are you kidding me?" then join the club. That's the typical reaction of parents who compare it to the actual screen time habits of today's kids. But science doesn't care about habits. It cares about drawing conclusions from scientific data, preferably long-term. Hard to come by with brand-new technologies.

To its credit, instead of waiting for long-term research to roll in, the good doctors of the AAP convened their symposium to study the data on hand. Then, after taking eighteen months to digest it, they released updated recommendations in October 2016.[34] You may recognize these guidelines for young children from Chapter 1:

- For children younger than eighteen months, avoid use of all screen media other than video chatting. Parents of children eighteen to twenty-four months of age who want to introduce digital media should choose high-quality programming and watch it with their children, to help them understand what they're seeing.
- For children ages two to five years, limit screen use to one hour per day of high-quality programs. Parents should co-view media with children, to help them understand what they are seeing and apply it to the world around them.

Regarding older children, the AAP decided to stay away from numbers altogether and focus on *limits, content,* and *communication*:

- For children ages six and older, place consistent limits on the time spent using media, and the types of media, and make sure media does not supplant adequate sleep, physical activity, and other behaviors essential to health.
- Designate media-free times together, such as dinner or driving, as well as media-free locations at home, such as bedrooms.
- Have ongoing communication about online citizenship and safety, including treating others with respect online and offline.

To make it "easy" for parents to follow these new recommendations, the AAP created an online *Family Media Use Tool* (https://www.healthychildren.org/English/media/Pages/default.aspx), to help parents manage the time each of their children spends online.

But here's the rub: Even with these new guidelines and this helpful tool, actual implementation requires parents to do the following:

- Find and choose the right programming.
- Co-view and discuss the right programming with their children.
- Limit and manage screen time for each child, based on her age.
- Ensure the essentials of daily living don't get lost in a Netflix binge.

As you know, *parents are busy.* It is difficult for even the most well intentioned to source the right programming, let alone squeeze in an hour here and there to co-view and discuss it with their children, especially when that media often offers a much-needed respite from the demanding job of parenting. But the consequences of *not* taking time to do this are too severe to ignore.

Effective day-to-day management of children's media use also requires some sleuthing skills, especially as kids get older and visit friends' homes and other places beyond your four walls. Sometimes it helps to use technology to manage technology.

Step 2: Use Technology to Manage Technology

Whenever I teach Cyber Civics at Journey School, I make it a practice, as is common in Waldorf schools, to shake the hands and look into the eyes of every student as they both arrive and leave the classroom. (A wise routine in the digital age—kids need practice at this!) In addition to allowing me to connect with every child, it offers the students an opportunity to share their thoughts with me. One day, a boy named Nathan paused on his way out the door. "You really ought to be teaching these lessons to our moms!" he suggested. "What a great idea," I thought. I ran the idea by Cynthia Lieberman, a former public relations executive at Sony, who teaches social media marketing to higher education students at UCLA and has raised two Millennial kids. We had both recently completed our graduate studies in media psychology and were wondering how to best put our education to work. Thanks to Nathan's suggestion, we decided to launch a website for parents called *Cyberwise,* and my husband came up with our snappy motto: *No Grownup Left Behind!*

As Cyberwise got rolling, we started visiting schools to talk to parents. One evening we were delivering a presentation at a school in Los Angeles, where parents were eager to discuss the amount of time their kids were spending online. As the parents took turns expressing their anguish over this issue, I watched their kids, who were sitting quietly in the rear of the auditorium. They were all busy on devices—tablets, laptops, smartphones—and completely oblivious to our conversation. When I pointed this out to their parents, they explained that their kids *had* to be online because they were "doing their homework."

Curious to see what they were really doing, Lieberman roamed the room. Surreptitiously glancing over the kids' shoulders, she spied Instagram posts, Snapchat Stories, and text messages (lots of text messages) . . . and some homework. "What they were actually doing is what former Apple and Microsoft executive Linda Stone coined as paying 'continuous partial attention,' where the brain switches back and forth quickly between tasks," says Lieberman. If you ask kids about it, they'll tell you they can successfully manage all the things their devices let them do at once. However, switching from one task to another causes both tasks to suffer. Contrary to what most kids think, it takes longer to finish multiple tasks when jumping back and forth between them than it does to finish each one separately.

When it came to her portion of the presentation, Lieberman asked the kids what they typically do on their devices, and what they were doing right then. Smirks and giggles erupted as a few chimed in, "Homework," "Yeah, homework, of course." When she pressed to find out if they were *only* doing homework, most squirmed uncomfortably in their seats before admitting, "Well, maybe we were doing some texting and playing games in between, too."

"The truth is, the constant barrage of digital distractions inside and outside of class are a tremendous challenge for kids to manage," says Lieberman. "Parents need help trying to keep their young learners on task."

Parental Monitoring Software Can Help

Today, loads of parental monitoring software options are available to help parents manage not only *what* their kids are doing online, but also *how much time* they spend doing it. Mobicip, Family Zone, Surfie, Net Nanny, Torch, Bark, Circle with Disney, and Qustodio are a few such products. They all offer similar bells and whistles and are inexpensive and easy to install and use. This software helps busy parents keep their kids safe, and most make it easy to set time limits, too. More and more, parents seek out these products for this feature alone.

Additionally, today's devices—iPhone, Android, Mac, or PC—come out of the box with many parental control features preinstalled, including time-management tools. Usually these are accessed via the device's system settings and are simple to figure out and use, even if you're not a tech expert. If you do need help, visit YouTube and search "parental controls _____" (fill in the blank with the type of device you and/or your child uses).

Of the five steps, please don't make this the only one you follow. Using technology to manage technology is an imperfect solution. As kids get older, they become savvy at circumventing the tech parents install to manage their tech. Parental monitoring software becomes less effective when a child reaches age twelve or thirteen, or even younger. That's why parents must help children learn how and why to put down their devices themselves. It's important to let kids experience the benefits of unplugging and to practice this skill. Remember, youth learn through repeated exposures and need to be exposed to an experience fewer times than adults do to learn. This applies to unplugging as well.

They also need adult role models who show them *how* to put down their devices.

Step 3: Be a Role Model

When I challenge students to give up screens for a day, I send their parents a letter asking them to do the same, so they can discuss the experience as a family. Last year, when I told my students I was going to do this, they warned me it was a terrible idea.

"There's *no way* my mom could do that."

"My dad *has* to get his email for work."

"My mom would *die* without being able to text me."

They were right. Parents' enthusiasm for this activity was as lackluster as their kids'. In their reflective paragraphs, many students wrote of their disappointment in their parents:

"My parents are so weak, they couldn't go five minutes without picking up their phones."

"I realized my mom can't separate from her device."

"It was hard to give up my phone for twenty-four hours, when my parents couldn't do it for twenty-four minutes."

Kids learn their media habits from their adult role models, which is bad news. Think about what they see from the time they are babies: adults everywhere prioritizing phone time over facetime. A 2016 Common Sense Media study discovered that adults spend as much, or more, time with screens as their kids. Parents of tweens and teens spend an average of more than nine hours per day using screen media, with 82 percent of that time devoted to personal screen media, not work. Yet 78 percent believe they are good media and technology role models for their children.[35]

In the same study, parents indicated that their top media concern was "the time their kids spend online." Parents said they were "moderately" or "extremely" worried about kids spending too much time online (43 percent) and over half expressed concern that their children may become addicted to technology.[36]

So here we are. Parents worried about their kids' screen time spend a big chunk of their own time on screens, while kids are observing this use. Sounds like we're trapped on a perpetual hamster wheel. The only way to pause it may be to pull the plug.

Step 4: Practice Unplugging

Last summer, I took a trip to Nicaragua with my family. Knowing I'd be away from my computer for two weeks, I prepared. I called AT&T and signed up for their "Passport" service for my phone, ensuring that I'd be able to use all my regular features—email, text, etc.— uninterrupted for only ten dollars per day. I left feeling confident I'd be able to stay plugged in, as I left to (somewhat) unplug.

The first day in Nicaragua, my iPhone was stolen. My kids found this hilarious. The woman who regularly preaches the benefits of unplugging was finally going to get a taste of her own medicine.

I'm not going to lie. It was a rough two weeks. What I missed most was being able to take pictures and share them. I'd almost forgotten that, a couple of short decades ago, I had to wait until I got home from a vacation to look at my pictures, let alone share them with family and friends. When we got lost, which was often, I couldn't rely on my navigation app to find our way. I had to talk to actual people, in Spanish, to get directions, also in Spanish. Without the aid of a language app, I couldn't use my compass to figure out which way we were going either. So I did something I hadn't done in ages: I navigated by landmarks—mountains, the Pacific Ocean, the sun's position in the sky. I felt like a modern-day Magellan.

Phoneless, I started noticing a lot more around me. One afternoon, we dined in a restaurant that was situated on a big public square in León, a picturesque town near the capital of Managua. The afternoon was resplendent with people-watching opportunities. At the table next to us sat a dozen or so American tourists, all teenage girls, staring down at their phones instead of enjoying the sights and sounds around them. I never would have noticed them if I had my own phone! By the time we returned to LAX, I'd become expert at looking at others looking at their screens. Waiting in line at customs, I realized that I was the only person, save a sleeping infant, not gazing down at a screen. If eyes truly are the window to the soul, I thought, what a soulless society we've become.

This Zenlike revelation was forgotten as soon as my new iPhone arrived in the mail.

But some of the benefits of my forced unplugging remain. I decided to disable all of my notifications when I got home, and they remain off today. It's nice to no longer jump out of my skin every time I get a text message, new tweet, or Facebook comment. I try not to look at my email every five minutes either. I'm no saint, as my kids will attest. Breaking addictive habits takes constant vigilance and practice. But for me, had the plug not been pulled, I would not have experienced or learned the benefits of unplugging. So, to the pickpocket who lifted the phone from my backpack, I say, "Gracias." (And to Apple I say, "Gracias a Dios," that I could erase my phone remotely!)

The Benefits of Getting Kids to Unplug

I wanted my reluctant seventh graders to experience the benefits of unplugging, too, so I gave them several months to complete their homework assignment. Even so, only nine out of twenty-eight students ever did unplug, despite repeated warnings that not doing so would affect their final grade. This would have been a huge failure except that one of the students who did complete the assignment was Nick, the boy who had jumped up and contested its legality. After a media-free day, he handed me the following paragraph:

Last Saturday I went twenty-four hours without media. It was difficult because my life revolves so much around media. Instead I had to do other things like play with my dogs or walk at the park or even go for a bike ride with my family. The best thing about doing this is after a while you start to feel calm and relaxed. I believe that all people should try to go twenty-four hours without media.

A few months after Nick turned this in, I asked him if he still believed the assignment had been beneficial. "Well, at first I thought it was stupid," he told me. "But it did help me learn that I can survive, and even have fun, without my phone."

Before walking out of the classroom, Nick turned to add, "Ms. Graber, you definitely need to assign this homework more than once."

College Students Benefit from Unplugging, Too

Despite her students' complaints, Siani held firm to the "Digital Cleanse" challenge. She had better luck than I did. "After a few days," she told me, "nearly every student started reporting positive things, even if it was hard for them to get there."

For example, Steve, the young man who thought he wouldn't be able to stand the anxiety of not having his phone, said, "It was actually invigorating to be out in the world. Usually I'm plugged in to my headphones when I'm walking to class, and I don't really talk to anybody. But I interacted with strangers, gave them a hello, a small wave, or whatever. It felt good."

Another student reported, "I thought I suffered from insomnia, but once I didn't have the distraction of the cell phone or computer I fell asleep in, like, fifteen minutes. It was really awesome to feel so good."

"Every student who has ever gone through with this assignment got benefits out of it and wanted to share them," said Siani. Whether they can sustain those benefits remains to be seen. "It'll be tough for them," she admits. "That's why it is critical to teach the benefits of authentic human connection at a young age."

Siani encouraged me to keep trying to get my young students to experience life without their phones. "Humans need to be understood by other humans; it's in our DNA," Siani told me. "An entire generation lost out on this message. The younger they know that there is a difference between the value of authentic interactions and the more they practice connecting in person, the better for all of us."[37]

Step 5: Connect with Nature

When I was barely two years old, my dad used to sit me on the handlebars of his old, rickety ten-speed and pedal nearly five miles from our house to the beach. This, as unsafe as it was, is one of my fondest memories and likely explains why I spend most of my free time on a bike and spent my early career working in outdoor sports. Today, I'm always looking for ways to get kids to love the outdoors as much as I do. With my own kids, this was easy. We spent tons of time traipsing around outside in the remote locations where their dad was working on one outdoor film or another. With my students, I encourage them to think of things they can do outdoors, away from technology. In return, they have encouraged me to think of the outdoors as a place where we might enjoy both nature and technology.

"In my perfect dream world, I would prefer it if kids did not bring their devices to public parks and nature spaces," writer Michele Whiteaker told me, "but I realize it's inevitable. Unfortunately, they really don't have guidelines to help them know how to maintain a healthy balance between enjoying tech and enjoying nature."[38]

Whiteaker, a certified interpretive guide and mom of two, founded her FunOrangeCountyParks.com blog over a decade ago, to promote play and empower families to get outside. A few years ago, she invited me to work with her on a project for the *Children & Nature Network* blog exploring how kids—and adults, for that matter—can find a healthy balance between tech and nature. I loved her idea and readily agreed. We came up with the following guidelines:

- **Research before, share after.** The time to use technology to enhance your nature experience is before you go and after you return. Whiteaker calls this strategy "bookending." It's okay to make some time and space to snap a few photos while you're out, but otherwise, replace that selfie stick with a walking stick, put your smartphone in your pocket, and be *present* in your nature experience.
- **Let why be your guide.** Always ask yourself if you *need* to be connected. For instance, are you blogging to inspire others? Keeping a nature photo album? Telling a story? Doing research? "Collecting"

flora and fauna through photographs? Navigating your way around? If the answer to these types of questions is no, then put away your tech and enjoy the moment.

- **Don't be distracted.** Ask yourself: Is your tech helping you see things, or is it making you miss the moment? If your goal is time in nature, then give nature 100 percent of your attention. A few years ago, an entire class missed the breaching of a whale because they were all on their phones, and another class almost walked into a deer right in front of them because they were distracted by their devices. Don't let yourself miss special moments like these.

- **An hour away is more than okay.** Always, always, always leave time for enjoyment and the purity of the moment. Don't let the constant beeping of text messages, tweets, and waiting Snaps interfere. They will be there later. As you get out more, you'll get better at this.

- **Turn off the sound and look around.** Part of the nature experience is being silent, so you can enjoy the sounds of the wild. No one wants to miss this because of the click, click, click of texting or taking photos. Nature is a sacred place to those who are enjoying it and to the wildlife that calls it home. Do your best not to interrupt this experience.

- **Tech is not terrible, but how you use it may be.** Technology is often vilified and placed into opposition with nature experiences, but tech *can* be a handy tool. Use it for identification, research, or the way you would use a field guide to enhance your outdoor experience. But remember that you don't have to know the name of something to enjoy it. And in case you get lost or run into trouble, having a phone handy is a good idea.

- **Don't trample the woods to share your goods.** A graffiti artist once defaced a rock formation in a national park to share his work on Instagram, while ex–Boy Scout leaders knocked over an ancient rock formation to shoot a video.[39] Getting that one-of-a-kind shot to share with "friends" doesn't mean you should trample or deface natural resources to get it. Don't get carried away just to share your experience with others, like the hiker who fell forty feet to his death while taking a selfie at a waterfall.[40] No shot is worth losing a life.

- **Nature is its own best teacher.** The intrinsic value of nature emerges when we can experience it for what it is. When you see something occur in nature that you've never seen before and may never see again (like the scene in New Zealand that I described at the beginning of this chapter), you've just experienced a dose of what Richard Louv, author of *Last Child in the Woods*, calls "Vitamin N."[41] Louv claims that Vitamin N helps us navigate struggles and makes us healthier, smarter, and happier.

CYBER CIVICS MOMENTS

It's inevitable that kids will want to spend time with their screens. Lots of time, if you let them. That's why it's vital to help them learn how to maintain a healthy balance between screen time and everything else that life has to offer. They might need to be reminded what offline life has to offer. Or they might need help combining their two lives, as in the tech/nature example above. But kids are smart and adaptable, and even if they resist at first, they will be grateful for your help in the end. I promise. Remember, it's all about balance—finding it and maintaining it. I hope these activities will help your family achieve this balance.

Make an Offline-Life List

Many kids today find their most pleasurable experiences online, and that's too bad because the real world offers lots of pleasurable experiences too. Dr. David Greenfield helps his own patients reconnect with offline life's pleasures by having them write down one hundred things they can do without a screen. Even though many find this activity challenging initially, once they get going it becomes easier, and their lists become road maps, full of real-time activities to choose from when the urge to plug in hits.

This is a great activity for families to do together. The goal is to make a list you can refer to when your children inevitably tell you they have *nothing* to do. (This list will be useful for the next activity as well.) Here's how to create your family's list:

1. Get a large piece of blank white paper. Write "100 Non-Screen Activities" at the top. Together with your children, think of all the things

you can do as a family, or that they can do alone, that do not involve a screen. Your family could go to the park, the beach, or the zoo. Your children could paint, draw, skateboard, or hike. (These activities will vary according to each child's age and interests.) They could write a letter to Grandma, make dinner with you, or walk the dog. The point is to come up with one hundred ideas and write them down.

2. Post this list in a prominent place in your house. Encourage your children to refer to it when they're tempted to pick up a device, or when they've been online too long. You also can refer to it when you find yourself doing something like scrolling mindlessly through your Facebook feed. Use the list to inspire your family to do fun, non-screen activities together and alone. Your kids may even find these new offline experiences so pleasurable and dopamine-inducing that they end up craving a good hike over a game of *Fortnite*. Who knows?

Weigh In

It is surprising how all the moments spent online—checking text messages, listening to podcasts, getting directions, looking at social media—add up. This activity will help your children (and you) *see* their digital diets. Getting a clear picture of how they spend their time—online and offline—helps kids discover how healthy, or unhealthy, their diets may be. You can "weigh in" by completing the following steps:

1. Select a typical weekend day, and have your children write down *everything* they do, from the time they wake up until the moment they go to sleep. (You should do this, too!) Remind them to notice what they do when they first wake up. (Ask, "Do you grab your phone and check for text messages?") Tell them to think about what they do in the car. (Ask, "Do you listen to music on a device? Check social media?") During dinner, remind them to notice where they place their attention. (Ask, "Are you watching TV? Playing a video game?")

2. Next, have your children sort all their activities into categories. Make this easy by suggesting they use the following categories to organize their data regarding where they spent their time:

- On a phone
- Watching television
- On a computer
- On an iPad, Kindle, e-reader
- On a video-game player
- Engaged in outdoor activities
- Sleeping or eating
- Other activities

3. Have your children add up the time in each category, and if they are ten or older, show them how to convert that data into a chart (a bar chart or pie chart works well). This is a terrific math skill! The result will help them visualize how their time was spent.
4. After you've analyzed this data, talk about it! Discuss their tech-life balance. (Ask, "Did you spend more time with digital media than you expected? Less time? What would you change?") Explain how technology is designed to capture and hold our attention. You'd be surprised at how kids respond to this information. No kid wants to be manipulated, whether by a parent, teacher, or device. They like having agency over their time, online and offline. Finally, remember to be nonjudgmental. Approach this as a scientific exploration, rather than an opportunity to give a lecture. Make decisions together about how they might improve their digital diets going forward.

Take the Unplug Challenge

By now, the purpose of unplugging should be obvious. Unless your children (and you) experience what it's like not to be plugged in 24/7, they won't know or remember what they're missing, or learn that they can survive. Taking this challenge may even help them (and you) discover things they like to do that have nothing to do with a screen. Anything could happen.

1. Challenge your children to give up all digital media for twenty-four hours. This includes smartphones, computers, tablets, television, games, etc. They should try to survive a full day without looking at a screen at home, school, or a friend's house.

2. Have your children keep track of all the non-screen activities they engage in during this twenty-four-hour period. If they need help thinking of non-screen activities to do, have them refer to the offline-life list they made during the activity above. They should also jot down all the challenges they face and opportunities presented by this activity.

3. Talk about the activity. Ask questions like the following: Was it difficult? Easy? What did you miss the most? The least? What did you learn? Would you do it again? What, if anything, will you change about your screen time in the future?

As Joni Siani told me, "We forget that today's kids have been totally socialized in a digital world. They really need opportunities to compare and contrast plugged-in and unplugged life, and maybe they'll like being unplugged better. The second a college kid says, 'Hey, talking is cooler than texting!' the thirteen-year-olds will want to be just like them, and next so will the fifty-year-olds. Now wouldn't that be something?"[42]

Chapter 5

Relationships

●

I love the feeling of having all my friends in my pocket.

—SEVENTH-GRADE STUDENT

"**M**s. Graber, we have a problem." This is how Journey School's sixth-grade teacher greeted me one Monday morning when I arrived to teach her class. "We had a cyberbullying incident over the weekend," she told me. "I'm hoping you will talk to the students about it during their lesson today."

"Dang," I thought to myself. That day we were scheduled to begin a five-lesson unit called "Cyberbullying and Digital Drama." I'd been looking forward to guiding her students through sequential activities that would help them identify online cruelty and give them strategies they could use if and when they encountered it. Now it appeared I'd be starting these lessons a day too late.

Here's what happened: A student in the class had opened a "fake" Instagram account. Kids call this a "Finsta" or "Finstagram," a combination of the words "fake" and "Instagram." It is not uncommon for kids to open fake social media accounts, in addition to "real" ones, to have a place to post and comment freely, unconstrained by the negative impact their activities might have upon their digital reputations. Eventually, their "friends"—online and offline—identify the owners of these fake accounts, but that doesn't stop kids from trying to be anonymous online. In this case, students had already figured out that the fake account's owner was someone in their class, and through that account had posted something mean and inappropriate on another kid's feed.

After being apprised of the situation, I took a deep breath, entered the classroom, and found a somber group of students. They confirmed what their teacher had told me—someone had cyberbullied a girl named Rosa,

95

and she had evidence to prove it. Rosa, a smart, confident preteen who any-one would think twice about bullying online or offline, told me that she had heeded advice I'd given the class a few weeks earlier. She'd taken a screen-shot of the evidence and even sent it to Instagram. Instagram, she reported with indignation, had not responded to her complaint. Then she asked me if I would like to see the evidence.

Bracing myself for what I imagined I was about to view, I said yes. Here is what she showed me:

Rosa is 🔥🔥🔥

Struggling to maintain a straight face, I explained to the class why this post, in which Rosa was being called "hot" (or "lit" as kids would say), falls short of "cyberbullying" (which, they were about to learn, is identifiable by these characteristics—it's *online, intentional, repeated,* and *harmful*). Even if the post felt hurtful to Rosa, I explained, chances are that was not the send-er's intent. Additionally, I told them that Instagram would not view this as "cyberbullying." Its terms of use state that users must not "defame, stalk, bully, abuse, harass, threaten, impersonate, or intimidate" one another.[1] Ins-tagram doesn't intervene when users comment on one another's "hotness."

The students seemed satisfied with my explanations, and I was able to start the day's lesson—"What Is Cyberbullying?"—with this incident pro-viding the perfect introduction.

But that's not the end of this story. The next week when I arrived to teach the same class, someone else was waiting for me at the door. This time it was a student named George. One of the smallest boys in the class, George had one of the biggest personalities and typically needed constant reminding to keep still or be quiet. Yet on this day he was subdued. "Ms. Graber," he asked in a hushed voice, "may I have a word with you in private?" I told him he could as we had a few free moments before class.

"I'm the one who opened the fake account on Instagram."

Embarrassed, he looked down at his feet and continued, "You see, I sort of like Rosa and was embarrassed to tell her in person."

Once again, I found myself desperately trying to maintain my compo-sure. I thanked George for trusting me with his secret, but also warned him it was likely his classmates would find out he had opened the fake account because "nothing online stays private for long."

"I know, they're already figuring it out," he said. "It was stupid. I won't do it again."

REAL PEOPLE, REAL FEELINGS

In addition to its excellent entertainment value, this incident provided three important lessons:

1. Cyberbullying is a serious digital-age issue (which we'll address in this chapter), yet the term is sometimes used too broadly. There's a difference between actual cyberbullying (remember, it's *online, intentional, repeated,* and *harmful*), digital drama ("mean" online behavior that falls short of *harmful*), old-fashioned teasing, and miscommunication. Consider a sleepover photo that lands on Instagram. To a child not invited to the event, this image might scream, "You got left out!" While this might *feel* like cyberbullying to the left-out child (or sometimes even to the parents of the left-out child), it would be inaccurate to label it as such. Even worse, it might be unfair to call the child who posted the photo a bully. All kids make mistakes, and labels can stick. It's important to remember that every child is different and how he responds to online cruelty, real or imagined, is unique to that child. Complicated? You bet.
2. Making and maintaining peer relationships has always been a tricky business. Today this developmental task is even *more* challenging, as it's taking place in an environment devoid of social cues, facial expressions, or adult role models to provide guidance.
3. Finally, and most importantly, the online activities of digital kids *always* provide teachable moments ideal for addressing all of the above, without being preachy or pedantic.

When George shared the secret of his crush with me, I was, coincidentally, about to teach his class a lesson called "Real People, Real Feelings." During our hour together, we explored how the internet provides ample opportunities for people to hide behind avatars, screen names, and even fake accounts. Psychologists call this *online disinhibition,* which is the "loosening (or complete abandonment) of social restrictions and inhibitions that would otherwise be present in normal face-to-face interactions."[2] George and his classmates learned that because digital media leaves out many of the real-life social cues and facial expressions that prompt us to know how someone is feeling, it's easy to forget that real people—with real feelings—lie behind all online interactions.

As if by magic, my students' social media lives often align perfectly with whatever I'm about to teach them that day. This serendipity makes our discussions all the more meaningful and memorable. This can happen at home, too! Granted, your children might not be as willing or eager to tell you about posting their innermost feelings on Instagram, but I bet they would tell you about a friend or classmate doing so. The trick is to open the door to discussions about online relationships, and to leave it wide open.

DIGITAL RELATIONSHIPS

What kids love most about social media—that it lets them socialize with others at almost any time of the day or night—is also what most frightens parents. Fear that their children might connect with unsavory characters online is fueled by the media, which is littered with stories about online relationships gone dangerously awry. Here are some headlines I ran across on just one day:

- "Swedish Man Convicted Over 'Online Rape' of Teens Groomed into Performing Webcam Sex Acts"[3]
- "A Fourteen-Year-Old Girl Sexted on Her Crush. She May Have to Register as a Sex Offender"[4]
- "Sutton Teen's Suicide Raises Awareness of Cyberbullying"[5]
- "Reports of Children Being Groomed on the Internet Have Increased Fivefold in Four Years"[6]
- "Top Health Concern for Parents: Bullying, Cyberbullying, and Internet Safety"[7]

Cyberbullying, sexting, online grooming, sextortion, predators, and more. These are the potential risks that make most parents want to take their kids' phones and bury them in the backyard. Thankfully, these are *not* activities most kids engage in when they are online. More commonly, online kids are doing what offline kids have done for eons—they are connecting with their peers.

SOCIALIZING IS THE WORK OF ADOLESCENCE

In 1959, renowned developmental psychologist Erik Erikson wrote, "The adolescent process . . . is conclusively complete only when the individual has subordinated his childhood identifications to a new kind of identification, achieved in absorbing sociability and in competitive apprenticeship with and among his age-mates."[8] To put this in contemporary vernacular, to grow into adults, teens need to socialize with their peers. This essential task of adolescence is called *separation-individuation*. As young teens begin to separate from their families of origin to construct their own unique identities, peer groups become *very* important. "The exploration of who they are in relation to their social environment is a way for youth to figure out where they fit in," explains Dr. Pamela Rutledge.[9]

Rutledge, whom you met in the book's introduction, is a professor of media psychology at Fielding Graduate University. She is also the director of the Media Psychology Research Center and coauthor of *Exploring Positive Psychology: The Science of Happiness and Well-Being* and is sought out regularly by the media to comment on technology's psychological impact. When it comes to how young people use social media, Rutledge is a firm believer that there are many positive benefits. "Social connections help teens develop emotionally and physically," she says.

"We are hardwired to be social animals," explains Rutledge. "How we interact with others and our attention to how others see us . . . that's a biological imperative. Young people have always focused on social activities that help them connect with the world outside their family of origin. Identity formation is a critical task of adolescence and young adulthood so that they have the psychological tools they need to leave the nest and successfully build a life of their own."[10]

While this much about adolescence has not changed, obviously the places where they do this socialization has. Digital media provides ample and easy opportunities for teens to satisfy their biological needs for socialization. It also provides a way for them to satisfy a trio of *other* psychological needs: *social comparison, self-disclosure,* and *impression management.* "While these terms probably strike fear into a parent's heart, there are very positive aspects of each," explains Rutledge. "*Social comparison* is how everyone observes and compares their behavior to others. It allows us to learn social norms and express affiliation. *Self-disclosure* is not always about oversharing; it's actually at the heart of relational closeness. By sharing experiences with friends, we feel closer and more connected to others. And finally, *impression management* is a fancy term for the actions one takes to control one's own image. This might mean highlighting positive traits, minimizing negative ones, or expressing connection with a group."

None of this was "invented by social media," says Rutledge. "Whether it's Facebook, Snapchat, cruising Main Street, or hanging out at the malt shop, people are biologically compelled to explore their social worlds."[11]

While this information doesn't make for captivating headlines, it does explain why it's so darn hard for teens to disconnect from their phones and why—when used safely and in moderation—socializing online might not be such a terrible thing, after all.

COULD SOCIAL MEDIA BE *GOOD* FOR YOUTH?

Snapchat, Instagram, YouTube, Xbox Live, WhatsApp, and so forth. Teen friendships thrive in these communities today. More than nine in ten teens spend time online with their real-life friends, and nearly one-third do so every single day. They are making new friends online, too. Nearly two-thirds report having forged at least one new friendship online.[12] Moreover, 67 percent of teens report that they would feel isolated if they couldn't talk to the their friends via technology.[13]

Research on the impact of all this digital connection is beginning to validate what media psychologists like Rutledge have long suspected:

- A large amount of time online is spent on strengthening existing bonds between friends.[14]
- Social media can help teens understand their friends' feelings.[15]
- Social media contributes to less peer-related loneliness.[16]
- Youth who struggle with their social lives offline can sometimes develop friendships and receive social support online that they are not receiving elsewhere.[17]

- Emerging research is showing an association between social media, increased self-esteem, and the development of social capital (resources available through social connections).[18]
- Media and internet-related activities can improve family relationships, when parents and children watch TV, stream content, play video games, and use educational apps together. They can also stay in touch by texting, using messaging apps, and making video calls.[19]
- The role of social networking in strengthening and maintaining friendships has been reported by over 90 percent of teens using mobile devices in countries as diverse as Egypt, India, Indonesia, Iraq, and Saudi Arabia.[20]

"Contrary to urban mythology," Rutledge adds, "online friendships do not replace offline relationships. For teens, there is no fundamental difference between online and offline in terms of their social lives."[21]

ONLINE GAMES CAN STRENGTHEN FRIENDSHIPS, TOO

It's a rare teen today who has not played a video game. A nationally representative sample of 1,102 young people, ages twelve to seventeen, found that 97 percent play video games. That's 99 percent of boys and 94 percent of girls, with little difference among various racial and ethnic groups and incomes.[22] Online gaming "handles" (the nicknames kids use while playing video games) are one of the first pieces of information that 38 percent of adolescent boys share when they meet someone in real life with whom they'd like to be friends.[23]

Online games are essentially social media sites, because youth are often connecting with existing friends and making new ones while playing massive multiplayer games. Numerous players compete, cooperate, and interact with one another in expansive virtual worlds.

I hear my young students talk about online games often. Actually, make that *constantly*. They describe their gaming friends in such fond and intimate detail that you'd think they lived right next door. But I guess when your friends live on your phone, computer, or gaming device, they feel even closer than a physical neighbor.

Recently during the holidays, I was curious what the most coveted "tech" gifts were among young teens, so I quizzed my classes. Overwhelmingly, they told me they wanted headsets, the "voice-activated kind that let you talk to your friends while gaming." Today over 71 percent of all gamers use headsets so they can converse and work together to solve challenges.[24] "If you watch kids playing games, they are playing together," says Dubit's David Kleeman. "As they play they are not just talking about what's in the game; they are actually talking about what we used to sit around and talk about on the telephone."[25]

Some of the skills kids learn while playing games with friends manifest in better offline relationships. In "The Benefits of Playing Video Games," researchers say that gamers can translate the prosocial skills learned from playing with others to "peer and family relations outside the gaming environment."[26] Another study suggests that kids who play multiplayer games are more likely to have a positive attitude toward people from different cultures because online gaming exposes them to a more diverse group of friends.[27]

These positive findings can't change the fact that many kids today spend too much time playing online games, and for some that's a real problem. In early 2018, the World Health Organization added gaming disorder to its latest draft of the International Classification of Diseases Manual, or ICD-11. "Gaming disorder is characterized by a pattern of persistent or recurrent gaming behavior ('digital gaming' or 'video gaming'), which may be online or offline," according to the ICD-11. "The behavior pattern is of sufficient severity to result in significant impairment in personal, family, social, educational, occupational, or other important areas of functioning."[28]

Several countries outside of the United States have already identified gaming addiction as a major public health issue. The South Korean government introduced a law banning access to games between midnight and 6:00 a.m. for kids under age sixteen. In Japan, gamers receive an alert if they spend too much time playing, and China's Tencent (the leading provider of internet value-added services) limits the hours per day that children can play its most popular games. Many of the parents I speak with in the U.S. believe we should follow suit.

Probably due to my experience with the New Zealand–bound snowboarders, I didn't let my own young kids play video games. But when my oldest daughter reached high school, she was introduced to *Minecraft* by the fifth-grade girl she was tutoring. "I can't believe you didn't let us play games like *Minecraft* when we were young!" she chastised me one evening after a "tutoring" session. "Do you have any idea how much kids learn playing it?" I didn't. But since then I've learned that *Minecraft*, a game where users build their own worlds and experiences, has been lauded for helping children develop spatial reasoning, problem solving, reading, writing, math skills, and more. So while there are *definitely* some valid concerns parents need to be aware of if their kids play online games—particularly when they are young—there are also positive benefits to be had. One of these is the opportunity to nurture friendships made in "real" life. We owe it our kids to know about the benefits *and* to protect them from downsides.

THE DOWNSIDES OF GAMING

One morning Jules, a twelve-year-old boy whose sweet face makes him look barely ten, arrived early to class. I asked him how his weekend was, and he told me he spent most of it playing *GTA* (*Grand Theft Auto*). *GTA* is an M-rated action-adventure video game. That means the Entertainment Software Rating Board has determined it is appropriate for "mature" players ages seventeen and older. In this game, players assume the role of one of three criminals (they can switch back and forth) who complete missions in a fictionalized version of Los Angeles or another fictionalized major city. According to a *GTA* game review on Common Sense Media's website (where you will find helpful reviews on nearly everything kids do online), "Players kill not only fellow gangsters but also police officers and innocent civilians, using both weapons and vehicles while conducting premeditated crimes, including a particularly disturbing scene involving torture. Women are frequently depicted as sexual objects, with a strip club mini-game allowing players to fondle strippers' bodies, which are nude from the waist up."[29]

I didn't know this at the time, so I responded to Jules offhandedly: "Maybe I'll check the game out sometime." He looked at me in abject horror. "Don't do that, Ms. Graber—there is a *lot* of cussing. You wouldn't be able to handle it."

Jules told me that many gamers cuss freely because, they figure, "Who's gonna hear me besides other players?" Plus, they are role-playing. How many violent criminals do you know who apologize politely before shooting someone into oblivion?

According to my young sources, foul language and bullying in video games is often directed at "squeakers," the youngest, newest, and most naive players.

"Yeah, this squeaker started playing *Call of Duty,*" said Ross, another twelve-year-old boy who had joined our conversation that morning, "and everyone was cussing at him and calling him names. I could hear him softly crying, so I taught him how to use his mute button."

While I commended Ross for this act of empathy, I couldn't shake the image of a young child somewhere, crying in front of his screen.

"By the way, what is *Call of Duty?*" I asked Ross.

That's when Troy, a wizened thirteen-year-old, chimed in. "It's a first-person shooter game with lots of violence and gore. I started out gaming on *Call of Duty* a long, long time ago." He told me he was nine years old when he first started playing the game.

"Yeah, I was a squeaker," he said. "I remember the first time I logged on. I said, 'Hi,' and then everyone started cussing and bullying me. I learned all the cuss words I know in the first hour of playing that game."

My morning conversation—a carbon copy of many I've had before and since at all sorts of schools—is the reason many adults hate all video games. But keeping teens from playing them, or talking about them, is an exercise in futility. A smarter approach is to find out *what* they're playing, because for every violent, first-person shooter game, there's a *Minecraft.* So please help your kids find appropriate games, ask who they are talking to, and what they are talking about. Most importantly, be mindful of age guidelines. It's easy to find recommended ages and reviews for nearly every game in the universe by going to Common Sense Media's website. Please don't let it be *your* nine-year-old silently crying in front of a screen.

Social Media: Any website or app that enables users to create content, share content, communicate, or participate in social networking.

DOES TOO MUCH SOCIAL MEDIA CAUSE DEPRESSION?

Yes. No. *Maybe.*

Teen anxiety and depression are on the rise. At least that's what many experts are reporting. Researchers at Columbia University's Mailman School of Public Health and the CUNY Graduate School of Public Health

and Health Policy report that from 2005 to 2015, depression rose significantly among Americans age twelve and older, with the most rapid increases
observed in young people.[30] In her book, Jean Twenge writes that adolescent
self-esteem, life satisfaction, and happiness have plunged since 2012, the
same year smartphone ownership reached the 50 percent mark in the
United States. By drawing upon massive databases, large national surveys
conducted over time that, in total, queried eleven million people, Twenge
makes a compelling case that the smartphone is to blame for this problem.
She extrapolates the following from the data:

> The results could not be clearer: teens who spend more time on screen
> activities are more likely to be unhappy, and those who spend more
> time on nonscreen activities are more likely to be happy. There's not a
> single exception: All screen activities are linked to less happiness, and
> all nonscreen activities are linked to more happiness.[31]

While her argument sounds convincing, some experts have questioned
these findings, primarily because the link Twenge draws between smartphones and teenage angst is *correlational*; that is, the data doesn't *prove* that
smartphones are directly responsible for teenage depression. Other factors
could be at work. It could be that depressed kids are spending more time on
social media (some studies suggest as much) or that nondepressed kids are
spending less time on social media.[32] Other things could be making them
depressed—like gun violence, global warming, college admissions, or the
news in general. Or we could be getting better at reporting and diagnosing
depression and anxiety. Researchers from Harvard who have been studying
youth and technology use for over a decade warn, "No single answer . . . can
be applied to explain the mental health and well-being of an entire
generation."[33]

As Dr. Rutledge points out, most research shows that "social connection
is an antidote to depression, not the cause of it."[34] She suggests it might be
more meaningful to ask teens themselves *why* they feel depressed, so that's
what I did. One thirteen-year-old looked at me quizzically when I asked her,
wondering why I was asking such a ridiculous question. "We're depressed
because we're teens," she told me matter-of-factly. I could almost hear the
"duh" she was too polite to add.

Other teens told me that connecting with their friends online makes
them feel "way less depressed."

"I often turn to my friends on social media when I feel bad," said Kelly, a shy fourteen-year-old. "It makes me feel better."

Although it's hard to dismiss Twenge's findings (believe me, I've tried), what good can come from dwelling on them? Eliminating the smartphone from teen life just ain't gonna happen.

Fortunately, the same data reveals that the happiest teens are those who spend a *small amount* of time on electronic communication activities, *not those who spend no time*.[35] Reducing screen time, not eliminating it, seems to be the best recipe for happy teens, and is a more realistic goal.

THE GOLDILOCKS HYPOTHESIS

In the child's fairy tale *Goldilocks and the Three Bears*, Goldilocks goes for a stroll in the forest and stumbles upon a house where she finds three bowls of porridge. The first one, she discovers, is too hot. The second is too cold. But the third bowl is just right, so she eats it all up. It turns out this fable might apply perfectly to technology.

Researchers Andrew Przybylski and Netta Weinstein speculate that a similar "sweet spot" might exist for how much time teens spend using technology. Their research reveals that screen time may benefit teens' well-being by providing opportunities to develop social connections and skills. Well-being increases as teen screen time increases, *up to a certain point*. After that point, increased screen time is associated with decreased well-being.

Like Goldilocks discovered with her three bears, these researchers discovered that a level of screen time use seems to correlate with mental well-being for youth, and this level differs depending on the day of the week. On weekdays, teens' well-being peaked at about the following:

- One hour and forty minutes of video game play
- One hour fifty-seven minutes of smartphone use
- Three hours and forty-one minutes of watching videos
- Four hours and seventeen minutes of using computers

However, on the weekends, teens could engage in digital activities between twenty-two minutes and two hours thirteen minutes longer than weekdays before demonstrating negative effects.[36]

The researchers also say that not all digital activities are created equal. Some activities help teens build life and social skills, which in turn fosters well-being. Researchers even suggest that some digital activities may *not* be displacing meaningful offline activities that contribute to social development, whereas—hold on for this one—solitary reading just might!

CAN YOU HAVE *TOO* MANY ONLINE "FRIENDS"?

With online friends, is it possible to overdo a good thing? The short answer is *yes*.

The average teen is said to have about three hundred online friends.[37] That number sounds low to me. A quick look at the social media accounts of my kids and their friends reveals a different story. The friend count I more commonly see ranges from three hundred to a thousand or more.

That's an awful lot of relationships for a teen to manage. Science agrees. The number of stable relationships the human brain can maintain is much, much lower: 150.[38]

British anthropologist Robin Dunbar figured that out. Judging from the size of an average human brain, he discovered that the number of people a person could effectively manage in a social group was 150. Any more than that, he postulated, would be too complicated for the brain to handle. Yet young humans juggle this many friends and often many, many more.

When Dunbar was asked if virtual social networks will prove wonderful for friends or will ultimately diminish the number of satisfying relationships one has, he couldn't answer. "This is the big imponderable," he said. "We haven't yet seen an entire generation that's grown up with things like Facebook go through adulthood yet."[39]

LIVING FOR "LIKES"

If I don't get one hundred likes in the first five minutes I put a picture up, I take it down.

—EIGHTH-GRADE STUDENT

When kids, or anyone for that matter, post something to a social media account, they're "speaking" to their large audience of friends and expecting, or hoping, that many will respond in turn, through comments or "likes." These likes—which for youth translate into positive affirmations—influence the kinds of posts teens put up and leave up.

For many teens, monitoring their social media feeds becomes a time-consuming task that includes tracking their likes. In 2015, Penn State University researchers found that most teens post a lot of photos but quickly delete them if they do not immediately receive a boatload of likes.[40] In another study, teens explicitly stated that a minimum threshold of likes was needed to convey popularity on Instagram. That threshold ranged from thirty to ninety in total.[41] Interestingly, studies indicate that, on average, males need fifty-nine likes on an Instagram post to "feel happy," whereas females only need forty-five.[42]

Here's something else that might surprise you—adults post more photos on Instagram than teens do.[43] This startling fact holds true in my own family. My husband, a cinematographer who posts beautiful photos on Instagram, has been chastised more than once by our teenage daughter for overposting! Today he tries to stick to the "one-a-day" rule she imposed on him.

How this quest for validation and positive affirmation from peers is affecting the well-being of youth (and adults) is a question just beginning to be answered. A Children's Commission for England study discovered that while younger children felt good when they received likes or comments from friends, at about Year 7 (early middle school), they start becoming overly dependent upon this affirmation.[44]

This is when kids start using techniques that will help them garner a high number of likes. What are some of these techniques? According to kids I've queried, they range anywhere from "liking and commenting a lot on their friends' posts," to "using the right hashtag," "tagging the right friends," "asking your friends to like and comment on your posts," and, most importantly, "choosing the right time to post." Kids say that "posting right before bedtime" is the "perfect" time to collect a lot of likes.

Kids have also told me it's important to "earn" your likes and followers fairly. Purchasing followers (yes, that's a thing) in the hopes of getting more likes makes users appear "desperate" (kids can "absolutely tell" when followers have been purchased). Using too many hashtags is "lame" as well. Our daughter advised my husband that using two hashtags per post was "just right." And the worst social media offense of all? Liking your own photos. That's akin to committing social media suicide!

ANXIETY AND FOMO

Many parents are concerned about the anxiety all this social media management must be causing in their kids. This, it turns out, is a valid concern. A 2017 survey of almost 1,500 teens and young adults found Instagram (along with Snapchat, Facebook, and Twitter) to be associated with high levels of depression, bullying, and FOMO, the "fear of missing out." Instagram, where personal photos or selfies (often carefully staged or touched up) rule, was the worst social media network for mental health and well-being. A teen respondent to the survey wrote, "Instagram easily makes girls and women feel as if their bodies aren't good enough, as people add filters and edit their pictures in order for them to look 'perfect.'"[45]

According to the #StatusOfMind survey, published by the United Kingdom's Royal Society for Public Health, "Seeing friends constantly on holiday or enjoying nights out can make young people feel like they are missing out while others enjoy life. These feelings can promote a 'compare and despair' attitude in young people. Individuals may view heavily photoshopped, edited, or staged photographs and videos and compare them to their seemingly mundane lives."[46]

But researchers found some benefits from social media use, too. All five networks surveyed—Instagram, Snapchat, YouTube, Twitter, and Facebook—received positive scores for self-identity, self-expression, community building, and emotional support. YouTube got high marks for providing access to trustworthy information, while Facebook was lauded for providing "groups" or "pages" where youth could surround themselves with like-minded friends. This was especially beneficial to the well-being of LGBTQ+ youth and those who belong to ethnic minorities, two populations that find it challenging to find like-minded peers in their offline communities.

ONCE AGAIN, AGE MATTERS

How children use and respond to social media is highly dependent upon their ages. While younger children use media in "playful, creative ways—often to play games"—this lighthearted attitude changes abruptly by middle school. As exposure to peers via social media ramps up, their well-being reaches a "cliff edge," according to a Children's Commission for England report. That's when kids need "lessons around digital literacy and online resilience," because "lessons around online safety learned at younger ages are insufficient."[47]

Amen to that! I heartily agree that kids at this stage need help with the difficult task of managing their online social lives. Talking with middle schoolers about their online lives gives them a chance to notice the ridiculousness of counting likes or posting at the right hour of the night. Often, they independently conclude, "Gosh, maybe it's really not worth all the trouble." Whether this revelation lasts more than a week or two is hard to say. But I do know this: It's unlikely kids are going to step back and even consider the possibility, unless adults provide the time and opportunity for them to do so.

My friend Liz Repking, founder and CEO of Cyber Safety Consulting, regularly visits schools to talk to kids about their digital lives, and she has three children of her own. "What really gets me is how deeply kids are craving help, and knowledge, and direction when it comes to all this stuff," says Repking. "They are craving it so, so deeply. We have to give these kids the help they need."[48]

Repking is right. Kids do need our help, especially to learn how to avoid the big risks that come with making and maintaining relationships online. So let's look at the big two they need our help with: sexting and cyberbullying.

SEXTING

Before Peter Kelley began helping me with Cyber Civics, he was an English teacher at a large public high school in Southern California. When we started working together in 2016, he told me a story that still haunts me.

At Kelly's school there was a popular, outgoing cheerleader named Carrie, who was a junior at the time of this story. Carrie appeared to have everything going for her. That is, until she made one terrible mistake. While in a committed relationship with a boy from the same school, she and the boy shot a sex video of themselves. Shortly after doing so, they broke up. Then, for whatever reason, or for no reason at all, the boy shared the video online with some friends, who shared it with their friends, and so on. Kelley told me that, before long, "There was not a single person at the school who had not seen or at least knew about that sex video."[49]

Because of her mistake, Carrie was kicked off the cheerleading squad. Her cheerleading friends stopped hanging out with her, and soon other students began pointing or laughing at her when she passed by. According to Kelley, who was also the school's tennis coach, "She tried everything to make new friends and get back into school life, even trying out for the tennis team without any prior experience. Of course, in high school it's hard to earn a position in a sport you've never played before, so she didn't make the team. She had a hard time finding any place to fit in."

"I watched this super-outgoing, confident girl turn into a sad, fearful one," Kelley told me. "It was heartbreaking to watch. It seemed like a high price to pay for one mistake."

That incident helped Kelley decide to quit his teaching job, and start working with me, though he said, "I'm sorry I didn't stick around long enough to see what ultimately happened with this girl." But before he quit, he asked the students in one of his English classes to raise their hands if they thought they would have benefited from lessons in digital literacy during middle school.

"Every hand went up," he said.[50]

WHAT EXACTLY IS SEXTING?

Sexting is the sending, receiving, or forwarding of any sexually explicit message, photograph, or image between digital devices (most commonly cell phones). Sending "sexts" of people under the age of eighteen, even between two teenagers in a relationship, is illegal in most states.

Teens are seldom aware of sexting's full definition and, more concerningly, its consequences. Every year when I deliver lessons on sexting to eighth-grade students and explain that if they create and share sexually explicit images of themselves, they are technically producing, distributing, or possessing child pornography, they are surprised, shocked even. I tell them they could get into as much trouble for *receiving* an unsolicited sext as for *sending* one. You should see their faces as they mentally calculate who, among their hundreds, sometimes thousands, of online "friends" might send them such a thing.

Most schools today don't give their students the courtesy of such lessons, even though the consequences for getting caught sexting are severe. In California, where I live, "individuals who distribute, possess, or produce a sexually explicit image of a minor could be charged under the State's child pornography statutes. If the individual is tried as an adult and is convicted, they could receive up to six years in jail and will generally be required to register as a sex offender."[51]

In states that have not enacted specific laws that address sexting by minors (which is most states), the possession of sexually explicit material portraying minors falls under their existing child pornography laws.

I hope that seems as unfair to you as it does to me.

My assistant, Anna, is a bright college student who helped me while I was writing this book. One day I asked her if she had ever been taught anything about sexting when she was in middle or high school. "No, never," she told me. "I had no idea you could get into as much trouble for receiving a sext as sending one. I learned about that from Piper, and it was really a surprise!" Piper is my daughter. She was a student in the first series of Cyber Civics classes I taught and thus had to suffer the embarrassment of her mother explaining sexting to her and her classmates when she was in eighth grade. Her discomfort aside, I was happy to hear that this lesson had spread beyond the walls of our small classroom.

WHO'S SEXTING?

In early 2018, a comprehensive study on teen sexting published in the *Journal of the American Medical Association* (*JAMA*) revealed that one in four teenagers reports having received a sext and one in seven reports having sent one. Considering the severity of getting caught for such an offense, these findings are startling.

The researchers who conducted this study analyzed a significant amount of data—thirty-nine previous studies with 110,000 participants, split evenly between girls and boys between the ages of eleven and eighteen. They discovered that the number of kids involved in sexting has risen significantly in recent years, due to the number of kids who have their own phones today. It's not just boys asking girls for "nudes" either. Researchers found no significant difference between the sexes pertaining to either sending or receiving sexting messages. The data also revealed that teens are more likely to send and receive sexts with each year of increasing age, a conclusion that "lends credence to the notion that youth sexting may be an emerging, and potentially normal, component of sexual behavior and development."[52]

This data does not surprise Dr. Michelle Drouin. "I would say sexting is a part of the normative teenage, early adulthood experience now," she told me. "So it is very, very common to send some type of sexually explicit message. That could be a text-only message. It could be a photo or video message. More than half of my young adult students have sent this type of message. And by the time they hit young adulthood, more than half have sent sexually explicit pictures."[53]

Dr. Drouin, a developmental psychologist, is a professor of psychology at Purdue University Fort Wayne. She is also an internationally recognized speaker who travels extensively to deliver talks on technology and relationships, including social media and sexting. There is comfort in talking with Drouin about sexting because she views it matter-of-factly and in the context of normal teenage behavior, and I think that's important. While the media and the laws that currently cover sexting (child pornography laws) sometimes paint it as a dangerous and illegal act, if you strip away the hysteria and look at it from a developmental viewpoint, it becomes something entirely different.

"It's not a bad kid thing," explains Drouin. "Rather, what you have is a perfect storm of budding sexuality combined with a child's first freedom on their own technological device. On top of all that, this budding sexuality happens well before the prefrontal cortex—the part of the brain responsible for impulse control—is fully developed. Young teens still have quite a bit of brain development to go in terms of the ability to think about consequences. So kids often send sext messages without thinking."[54]

They also don't think they'll get caught. But for those few unlucky ones who do, the consequences can be devastating, as in these cases:

- Seven students in Iowa's Storm Lake School District, ranging from fifteen to seventeen years old, faced criminal charges for sharing phone text messages that contained nude photos. Three faced felony charges, while another four faced serious misdemeanor charges.[55]

- A seventeen-year-old star football player in Michigan who exchanged nude photos with his sixteen-year-old girlfriend was charged with two counts of second-degree sexual exploitation and three counts of third-degree exploitation. If convicted, he could spend ten years behind bars and be forced to register as a sex offender. As he awaited trial, he was dropped from his high school football team. His girlfriend opted for a plea deal and was sentenced to one year of probation without access to a cell phone, had to enroll in a class on making smarter life decisions, and had to pay a $200 fine.[56]

- Twenty high-school students in Long Island, New York, were suspended for up to five days for simply receiving or forwarding a sex video that was sent to them via a group text. Suspended students included those who received the video and didn't even know what it was.[57]

Several of the experts I spoke to while writing this book told me sexting has become one of the most serious problems at the schools they work with. Even teens who have not engaged in sexting themselves either know or have heard of a friend who's sent, been asked for, or has received a sexually explicit message via electronic device. That's what I hear, too. In the words of one of my students, "In high school, *everyone* does it." Or at least that's what everyone *thinks*.

It doesn't appear that the number of kids who engage in sexting is likely to decrease, especially without education as to its possible consequences. As Jeff Temple, one of the researchers of the *JAMA* study, told the *Washington Post*, "As tweens and kid smartphone ownership gets younger and younger, we are going to see an increase in the number of teens who are sexting."[58]

WHAT TO TELL KIDS ABOUT SEXTING

When I first started teaching Cyber Civics, I struggled to find the right advice to give students about sexting. After all, it would have to be the exact opposite of what I'd told them about nearly every other online danger: "Take a screenshot of the evidence." Obviously, encouraging students to keep child pornography on their phones was not the best guidance. Fortunately, I found the advice I'd been searching for, in language students would understand, in a blog post written by Dr. Justin Patchin of the

Cyberbullying Research Center (more about this organization in a moment). I share this excerpt with students and teachers today:

If you do receive [a sext] image, odds are that it was sent by a good friend (or a boyfriend or girlfriend). As a result, you probably don't want to get this person into too much trouble, but you also know that peddling in these kinds of pictures is probably not going to lead to great things in life. If you think about it, it is highly inappropriate, morally wrong, and potentially illegal. So what do you do? Most adults might advise you to "tell an adult you trust." This is generally good advice for a lot of problems you run into. However, in the case of a naked photo of an underaged youth, this can be devastating for all involved. If you show the image to a teacher, he or she is likely required by law to report it to the police. Teachers who don't can lose their teaching license and/or be fired. If they don't know what to do and seek guidance from a fellow teacher, they could get into even more trouble. If you give the teacher your cell phone with the nude image, and he or she shows another teacher, both teachers (and you) could be charged with "possession" of child pornography, since they had possession of your phone. That's because the police often treat these images as child pornography—irrespective of the sender's intent or the relationship of those involved. This means that if you took the picture, you can be charged with the "creation of child pornography." If you send or forward the pic, you can be charged with "distribution of child pornography." If you keep it on your phone, you can be charged with "possession of child pornography." In some cases, you could even end up on state sex offender registries.

My advice to teens who receive a nude or seminude image of a classmate is simple: Immediately delete it. Don't tell anyone about it. If there is an investigation, and someone asks if you received the image, you should tell them yes, but that you immediately deleted it. If necessary, they can get your cell phone records from your service provider and search your phone's contents, which will show that you deleted it within seconds of receiving it. This is the best situation for you. Some adults aren't going to like this advice because they want to be "in the know" to attempt to deal with the problem, but I think this is the only safe advice I can offer youth at this point.[59]

CYBERBULLYING

Although this chapter begins with a lighthearted anecdote about a situation mischaracterized as "cyberbullying," it's important to acknowledge that *actual* cyberbullying is a serious, unsolved, digital-age problem. If you want a comprehensive education on cyberbullying—a wise expenditure of time for any parent with a connected kid—I strongly urge you to visit the Cyberbullying Research Center (https://cyberbullying.org), founded by Dr. Sameer Hinduja and Dr. Justin Patchin. The site, launched while the pair was studying cyberbullying in graduate school at Michigan State, provides a wealth of reliable research and other resources about cyberbullying prevention and response.

Hinduja defines cyberbullying as "willful and repeated harm inflicted through the use of computers, cell phones, and other electronic devices," which aligns with the four indicators I give students: It's *online, intentional, repeated,* and *harmful.*[60] In terms of prevalence, he says that based on their nationally representative data of U.S. youth between the ages of twelve and seventeen:

- Seventy-three percent of students reported that they had been bullied at school at some point in their lifetime (44 percent said it happened in the last thirty days).
- Thirty-four percent of students had experienced cyberbullying in their lifetime (17 percent within the last thirty days).

Each year, I ask students to raise their hands if they have ever been bullied. About half raise their hands. Then I ask if they *know* anyone who has ever been bullied. Every kid raises a hand at this question. Every kid.

By any account, the number of kids who have experienced or witnessed bullying is alarming. The fact that, according to Hinduja's research, nearly three out of four kids are being bullied in person at school—a problem that has existed since there was school—is bad enough. But when you realize that new technologies enable a whole new type of cruelty, cyberbullying, and that one out of three kids has experienced it, that should be a wake-up call for all of us. It's often the same kids who endure both types of bullying. A Cyberbullying Research Center project discovered that 42.4 percent of cyberbullying victims were also victims of offline bullying.

It is important to note that while lots of kids have experienced or witnessed cruelty online, lots of kids have experienced or witnessed kindness, too. A report from the Pew Research Center finds that "69 percent of social media-using teens think that peers are mostly kind to each other on social network sites."[61] Proving, yet again, that kids' digital lives are confusing and complicated.

This positive data should not let us off the hook. No words can express the anguish in the eyes of a bullied child. We must solve this problem.

UNDERSTANDING CYBERBULLYING

While in-person bullying remains more prevalent than cyberbullying, some characteristics of cyberbullying make it particularly intense:

1. **There is no delete button online.** Targets often live with the constant reminder of cruelty when it's online. Even if they block the sender or delete the evidence from their own devices, other kids may see, save, or share it.
2. **It's constant.** While kids can walk away from physical bullying, there is no hiding from cyberbullying when they go home. Most kids carry their devices around 24/7.
3. **It's public.** *Everyone* sees bullying when its online.

This last factor—that cyberbullying is visible to many—can work in the target's favor! Imagine if every young "bystander" (someone who witnesses online cruelty) learned how to be an "upstander" (someone who *does* something about online cruelty). This could go a long way toward ending cyberbullying. Please see the activity at the end of this chapter that shows you how to teach your children to be upstanders.

EVERY CHILD IS DIFFERENT

There is no way of knowing how a child on the receiving end of cruelty—the target—will react. Some kids are resilient, while others are more sensitive to cruelty of any kind. As I write these words, stories of young children who have tragically taken their own lives (the digital-age name for this is *bully-cide*) litter the internet:

- Twelve-year-old Gabriella Green of Panama City Beach, Florida, committed suicide after enduring cyberbullying from two twelve-year-old classmates.[62]
- Ten-year-old Ashawnty Davis hung herself after a video of her fighting another girl was posted to the social media site Musical.ly.[63]
- Twelve-year-old Rebecca Sedwick of Lakeland, Florida, jumped to her death, after she had been bullied online by two teens, a twelve-year-old and a fourteen-year-old.[64]

Each of these tragic incidents, equal in their heartbreak, share another commonality. The targets and most of the perpetrators are twelve years of age or younger—technically too young to have accounts on the social media sites where most of the bullying took place. Respecting the minimum age requirements of social media sites seems like a painfully obvious, and simple, solution to at least reducing online cruelty.

I asked Ross Ellis about this. She is the passionate founder and CEO of STOMP Out Bullying,™ the leading national nonprofit dedicated to reducing and preventing bullying, cyberbullying, and cruelty of all kinds. Her website is another one you must visit (https://www.stompoutbullying.org), because in addition to providing excellent resources about cyberbullying and other types of cruelty, it offers a live HelpChat line, staffed by counselors trained to assist young people being bullied online.

"I'm always surprised when parents let a young child open a social media account because 'all their friends have one,' or when they hand their young child a $600 phone with every app on it, yet don't teach them the responsible digital citizenship that will keep them safe," Ellis told me. "It is so important to talk to kids early about online bullying. Even seven-year-olds today know about suicide."[65]

WHAT CAN PARENTS DO?

In addition to being mindful of age restrictions and teaching device responsibility, what can parents do to protect their children from cyberbullying? "First and foremost, parents must make sure their children feel safe," advises

Hinduja. Sadly, "nearly two-thirds (64 percent) of the students who experienced cyberbullying stated that it really affected their ability to learn and feel safe at school," he says.[66] Parents must be their children's advocates. They must take time to talk and listen. And they must inform their schools when and if their children are involved in an incident.

Parents can also help their children collect evidence when and if online cruelty occurs (find out how to do this at the end of this chapter) and help their children get this evidence into the right hands—the school, the social media network, gaming site, service provider, or whatever other entity might be involved.

Finally, parents should ask their children's schools if and how they teach bullying and cyberbullying prevention. Every school must make time for this.

WHEN PREDATORS SEEK ONLINE RELATIONSHIPS WITH KIDS

In late 2016, I began fielding questions from parents about a new app called Musical.ly. Launched in 2014 by a Shanghai-based company, Musical.ly (now called TikTok) amassed two hundred million registered users almost overnight, and many of these were kids—very young kids.[67] They love the app because it lets them make short videos in which they lip-sync and dance to popular songs. Think karaoke meets YouTube. Then they post their creations, sit back, and wait to be showered with hearts. What's not to love?

According to social media advertising agency executive Gary Vaynerchuck, "I would say that Snapchat and Instagram, they skew a little bit young." He adds that "with Musical.ly, you're talking about first, second, third grade."[68]

That's what I was hearing from parents, too. Many were visibly distraught as they recounted stories of their young kids talking them into letting them download Musical.ly, convincing them it was "just a music app." One mom told me, "I figured, 'What's the harm?' Next thing I know, my daughter has 2,200 followers. That freaked me out, so I tried to delete her account and discovered it was impossible to do."

The social nature of this app encourages users, many too young to know better, to share personal and identifying information with strangers. When I downloaded the app, it was relentless in its pursuit of my age, phone number, contacts, email address, and more. The app also lets users perform for and connect with strangers, and sometimes these strangers are not who they appear to be.

Here's an example: An Australian mother let her nine-year-old daughter, Lilly, download Musical.ly. Lilly was a fan of a U.S. teen dance star named JoJo Siwa, who starred in the reality show *Dance Moms*. Understandably, Lilly was beside herself with joy when she received what she thought was a message from JoJo on the app.

This concerned her mom. Pretending to be Lilly, she responded to a message from "JoJo" that asked what she was doing and what she was wearing. After Lilly's mom answered that she was in her room dancing in her pajamas, "JoJo" asked her to send a video "without clothes, showing off your body."

Lilly's mom, still pretending to be Lilly, said she might get in trouble for doing this. So "JoJo" responded, "Delete it afterward, silly."

Following this disturbing exchange, Lilly's mother contacted the parents of one of Lilly's friends, only to hear that child had been contacted by "JoJo," too. The friend had received a message asking her to send a video of herself removing her underwear.

Lilly's mom reported this incident to the Australian Federal Police (AFP) and learned that predators commonly use fake celebrity profiles to form online relationships with children. In one year alone, the AFP received more than nine thousand reports related to child exploitation, including online grooming.[69]

CYBER CIVICS MOMENTS
Have "The Talk" (About Sexting)

As uncomfortable as it might be, you *must* talk to your children about sexting. If you think your children are too young to discuss sexting, then they are definitely too young to own a connected device with a camera. Here are your talking points:

- **Define sexting.** Don't assume your children know what sexting is. Tell them it is the *sending, receiving,* or *forwarding* of sexually explicit or sexually suggestive images, messages, or video via a cell phone or the internet. Don't be surprised when they ask you to define "sexually suggestive." Explain that sending such images of or between minors is a crime in most states. (Look up the laws in your own state here and share them with your child: https:// cyberbullying.org/state-sexting-laws). These examples will help your children understand what kinds of things might be categorized as "sexting":

Nude or nearly nude selfies
Videos showing nudity or sex acts
Text messages that propose sex or refer to sexual acts

- **Ignore and don't ask.** Tell your children that if anyone ever asks them for a sexually explicit image, their answer is no. Explain that they should never, under any circumstances, ask for one either.
- **Delete and don't repeat.** If someone sends your children a sexually explicit image, tell them to immediately delete it. Never, under any circumstances, should they share a sexually explicit image with others, no matter how tempting it may be to do so.
- **Speak up.** Tell your children to speak up if they know or hear that a sexually explicit image of someone is being circulated. They should tell the person whose image it is first, because they would want someone to tell them, right?
- **Think twice before hitting send.** Explain to your children, early and often, that the moment an image or message is sent via electronic device, it is no longer in their control. It can never be taken back. It will likely spread beyond the person who was meant to see it.
- **Share a cautionary tale.** The easiest way to reinforce these points is through a cautionary tale, which are easy to find online. If you search "sexting" and "high school," you will have abundant sorrowful tales to share. Select stories that are appropriate for your children to hear. Don't preach, but ask leading questions, such as, "What did you think about this story?" and "What would you do if you were in this situation?"

Cultivate Kindness

The most effective way to curb cyberbullying is to stop it before it starts. This is how cultivating empathy can help.

This simple activity is an extension of one recommended in Chapter 2, "Tell Stories." Even as children move through elementary school and beyond, they will crave good stories and will learn a lot more from a captivating tale than a boring lecture. Journey School's cyberbullying prevention program centers around rich stories about heroes, honorable people, role models, and other real-life upstanders. Hinduja says he and Patchin are fans of stories, too, because they "cultivate empathy among youth to make sure they can emotionally understand the harm they can inflict with some of their actions online."[70] Here are some of the books they recommend: *El Deafo, Wonder, Same Sun Here, Inside Out and Back Again, Night* (by Elie Wiesel), *Where the Red Fern Grows,* and *Out of My Mind.*

Utilize Common Sense Media's rating system to find out what books and other media are appropriate for your children: https://www.commonsensemedia.org/reviews.

See Cyberbullying? Here's What to Do

Many students have told me they would not know what to do if they were treated cruelly online, or if they saw someone else being treated cruelly online.

This is unacceptable, especially considering that 88 percent of social media–using teens have witnessed other people being mean or cruel on social network sites.[71] Not to mention that 90 percent of social media–using teens who have witnessed online cruelty say they have ignored it; more than a third have done this frequently.[72]

Imagine if all children knew what to do if they or their friends were being cyberbullied, and they did it. The steps are so simple: *Take stock, block,* and *talk:*

1. **Take stock.** Take a screenshot of the evidence. Make sure your children know how to use their connected devices to take a screenshot of any harmful messages and save them. If you don't know how to take a

screenshot yourself, search for "how to take a screenshot with [type of device]." Taking a screenshot will enable your children to save any cruel comments as evidence to share with a trusted adult, or to report the incident to the social media network where the cruelty occurred.

2. **Block.** Tell your children they need not be subjected to online cruelty. Such activity is easy to block. Hinduja shares this invaluable advice: Children can control their online experience by blocking and reporting other users who have harassed or annoyed them. Every major social media app and online multiplayer game has that functionality built in, and youth don't need to subject themselves to interactions with people who are mean. Also, they should not hesitate to unfollow or unfriend anyone who compromises the quality of their online experience. It's hard to do so sometimes—even for adults—but we must.[73]

3. **Talk.** Encourage your children to talk to a trusted adult about anything online that makes them feel uncomfortable. Hopefully, that trusted adult is you! Even if it's not, encourage your children to turn to a teacher, coach, family friend, or relative. Additionally, tell your children to contact the social media company, website, gaming network, or service provider involved in the incident. Most have strict policies forbidding cruelty of any kind. The Cyberbullying Research Center has compiled an ever-growing list of contact information here: https://cyberbullying.org/report. If your children don't have a trusted adult they feel comfortable talking to, let them know about the free and confidential live Help-Chat line for youth ages thirteen to twenty-four offered by STOMP Out Bullying™ (http://www.stompoutbullying.org/information-and-resources/helpchat-line/). Kids being bullied or who may be contemplating suicide can get help from trained volunteers. To date, this chatline has helped over five million students resolve bullying and cyberbullying situations and has saved over six thousand lives. "Yes, we've helped a lot of kids," says Ellis. "But even that is not enough. I know that any day I'm going to go online and read about a child I wasn't able to save."[74]

Be Upstanding!

Recently, when visiting a middle school, I asked the students if they knew what the term *upstander* meant. Perhaps they were being bashful, but not a single kid offered a definition. Finally, after a long, awkward pause, a boy in the back of the room raised his hand. "It sounds like something my mom always says: 'Be the helper.'" "What a great definition," I thought!

Here are three easy ways for a kid to "be the helper" online:

1. **Give comfort.** Tell your children they don't have to stand up to the perpetrator of online cruelty to be an upstander. Often confrontation is difficult for children, online or offline, and that's okay. Tell them that giving support to or sharing a kind word with the target may be just the help needed!

2. **Report the incident.** Tell your children that they don't have to be the target of online cruelty to report it. They can take a screenshot, tell a trusted adult, or report the incident to the social media network where it took place.

3. **Stand up, but be kind.** Some kids do have the courage to stand up to perpetrators of online cruelty. To these children I say, "Fight cruelty with kindness." Advise your children not to sink to the level of online cruelty. Instead, they might try disarming the sender with a message of concern or kindness. Comedian Sarah Silverman did this expertly by responding to an online troll with this message: "Your rage is thinly veiled pain . . . see what happens when you choose love."[75] Imagine an online world filled with such kindness and concern. Now *that* would be upstanding!

Chapter 6

Privacy

•

Facebook is changing the norms of what it means to be private, what it means to be a kid, and what it means to be a "human product." As the phrase goes, if you are not paying for it, then you are not the customer, you are the product.

—JONATHAN TAPLIN, *MOVE FAST AND BREAK THINGS*[1]

E
very year I play a trick on my seventh-grade classes. Instead of launching into one of our regularly scheduled lessons, I deliver the following special announcement: "The school principal just hired a research firm to help him customize the school to better meet your needs. To accomplish this task, researchers will be on campus for one week. During this time, they'll be collecting personal information about you, such as your name, age, address, and so forth. They'll also be following you around and tracking your habits, like where you go (including the restroom, lunch area, playground, etc.), how long you spend there, who you spend time with, and basically everything you do all day."

As you have probably guessed, this ploy aims to make kids realize that every time they go online, to download an app, play a game, fill out a form, visit a website, buy a product, or do just about anything, their personal information and habits are being collected, sometimes without their knowledge or consent. I discovered this ingenious method of introducing students to the concept of "personal information and online privacy" in Common Sense Media's Digital Citizenship lessons, which they offer free online. This lesson works every time.

You can imagine how indignant twelve- and thirteen-year-olds become when they hear this announcement. They complain bitterly about this egregious violation of their privacy. And when they do, I'm ready. Handing every student a piece of paper, I invite them to express their concerns in a letter to the school principal. For many, this is the first letter they've ever written! What they put down on paper is striking:

> "This to me is an invasion of privacy and stalking."
>
> "They call it 'personal info' for a reason. If we gave it away, it would not be 'personal' anymore."
>
> "I don't want to feel like a lab rat. Also, my mom said not to give personal information to strangers."
>
> "Who follows you around everywhere and keeps track of your every move? This is kind of creepy. Let me make this more clear: *It is a lot creepy!*"
>
> "You know it's illegal to ask children for their personal information without asking their legal guardians first."
>
> "I would like to know what they are going to do with this information."
>
> "I strongly believe in children's rights to be safe."
>
> "These people have no right to know my habits or personal information."
>
> "I will not do this without my mother's approval."
>
> "Just no. It's creepy."

Don't you think it's astonishing that kids who so readily sign up for apps and services without a care to either privacy or parental approval are so eager for it in this situation? Nevertheless, when I explain that no researchers will be coming to the school, but that whenever they go online, their personal information and habits are being collected as though researchers were living in their phones, they are stunned. Then I read their own words back to them. That's what really gets them. As one seventh-grade boy put it, "Wow. Mind blown."

REALITY IS STRANGER THAN FICTION

If kids knew how close to reality this scenario is, their young minds would be blown. Attorney Bradley Shear, whom you met in Chapter 3, explains how personal information is being collected from schoolchildren in his blog, *Shear on Social Media Law & Tech*:

The type and amount of data being accumulated and stored by K–12 schools and third-party vendors is staggering. For example, some elementary schools deploy identification cards with RFID [radio-frequency identification] chips that track when and how many times our kids go to the bathroom, how long they spend inside a bathroom stall while taking care of their personal business, and how many times they go to the water fountain, along with all of their daily movements in and within the school's property. Other schools utilize biometric palm readers that scan our kids' hands or fingerprints to track everything our kids buy in the school cafeteria. All of this cumulative data is a honeypot for colleges, employers, insurance companies, data brokers, cybercriminals, foreign governments, etc.[2]

Shear, the father of two children in elementary school, says an immense amount of data is being collected from today's students. "Schools are using free apps, and the personal data these apps collect is being sold, literally right under a parent's nose," says Shear.[3] When *Education Week* interviewed him on this topic, he told them, "When I was young, I went to the library, I took out books on all kinds of crazy stuff, and that information wasn't stored in the cloud to be analyzed by algorithms or sold to third-party advertisers. Our kids should have the same freedom."[4]

Yet they don't. Students today routinely divulge personal information, a task made easy thanks to technology, without fully understanding the possible consequences. Many seventh and eighth graders take the PSAT 8/9 Assessment. This is the precursor to the popular SAT, the College Board test that most college-bound high school students take. The personal information collected by the College Board includes name, grade level, sex, date of birth, student ID number or Social Security number, racial/ethnic group, military relation, home address, email address, mobile phone, grade point average, courses taken, and parents' highest education levels. While it is not mandatory that students provide all this information (good luck collecting this data from my now-skeptical students next year, College Board!), most kids obediently and willingly do so anyway. What does the College Board do with this sensitive information? In a letter published in the *Washington Post*, Cheri Kiesecker, a Colorado parent and member of the Parent Coalition for Student Privacy, writes:

[T]he College Board's privacy policy to parents and students claims they do not sell student data. Rather, they sell a license to access a student's personal data. What is the difference? Indeed, this distinction seems only semantical.[5]

Consider the dozens, possibly hundreds or thousands, of free educational services and apps available to schools today. For instance, one of the most popular is Google's G Suite for Education (formerly Google Apps for Education), an online learning management system designed specifically for schools. It incorporates Google Classroom (a free web service that lets teachers and students easily share work and assignments) with other free Google products like Gmail, Calendar, Docs, Sheets, and Slides. It's an amazing resource that helps teachers stay organized, conduct quizzes, share information, and communicate with students—and the best part is, it's entirely free! Who can fault a cash-strapped school or teacher for taking full advantage of such a deal? More than seventy million people actively use G Suite for Education today. Perhaps not surprisingly, Google openly acknowledged in 2016 that it "collects and data mines for some commercial purposes a wide range of personal information on student users who log in through its popular Apps for Education service, then venture to the company's search engine and other products."[6] It's not just apps that collect student data. Software on laptops, tablets, and computers used in school collect personal information, too—everything from birth dates to search histories.

Google tracks its users across other services it offers, including YouTube. In early 2018, a complaint filed with the FTC by twenty advocacy groups claimed YouTube routinely collects data on children under age thirteen. In its defense, YouTube says its terms of service state the site is not for viewers under age thirteen. Which is hard to believe, as it offers "cartoons, nursery rhyme videos, and those ever-popular toy-unboxing clips" that garner millions of views.[7]

In and out of school, kids give personal information to the apps, games, websites, and anything else they use. "All of this data may be used in ways never imagined," says Shear. "We need to educate our kids about what is actually happening with their personal information when they use so-called 'free' digital products and services."[8]

TEACHING KIDS ABOUT PERSONAL
INFORMATION AND PRIVACY—PART 1

With all the possible perils the internet poses to minors, data mining of their personal information might seem low on the list of parental concerns, but it's not. A 2015 report released by the Family Online Safety Institute (FOSI) states that while most parents believe technology affects their children's lives in positive ways, they remain concerned about their children's personal safety and privacy. FOSI found that parents are more concerned about privacy than about performance in school, social relationships, physical health, technology use, and behavior.[9]

Privacy isn't just important to parents. "It's very important to kids, too," says Shauna Leff, vice president of marketing and communications of PRIVO, a company that provides a suite of privacy solutions for companies. "Starting in middle school, privacy becomes very important to kids," she told me. "Their online lives become like their bedrooms. They want, and expect, to find privacy there."

According to Leff, kids want something else, too. "They want engagement; they want customization. They want to be able to use free sites, like YouTube," she explains. "But think about it: What does Google get out of it? Kids have to understand that everything online can't just be free. There is a price to be paid."[10]

That price is their personal information.

Learning the Price of "Free"

Learning that their personal information is a valuable commodity may be the most important lesson for children starting to use connected devices. I try to drive home this concept with my students through various activities that follow the introductory "announcement" at the beginning of this chapter. They are required to read the privacy policies and terms of service of the apps they use most: Snapchat, Instagram, etc. This comes after a basic vocabulary lesson that teaches them the meanings of words and phrases they'll find in the fine print of every app or web service they will ever use—*personal information, cookies, third parties, license, user content, location information, log file information, monetization,* and so forth. Many adults don't even fully understand these terms, even though they routinely see these words in the policies they skim and agree to when downloading apps and services to their own phones and computers.

COMMON PRIVACY POLICY TERMS

- **Personal information:** Includes your name, address, email address, phone number, age, etc.
- **Cookies:** Small files placed on your device by some sites you visit. Cookies enable sites to "remember" your data.
- **Third party:** "Party" is a legal term for a person or entity. A "third party" is a person or entity other than the one you may have entered into an agreement with.
- **License:** Official permission to do, use, or own something.
- **User content:** Includes words, images, videos, audio, memes, or anything else you post online.
- **Location information:** Information about where a device user is located. Apps and websites can determine location by using cellular, WiFi, GPS, Bluetooth, etc.
- **Log file information:** A log file records events that occur on a device and may include search queries, how web services were used, and information about crashes, hardware settings, browser type, and more.
- **Monetization:** The process of making money.

You'd think students would complain bitterly about the tedium of reading these excruciatingly long and boring policies. Instead, they attack them with zeal and are often appalled at what they find. Some of my students found this buried within the Snap Inc. terms of service: "Many of our Services let you create, upload, post, send, receive, and store content. When you do that, you retain whatever ownership rights in that content you had to begin with. But *you grant us a license to use that content.* How broad that license is depends on which Services you use and the Settings you have selected."[11] (emphasis added)

The part in italics grabbed their attention. "Snap" is short for Snapchat, the app they know and love because user content supposedly "disappears" after it is viewed by whomever it's been shared with. Sure, most kids realize that friends can screenshot the content to keep and use elsewhere, but few suspected Snapchat of using their content. Upon further scrutiny, students discovered that for all content uploaded to the app, "you grant Snap Inc. and our affiliates a worldwide, royalty-free, sublicensable, and transferable license to host, store, use, display, reproduce, modify, adapt, edit, publish, and distribute that content."[12]

Additionally, students learned that if their "Snapchat Stories" were set to be viewable by "everyone," any content in that story is "public content," which means:

> [T]he license you grant us for this content is broader. In addition to granting us the rights mentioned in the previous paragraph, you also grant us a perpetual license to create derivative works from, promote, exhibit, broadcast, syndicate, sublicense, publicly perform, and publicly display Public Content in any form and in any and all media or distribution methods (now known or later developed). To the extent it's necessary, when you appear in, create, upload, post, or send Public Content, you also grant Snap Inc., our affiliates, and our business partners the unrestricted, worldwide, perpetual right and license to *use your name, likeness, and voice, including in connection with commercial or sponsored content.*[13] (emphasis added)

You might have to read these excerpts a couple of times to get the point. My students got it right away. They discovered that, even on this so-called "disappearing" app, the personal information and content they share doesn't disappear at all.

A Third Party Asks What Students Think

A couple of weeks into these lessons, I was contacted by a producer from NBC's *Today Show,* who asked if he could send a film crew to Journey School. He wanted to include us in a series they were producing about kids and technology. When I delivered this exciting news to the seventh graders, they didn't believe me. I'd lost all credibility with that class after my "special announcement!"

Nevertheless, a few weeks later, a news crew did show up at school, and when NBC correspondent Jacob Soboroff asked a group of five students what they'd been learning in Cyber Civics, they wasted no time responding. "We've been learning about privacy policies and terms of agreement," a bright young boy named Nicolas answered. I was surprised at how eager they were to tell Soboroff all about the boring legalese they'd been reading, and I think he was surprised, too. Especially when they told him that what they discovered "freaked them out" so much, they'd decided to delete some of their apps.

"You guys have friends obviously outside of this school and outside of this class. Do any of them read the terms of agreement on social media?" asked Soboroff.

"No," they responded, laughing.[14]

When asked if they thought they knew more about the apps they use than their friends, all five heads bobbed up and down. "Absolutely," one student answered. "I can't believe how little most kids know."

Understanding Personal
Information = Smart Choices

NBC aired this segment the same day that Facebook's Mark Zuckerberg broke his silence about the privacy scandal involving his social network and Cambridge Analytica, a voter-profiling company that collected and used the personal information of tens of millions of Facebookers. When the *New York Times* and *The Guardian* broke this story, Facebook's stock quickly plunged by 7 percent (that's a $37 billion hit, by the way). Even worse for the social media app, many considered quitting Facebook as the hashtag #DeleteFacebook started trending across the web. It was a big deal. But if you dig into this story, it makes you wonder if things would have been different had Facebook users been better educated, or at least curious, about how the personal information they willingly provided the social media network might be used. Here's what happened: "A researcher named Aleksandr Kogan developed a personality-quiz app for Facebook. . . . About 270,000 people installed Kogan's app on their Facebook account. But as with any Facebook developer at the time, Kogan could access data on users *or their friends*."[15] (emphasis original)

There's more to the story than this, but the salient fact is that users whose personal information was shared likely didn't read Facebook's privacy policies carefully. Or understand they had the choice not to take the quiz. Or know how to customize their privacy settings. It's becoming apparent that these are basic survival skills for citizens in a digital age.

That's why it's essential to teach kids that "free" has a price: their personal information. But, even more importantly, they should know that they can and should decide how much of their personal information to share on the web.

Be Aware: Kids Will Still Share

Even armed with this knowledge, kids will be tempted to share personal information online. "We are living in a Facebook era, where people are so excited to share everything, their every moment," says Leff. "That's fine, that's great—if people have made a choice to do that. But everyone should be able to choose what they want to share and what they want to get in exchange."[16]

Personally, I've made the choice, time and again, to share personal information in exchange for awesome services. I share my listening history with Spotify (a music app), and in exchange it gives me a tailored "daily mix" of songs it thinks I will like, based on my data. Strava, an exercise app that tracks my bike rides, asks me to share my age, which I readily do (even though I don't do this nearly as readily in real life!). In exchange, it compares my performance to other riders that fall within my age range. That way, I don't have to suffer the humiliation of being mercilessly outridden by nineteen-year-old "Mach 1 Racer." Entirely worth it.

But like all fair exchanges, both parties should be fully aware of how the exchange works, even if one of those parties is a nine-year-old kid you've decided is old enough to play *Roblox* or *Minecraft*. When children download or sign up to use games, apps, music, or other services, they are inevitably going to be asked to share personal information. Most children will share their personal information, or yours. That's right. When children use a parent's device, which many do, the stored passwords, email addresses, credit card numbers, birth date, address, contacts, and other data on that device are often a quick click away from being shared by the child using that device.

Do I have your attention now? Good. Because helping your children understand that personal information should be protected and shared sparingly is really important. And this is only the beginning of what they should know about privacy and personal information. Why? Because not knowing about this next part puts our democracy at risk.

TEACHING KIDS ABOUT PRIVACY AND PERSONAL INFORMATION—PART 2

Way back in the days of a nascent internet, a short twenty-five years or so ago, many believed this magnificent new platform would be a boon for humankind because it would give everyone and anyone—regardless of race, age, gender, social status, or political persuasion—a voice. This "new public square," as many called it, would be teeming with new ideas, divergent worldviews, and alternative solutions to problems—unfiltered and unedited—and the world was going to be better for it.

In 2001, legal scholar Cass Sunstein, later head of President Obama's Office of Information and Regulatory Affairs, explained that such an internet would benefit democracy:

> [P]eople should be exposed to materials that they would not have chosen in advance. Unplanned, unanticipated encounters are central to democracy itself. Such encounters often involve topics and points of view that people have not sought out and perhaps find quite irritating. They are important partly to ensure against fragmentation and extremism, which are predictable outcomes of any situation in which like-minded people speak only with themselves.[17]

This idealistic vision of the internet never quite materialized. Instead, because of the business model explored in Part 1 (the internet extracts personal information and provides customized and free experiences in exchange), humankind ended up with something entirely different from what the optimists imagined. Today, we have an internet that largely decides for us what we want and like.

While this might sound like an overstatement, think about it. Sophisticated algorithms embedded in nearly every online experience track what we like and do, based on the information we give them. Not only does this include the personal information we willingly hand over, but also our searching, buying, and browsing habits. This is personal information, too. Now consider this: The internet is getting better and better at analyzing all the data it gobbles up. It knows what we like and want, sometimes better than we do. For example, did you happen to search for a new pair of shoes online? Bingo—now shoe advertisements are probably popping up on sites you visit. Did you like or share a left-leaning news article or two on Facebook? That explains why you're getting more stories from the *Huffington Post* and *Mother Jones* on your feed instead of Fox News and *The Weekly Standard.*

Welcome to the world of "filter bubbles" and "echo chambers." You've arrived at the *really* important part of personal information.

Help, I'm Trapped in a Filter Bubble!

In a compelling 2011 TED Talk, Eli Pariser, the former executive director of MoveOn.org, introduced the world to the term "filter bubble." "Your filter bubble is your own personal, unique universe of information that you live in online. And what's in your filter bubble depends on who you are, and it depends on what you do."[18] Additionally, Pariser warned, "if we don't pay attention to it, it could be a real problem."[19]

Google is particularly adept at this filter bubble business. Whenever you use the search engine, "there are fifty-seven signals that Google looks at—everything from what kind of computer you're on to what kind of browser you're using to where you're located—that it uses to personally tailor your query results."[20]

Google carefully analyzes your previous searches, plus a host of other data, to determine what it thinks you are looking for or what you might like, and *voila!* That's what you get. You may never even know what Google decides to filter out for you. To illustrate this point, here's an exercise I have my students try at home: Pick any word or phrase, though somewhat controversial topics works best (e.g., Iran, climate change, presidential). Next, ask five different family members or friends to Google the word or phrase on their own devices—mobile or desktop—and then to compare results. Likely, you will find each person's results to be unique. They will be tailored and customized to the person who conducted the search (notice that the ads will be customized as well).

Why does this matter pertain to today's youth? Because young people are supposed to be hard at work figuring out who they are, what they like, and what they believe in. This task is arguably more successfully accomplished when they are exposed to a broad spectrum of ideas and information. If Google, Facebook, Instagram, or other sites feed them a customized stream of information based on previous searches and personal information, to borrow the words of one of my students, "that's just creepy."

Pariser puts it in more thoughtful terms: "We need to make sure that they [internet services] also show us things that are uncomfortable or challenging or important. . . . We really need the internet to be that thing that we all dreamed of it being. We need it to connect us all together. We need it to introduce us to new ideas and new people and different perspectives. And it's not going to do that if it leaves us all isolated in a web of one."[21]

Avoiding Filter Bubbles

While Google and Facebook have drawn the most ire for data mining users' information in exchange for customized experiences, this phenomenon happens all over the web. Netflix and YouTube queue up movies and videos they think we'll like, based on our previous viewings. So if you just watched *Wedding Crashers*, it's more likely Netflix will offer you *The 40-Year-Old Virgin*, rather than *The Civil War*. Amazon has customized its offerings for years, starting with books. Today, the world's largest online retailer suggests all kinds of products based on whatever we bought or searched for last.

Granted, most young people aren't using Facebook or shopping on Amazon (too much) yet, but they are watching Netflix and YouTube. They're also using Instagram, which Facebook owns. A 2017 survey found that 76 percent of American teens, ages thirteen to seventeen, use this social network.[22] Instagram employs many of the same successful customization techniques as Facebook. In 2016, Instagram announced, "To improve your experience, your feed will soon be ordered to show the moments we believe you will care about the most. The order of photos and videos in your feed will be based on the likelihood you'll be interested in the content, your relationship with the person posting, and the timeliness of the post."[23]

Unless you happened to be one of my students and were required to read this, you probably missed this announcement entirely. In short, Instagram decided to follow parent Facebook's lead of reordering posts based on factors such as how recently the post was shared, interactions with the person who shared it, and whether or not the user found the post interesting. Based on this data, Instagram decides what it thinks a young user should see.

Judging from the grumbling I've heard among teens, they aren't crazy about algorithms making decisions for them, just like they don't relish Mom deciding what they should wear to school. But I'm hearing mostly from kids who are learning what to look out for. For each of these students, millions more have not learned why or how personal information is collected and how algorithms work. If they don't know or understand the process, they certainly aren't going to give a flying hoot about it.

Microsoft's Bill Gates is one of a growing number of technologists who have expressed concerns about filter bubbles. He told a *Quartz* reporter that there *is* a solution: "Education is a counterbalance to filter bubbles... since it exposes people 'to a common base of knowledge.'"[24]

For now, the opportunity the internet provides for everyone to be heard might outweigh the negative impact of filter bubbles, but it's critical for kids to understand how they work and, more importantly, how to avoid falling prey to their influence. It might sound hyperbolic to claim that our very democracy is at stake, but consider the long-term consequences of ignoring this problem. What if kids end up consuming only a narrow, and predetermined, slice of the vast array of ideas, information, and worldviews the internet has to offer? That doesn't sound like a wise use of this powerful and amazing resource to me.

The Paradoxical Privacy Practices of Teens

Andie is a fourteen-year-old girl I met one brisk February morning while visiting a K–12 school in Los Angeles. I was there to deliver lessons to their elementary- and middle-school students, but in the afternoon, I spent some time with their ninth graders. I planned to talk to them about online privacy, but these students weren't at all interested in what *not* to post online. They'd "already heard that lecture," they told me. What they really wanted to talk about was what they *should* be sharing online. They peppered me with questions:

- Do I need to have a LinkedIn account to get a job?
- I play club soccer, and I'd like college recruiters to see me play. Should I make a video? How long should it be? Where should I post it?
- In my spare time I tutor young kids. Would it be an invasion of their privacy to post their photos online?
- I'm performing in a lot of plays. Do you think I should videotape them for YouTube? Should I make my own channel?

I was impressed with their questions and at how eager they were to talk. The hour we had together wasn't nearly enough.

When class ended, Andie lingered and introduced herself to me. A petite girl with a cascading mane of jet black hair, she was one of the only students who hadn't uttered a word during the entire class. But once we started chatting, it didn't take long for her bubbly personality to reveal itself. She even asked if she could show me her Instagram feed. When I said yes, she proudly revealed an account with 3,800 followers. Then she told me her story:

> About a year ago my mom's friend started a clothing line. She was just making T-shirts, swimsuits, and stuff for teens. Since her company was brand new, she couldn't afford a model, so she asked my mom if I'd model for her. My mom asked me, and I agreed, and then I started putting some of the photos on my Instagram feed, and before long a bunch of kids from school found out about it and wanted to follow me.

Andie told me how much this boosted her self-esteem. Soon some of her new online friends became offline friends, and she said this is "helping me become less shy at school."

"I think it's good that you talk to kids about posting positive stuff online," Andie said. "Usually adults just tell us social media is bad. Kids hear that and just keep posting the bad stuff anyway, but on private or fake accounts. Adults forget that not using social media, for us, is not an option."

As I was driving home, I thought about what Andie said. What a delicate balancing act kids have to perform today between satisfying their need (and desire) to present themselves online while also preserving some privacy. It takes a lot of wisdom to get the balance just right.

To Share or Not to Share?

In 2015, a comprehensive study on the relationship between youth and online privacy revealed that teens "care more about social privacy than they do about privacy in the context of third-parties and big data/information privacy."[25] Researchers figured this is due to the fact that teens "fail to grasp what happens with that data after it has been posted." And I figure this is due to lack of education. Paradoxically, according to this report, even though teens care deeply about their social privacy, they still share a lot of personal information online. Teens share real names (92 percent), photos of themselves (91 percent), interests (84 percent), birth date (82 percent), and school name and city/town where they live (71 percent) through social media platforms. At the same time, they go to great lengths to keep this information private from certain audiences by using a combination of non-technical measures (creating fake identities and accounts) as well as technical ones (using privacy settings). Teens also employ other creative methods to maintain privacy online, particularly to avoid parental surveillance, like moving to new sites or encoding hidden meaning into their posts by using cultural references, slang, and emojis.

Teen privacy practices are a study in contradictions. On one hand it looks like they're indiscriminately sharing *waaaay* too much information, while on the other hand they seem to be going to great lengths to limit what gets seen, using methods that completely perplex adult onlookers. But as with every new digital activity, one's perspective depends on which generation you're viewing it from.

A perfect example of this perspective problem is the "selfie." In case you've been living under a rock for the past ten years, a selfie is a self-portrait one takes with a phone. While adults commonly worry that the numerous selfies kids take and post reveal TMI (too much information), both literally and figuratively, kids don't see them that way at all. For most cell phone–wielding kids, selfies are a normal part of their lives. And why shouldn't they be? Self-image sharing is nothing new. It used to be considered high art. Rembrandt did it, as did Claude Monet, and Vincent van Gogh, too (he painted more than thirty self-portraits between 1886–1889). Mexican painter Frida Kahlo created fifty-five self-portraits in her lifetime, often documenting the personal tragedies she endured. When asked why she painted so many pictures of herself, she answered, "Because I am the subject I know best."[26]

Technology has merely simplified the age-old act of self-disclosure. "It used to be that portraits were only available to people that were wealthy enough to hire Leonardo da Vinci to paint their picture or to hire a portrait photographer," says Dr. Pamela Rutledge. "But with the cell phone and the ability to upload to Facebook or Instagram at no cost, it has totally democ-ratized portraiture."[27]

I'd wager that if someone like van Gogh were alive today, he'd be snap-ping selfies, particularly if reincarnated as a teenager smack in the middle of the task of figuring out who he is and how to present that self to the world. What better way to document this process than by taking and sharing self-images?

"With selfie-taking, it puts people in charge of their own self-image," says Rutledge. "I think selfies play a big role in letting people document their growth and their progress. And explore identities. And think about them-selves. So, I think that part of it is very positive."[28]

Nevertheless, most parents worry, and rightfully so, that self-images posted online might reveal too much personal information that could dam-age their children's digital reputations or put them in harm's way, while kids don't worry about this at all. And *that* is my point.

When viewed through the rose-colored lens of youth, digital activities seem full of possibility and promise. Seldom do they look as rosy to parents. This applies to all the topics we've covered thus far—reputation, screen time, relationships, and privacy. Each of these—the four cornerstones of a sturdy structure that will keep your children safely protected in their digital world—are complex and sometimes confusing. Kids need conversation and education surrounding each one.

They need us to look at the digital world through their lens once in a while, too!

CYBER CIVICS MOMENTS

Virtual Stranger Danger

Children everywhere are taught about real world "stranger danger," but what about virtual stranger danger? They will come into contact with many, many more strangers online than they ever will in real life. Even though students

I've met represent a small sampling of the world at large, you would not believe how many have told me they have been asked for personal information from a stranger online. Even more disconcerting is how many say they know kids who have willingly provided such information to strangers.

The moment you hand your children a connected device, it is vital to share these hard, fast rules regarding personal information. Tape these to your refrigerator, your laptop, desktop computer, or your kids' foreheads. Whatever it takes.

1. Tell your children they should never, *ever* share the following information (their own or another's) with a stranger online without your express consent:

   - Full name
   - Physical address
   - Email address
   - Phone number
   - School name
   - Current location
   - Clues to future locations
   - Password
   - Photos

   As your children get older, they will start using their own best judgment about if and when it is safe to share any of the above. Until then, make sure they understand and agree to your rules.

2. Tell your children they should never, *ever* engage with strangers online. Explain that, on the internet, it's Halloween every day. People are hiding their identities behind masks otherwise known as their screens. While most of these people are nice, some may not be. As your children get older, they will start using their own best judgment as to if and when to engage with online strangers, but until then make sure they follow your rules.

3. Tell your children they should never, *ever* meet someone in real life that they have first met online. It may take longer for your children to develop the good judgment they'll need to decide when it is okay to

bend this rule, so keep open communication about their friendships, online and offline.

Password Perfect

Passwords are our first line of defense to protect our personal information online. Even though there are a lot of online programs that will make and remember passwords for them, teaching children how to make and remember their own is important. It underscores how critical it is to have safe and strong passwords and can also be a lot of fun.

1. Teach your children these seven rules for making a great password. A great password should:

   - Be at least eight characters in length.
   - Include a combination of lower and uppercase letters, symbols, and numbers.
   - Never include personal information (like a birth date or Social Security number).
   - Never include the name of family members, friends, or pets.
   - Never include sequences, such as *abcde* or *12345*.
   - Never include a dictionary word (unless a letter has been changed into a symbol).
   - Be changed regularly—at least every six months.

2. Explain the term "mnemonic" to your children. Simply put, a mnemonic is a memory device that aids in the retention of information.
3. Ask your children to think of their favorite celebrity, athlete, musician, or historical figure (make sure they do not tell you who it is). This will be their mnemonic.
4. Teach your children how to use a mnemonic to make a great password. Here's an example: Tell them your mnemonic is Taylor Swift (work with me here) and that your favorite song of hers is "We Are Never Ever Getting Back Together." Use the first letter of each word of this song title to begin your password (WANEGBT). Next, convert this into a mix of upper and lowercase letters (WaNeGbT). Because you

need to add a number or symbol, change the last word, "together," to "2gether" (WaNeGb2). Finally, since you need to add one more character to make your password the right length and Swift seemed emphatic about never ever getting back together, add an exclamation point at the end. Here is your password: WaNeGb2!

5. Have your children follow your example, creating their own great password. When they finish, try to guess who their mnemonics are based on the passwords they've made. Make another password yourself, and have them try to guess yours, or their siblings' or friends' mnemonics. I have done this in the classroom numerous times and am always amazed at how good kids are at this game. Plus, they will *never ever* forget how to make and remember great passwords!

Pitch Me!

Credit for this activity goes to one of my students, who told me that if she wants to download an app, her dad makes her first research it thoroughly. Then she has to make a PowerPoint presentation and use it to pitch him on the app. "Brilliant!" I thought. I loved this idea so much, I've made it easy for you to do it at home.

1. So, your children (who are at least thirteen years of age) want to download Snapchat. Invite them to research the app first. This is easy to do; Snapchat's privacy policy and terms of service are accessible via a Google search.

2. Have your children create a presentation for you about the app. They don't have to use Microsoft PowerPoint for this task. This is a wonderful opportunity for them to practice using one of the many free presentation tools available online. One of my favorites is Prezi. Tell your children to use the following questions as a guide when they create their presentation:

- What is the minimum user age for the app?
- What personal information will the app ask for?
- What will you receive in exchange for the personal information you provide?

- Will you share user content on this app? If so, who will own that content?
- Will the app share your information with third parties? If so, how?
- Will it track your location?
- What conduct does the app expect from users? Is there a way to report bad behavior?
- Will there be ads on the app? How else might the app be monetized?
- What kind of privacy settings does the app offer?

If this seems like too much work for your teens, please consider the amount of work they'll be putting into that app in the coming years. It takes time and effort to snap, curate, and post photos. Tagging, commenting, liking, and reading what others post takes time, too. If your teens don't have time to research this app, then they surely don't have time to use it!

My Self, My Selfie

If a picture is worth a thousand words, what's a selfie worth? That's the million-dollar question today, as young people indiscriminately share tons of information about themselves through the selfies they take and share. Explore this phenomenon with your children and come to a shared understanding of what personal information is or is not okay to share online.

1. Ask your children to tell *you* what a selfie is. They will probably know that this is "a photo one has taken of oneself," but ask them: What do you think the purpose of a selfie is? How often do you take and post pictures of yourself? Why do you think selfies have become so popular? Tell your children that, in 2012, *Time* named "selfie" one of the top ten buzzwords of the year, and that it was added to the Oxford English Dictionary in 2013.[29] They might be impressed about how much you know!

2. Ask your children if they have ever judged someone they didn't know by the person's selfie. Ask for examples.

3. Tell your children that, while taking selfies can be a lot of fun, it's important to think about what these images convey to others. Discuss

what personal information they may be sharing. (Do their selfies tell others where they are? Where they live? Or that no one is at home?) *How* they share their selfies and *who* they share them with are important discussion topics.

4. Explain that long before there were selfies, famous artists like van Gogh and Rembrandt, among others, shared their self-imagery through self-portraits.

5. Next is the fun part. Google some of these artists and view their self-portraits. Ask your children what they think these artists were trying to convey. Find out what they can ascertain about the artist by looking at the pictures you find.

6. Consider visiting your local art museum or gallery to do the above. It might inspire your children to see a museum or gallery you've visited before in a whole new light!

PART THREE

A
Vibrant
Community

Chapter 7

Thinking Critically

●

Misinformation and fake news will exist as long as humans do; they have existed ever since language was invented. Relying on algorithms and automated measures will result in various unwanted consequences. Unless we equip people with media literacy and critical-thinking skills, the spread of misinformation will prevail.

—SU SONIA HERRING[1]

A few years ago, Erin Reilly paid a visit to one of my classes at Journey School. She'd just landed a new project that required collecting data from flesh-and-blood students. While she cleverly disguised her objective as an engaging digital literacy activity, my students saw right through it. Instead of placidly acquiescing to her plan, they assaulted her with questions: Who created your lesson? Who is going to see our answers? Are you being paid to be here? Who is paying you? Why should we help you for free?

Though somewhat embarrassed at how forcefully my students grilled poor Reilly, I was also proud of them for flexing their emerging media literacy muscles. Media literate people ask questions about the messages they receive. Frankly, I think Reilly enjoyed the grilling as well. She has been an instrumental figure in the media literacy movement for years and is currently the president of NAMLE, the National Association of Media Literacy Education. She knows all too well how important it is for students to develop critical media literacy skills.

"I walked away that day thinking, 'Good for them!'" says Reilly. "One thing we don't want is for kids to just say yes and agree to everything we say. We want them to be critical consumers of information. We want them to be media literate."[2]

WHAT IS MEDIA LITERACY?

"We define media literacy as the ability to access, analyze, create, evaluate, and act using all forms of communication, meaning it's an expanded definition of literacy today," says Michelle Ciulla Lipkin, executive director of NAMLE.[3] Under her leadership, this organization has become the leading convener, thought leader, and resource for media literacy in the United States. Ciulla Lipkin is a force of enthusiasm, and within five minutes will have you convinced that media literacy may be the most important thing your kids should be learning in school.

While I share Lipkin's enthusiasm for media literacy—the entire final level of Cyber Civics is devoted to it—I don't think its long, academic definition comes close to capturing the urgency of teaching kids how to understand and contribute to the media assault that comes at them via their phones, televisions, computers, smartwatches, gaming consoles, etc. Until media literacy is fully appreciated and fully understood, it won't receive the emphasis it deserves. Math, English, history, and science will be what students, particularly in middle school, spend most of their time studying. Ironic when you consider that what they learn in school will likely be used online, and to be a vital online community member you've gotta be media literate.

I thought about this one day as I was leading an eighth-grade class through a media literacy lesson. They were learning how to distinguish fake websites from real ones, not an easy task, when I overheard two girls talking.

"I don't get why we only have Cyber Civics once a week, but we have algebra every day," one girl said to the other. "I'll use this stuff way, way more."

While I don't want to discount the importance of solving equations by using square and cubic root symbols, I do agree with this student that she will probably encounter more websites than algebraic equations in her future. But that's not how most schools or parents see it. At least they didn't up until 2016, the year that fake news catapulted media literacy into the real news.

FAKE NEWS

In 2016, Oxford Dictionaries declared "post-truth" the word of the year, defining it as "relating to or denoting circumstances in which objective facts are less influential in shaping public opinion than appeals to emotion and personal belief."[4] Although the term first appeared in 1992, in 2016 its use spiked by 2,000 percent, thanks to two events—Brexit and the U.S. presidential election. A tumultuous political environment, combined with huge numbers of people getting their news from social media—within their private filter bubbles—fostered a landscape ripe for hoaxes, falsities, and conspiracy theories, otherwise known as "fake news." You are undoubtedly familiar with this term.

I asked Ciulla Lipkin if fake news had finally provided media literacy its moment.

"Yes, fake news certainly put a spotlight on the conversation," she told me. "Suddenly issues about 'How do we understand information?' 'How do we decipher information?' were in such a public cultural conversation. In that way, the fake news conversation has been a really, really important one for media literacy."

But with the attention, she warns, comes a downside. "The danger is that it's so limiting. We can't just focus on what is true and what is false, because most information is somewhere in between. The majority of information that exists right now is opinion. So, we need to understand how to weigh opinions and agenda and all those things."

This, by the way, is what media literacy teaches kids to do. So, you'd think teaching it would be the obvious solution to "fake news"—one of today's biggest issues. But it's not.

"My biggest frustration is that most of the solutions being proposed are not educational solutions. They are more about 'How do we get social media sites to determine what is fake and make sure it doesn't trend?' or 'How do we create an app that will identify the good sites and the bad sites?' Where the money should be going is into our education system."[5]

TEACHABLE MOMENTS IN MEDIA LITERACY

Rather than waiting for money to flow into media literacy education, there's a better way to prepare kids for a media-filled world. Take matters into your own hands by availing yourself of the abundant teachable moments the media provides. While fake news might be bad for media, it's great for teaching media literacy. You don't have to search long to find a riveting fake news story to tell your kids, like this one that I shared with my students:

Once upon a time, in a town of only forty-five thousand residents called Veles, in the former Yugoslav Republic of Macedonia, lived some web-savvy teenagers and young adults. During the months leading up to the 2016 U.S. presidential election, these young people discovered an ingenious method of making fast, easy money by spreading fake news to Americans. The outcome of our election didn't matter to them one bit; their interest was purely economic. In a town where the average annual wage is the equivalent of $4,800, the possibility of earning thousands of dollars by simply reposting American news stories seemed almost too good to be true. So the young people in Veles took advantage of our existing, and entirely legal, social media and revenue-generating advertising systems, and most Americans were none the wiser.

To start, enterprising young Macedonians would create a website that looked as much like a legitimate American news site as possible (self-hosted WordPress sites are free for the making). Then, they'd give their site an American-sounding name. Some of the most popular names used were WorldPoliticus.com, TrumpVision365.com, USConservativeToday.com, and USADailyPolitics.com. Next, they'd go on the hunt for news stories. They searched mostly for pro-Trump content because, as they had discovered through trial and error, Trump content performed better than the left-leaning stories they'd tested. It didn't matter if these stories were true or not; mostly they were not. The only real criteria was that they had to be sensational. The youth would copy the stories, give them catchy headlines, like "Pope Francis Forbids Catholics from Voting for Hilary," and post them to their own websites.

Because two-thirds of U.S. adults were getting their news from social media networks, especially Facebook, the Macedonian youth decided to share their stories there.[6] They paid the social media network to target and share their fake news with the perfect audience, easy to do using Facebook's cheap, audience-targeting tools, or they'd post their stories directly on the pages of right-leaning Facebook groups. When Facebook users saw a catchy headline, they'd assume it was legitimate news, click on the story, and like and share it with other users who would do the same. This would generate traffic *back* to the websites where the stories were hosted, and that's how the youths made their money. Their income came from the Google AdSense ads they'd placed on their sites. Many websites make money using this online advertising service. The more people who clicked on these ads, the more money the Macedonian kids would make.

At one point, U.S. news organizations identified over 140 such websites being operated out of Veles. One seventeen-year-old Macedonian who had mastered this scheme told BuzzFeed News, "I started the site for an easy way to make money. In Macedonia the economy is very weak, and teenagers are not allowed to work, so we need to find creative ways to make some money. I'm a musician, but I can't afford music gear. Here in Macedonia the revenue from a small site is enough to afford many things."[7]

I remember seeing some of the fake news headlines generated by Macedonian youth on my own Facebook feed. They included these gems:

"Breaking: Proof Surfaces that Obama Was Born in Kenya—Trump Was Right All Along!"

"Rush Reveals Michelle's Perverted Past after She Dumps on Trump."

"JUST IN: Obama Illegally Transferred DOJ Money to Clinton Campaign!"

A BuzzFeed News analysis found that, during the months prior to the 2016 election, the top twenty fake news stories outperformed the top twenty legitimate news stories on Facebook—i.e., they received more shares, reactions, and comments.[8] Not only did fake stories spread by Macedonian youth claim that the pope endorsed Trump, but also that Mike Pence said Michelle Obama was the "most vulgar first lady we've ever had," a debunked story you can still find on a fake-news-site-that-looks-real.[9] Posts like these generated millions of shares, reactions, and comments on Facebook. That pushed huge amount of traffic to these fake websites, resulting in significant ad revenue for their owners. Losers in this exchange were unsuspecting Facebook users who fell for fake news.

When I finished telling my class this story, they sat in silence, highly unusual for this talkative group. One girl finally broke the spell. "Wow," she said, "that would have been a much better fund-raiser than our bake sale."

I hope she was kidding.

CRITICAL THINKING SKILLS NEEDED

The only surefire way to solve the problem of internet users falling for and sharing false information is to teach the next generation of users to be critical thinkers. This is a task we have to work on, fast, because today's kids aren't any better at critically evaluating online information than we adults are.

In 2016, researchers from the Stanford Graduate School of Education discovered that young people's ability to effectively evaluate the information they find online is, in a word, "bleak." Their study, which focused on the "civic online reasoning" of middle school, high school, and college students in twelve states, revealed, "Our 'digital natives' may be able to flit between Facebook and Twitter while simultaneously uploading a selfie to Instagram and texting a friend. But when they evaluate information that flows through social media channels, they are easily duped."[10]

Here's a summary of what researchers discovered:

- More than 80 percent of middle-school students were unable to distinguish a paid story branded as "sponsored content" from a real news story.
- When presented with a post that included a picture of daisies along with the claim that the flowers had "birth defects" from the Fukushima nuclear disaster, most high-school students failed to question the dubious photo or look for its source.
- High-school students did not recognize the difference between two posts, one from the real Fox News and one from an account that looked like Fox News.
- When shown a tweet from the liberal advocacy organization MoveOn.org, college students could not detect bias.
- Most Stanford college students could not tell the difference between a mainstream news source, The American Academy of Pediatrics, and a fringe news source, a group that splintered off from the AAP, called ACPeds.

From middle school through college, students involved in this study displayed an appalling inability to assess the credibility of online information.

Are you starting to see the need for media literacy education?

TEACHING MEDIA LITERACY

Long ago, after our first year of teaching Cyber Civics at Journey School, Principal Shaheer Faltas and I felt pretty smug about our results. Incidents of poor online behavior, cyberbullying, or even digital drama had virtually disappeared. Plus, we'd been honored at an awards ceremony given by the Orange County Tech Alliance and Project Tomorrow, two organizations that recognize "innovation in education." It was tempting to congratulate ourselves and call it a day.

However, near the end of the school year, a boy named Jamal rained on our self-congratulatory parade. One of the most social kids in the school, Jamal announced, "After everything I've learned this year, I've decided to go off the grid. No more phone, internet, nothing for me. It just ain't worth it."

"Yikes," I thought to myself, "this was not the outcome I'd hoped for!" I love tech and all the positive opportunities it enables, and I had hoped my students would feel the same.

That's when it dawned on us that we needed to add a second and third year to the program. Now that they knew how to use technology safely and wisely, it was time to address the *really* important topics: information literacy (how to find, retrieve, analyze, and use online information) and media literacy (which you just read about here). We couldn't leave students dangling with the bare minimum. It would be like showing them a picture of a Formula One racing car, handing them the keys, and suggesting they take a cross-country trip. With "digital citizenship" under their belts, they were clearly ready—and needed—to learn how to use technology to its full capacity. This is the real icing on the digital literacy cake, the crowning roof to their sturdy structure.

There are so many important lessons beyond learning how to use technology safely and wisely—which is where most schools and parents stop—that we could barely fit them into two years. Kids need to learn that conducting a Google search doesn't mean using the first result you see. They must learn how to write effective search queries, use meaningful keywords, analyze a results page, and distinguish ads from real content. They need to understand how Wikipedia works and how to use it, what copyright is, how to avoid plagiarism, use Creative Commons, stay out of filter bubbles, cite online sources, and much more.

But perhaps the single most important thing they need to learn is how to identify crap.

DETECTING CRAP ONLINE

If you're at all familiar with middle school kids, then you know they love anything remotely scatological (think fart jokes). That's why I love telling kids I'm going to teach them about crap. It gets their attention every time.

I learned about "crap detection" from cyberculture expert Howard Rheingold in his book, *Net Smart: How to Thrive Online*. Rheingold is a brilliant and somewhat quirky author, journalist, editor, and futurist who has written numerous compelling books about digital culture. I became a die-hard Rheingold fan while reading *Smart Mobs: The Next Social Revolution*, published in 2002. I devoured that book in almost one sitting, all the while wondering if I'd mistakenly picked up a sci-fi novel. Rheingold described, with stunning detail, the social and technological future we're living in now, addressing everything from wearable technology to the mobile telephone, which would be a like a "remote control" for people's lives.[11] This was long before either the smartwatch or the iPhone debuted.

In *Net Smart*, something of a guidebook for the digital age, Rheingold suggests that a crucial "digital know-how" skill needed today is "crap detection." He defines "crap" as "information tainted by ignorance, inept communication, or deliberate deception."[12] According to Rheingold, "Learning to be a critical consumer of web info is not rocket science. It's not even algebra. Becoming acquainted with the fundamentals of web credibility testing is easier than learning the multiplication tables. The hard part, as always, is the exercise of flabby think-for-yourself muscles."[13]

I try to help my students exercise these muscles by using crap detection's handy acronym, C.R.A.P. An unforgettable tool to assess the veracity of online information, C.R.A.P. is a set of four questions you can ask yourself whenever you encounter something dubious online. Variations can be found all over the internet, and here are mine:

Currency
- How current is the information?
- How recently was it was posted? Has it been updated?

Reliability
- How reliable is the information?
- Does the author provide references or sources?
- What proof do you have that the information is reliable?

Author
- Who is the creator or author of the information? What are her credentials?

- Who is the publisher or sponsor of the information? Is this a reputable information source?

Purpose/Point of view
- What is the purpose of this information? Is it intended to inform, entertain, or persuade?
- Does the information sound like fact or opinion? Is it biased?
- Is the creator or author trying to sell you something?

Personally, I rely on the C.R.A.P. test a lot. Like most people, I'm a sucker for salacious headlines. But if they seem suspicious, I give them the test (please bear in mind, online misinformation is nonpartisan, examples exist on both sides of the political aisle). Here's one example:

One day while scrolling through my Facebook feed, a friend's post caught my eye. The headline she shared read: "Shock Revelation: Obama Admin Actively Sabotaged Gun Background Check System." Intrigued, I clicked on the article and discovered it was posted on a website called Conservative Tribune.[14] While the website and article appeared *current* enough, neither seemed entirely *reliable*. The site was full of clickbait headlines sporting words like "vile," "stunner," and "disgraced." I checked out the *author*, and his humorous bio and few Twitter followers (only three people when I checked) made me wonder if he was a true journalist. So, I looked up Conservative Tribune on Media Bias/Fact Check. This is a media bias resource site—one of many online—that claims to be an independent outlet "dedicated to educating the public on media bias and deceptive news practices."[15] There I learned that Conservative Tribune is a "questionable source" that "exhibits one or more of the following: extreme bias, overt propaganda, poor or no sourcing to credible information and/or is fake news." I also discovered that the site "consistently fails fact checks, glorifies violence against Americans and Muslims," and more.[16] Finally, a scroll back through the Conservative Tribune website revealed a distinct *purpose and point of view*.

The article seemed like crap to me.

Back on Facebook, I returned to where the article was posted and in the upper right-hand corner selected "Report Post." A box popped up that read, "Help us understand what's happening," under which I selected "It's a false news story." Facebook presented me with some options. I could block, unfollow, or unfriend the person who posted the story. I didn't select any of those options, because I don't want to end up in a filter bubble. Instead I selected "Mark this post as false news" and was done.

This entire process didn't take much longer than it took you to read what steps I completed. It felt good, too! It's the small part I can play to help curb the flow of fake news stories online. I encourage my students to take action when they see false information online, too. It's important for them to use their critical thinking muscles *and* to feel like empowered digital citizens.

BEYOND CRITICAL THINKING

Years ago, after my husband and I signed Journey School's strict media contract, I read Stephen Johnson's book *Everything Bad Is Good for You*. Boy, was that a buzzkill. Despite a few transgressions, I'd begun to feel pretty comfortable on the "no media" high horse I was riding. As time went on, more and more people were coming around to what the Waldorf folks have espoused for years—that technology and young kids are a bad mix. At first, just a handful of tech insiders were saying as much, but soon more voices chimed in, from Apple's Tim Cook (who said he didn't want his nephew on social media) to Microsoft's Melinda Gates ("I probably would have waited longer before putting a computer in my children's pockets").[17] It was becoming vogue to think of media as the enemy of childhood.

Then Johnson introduced me to the "Sleeper Curve" theory, a term he derived from the Woody Allen film *Sleeper*, a mock sci-fi movie "where a team of scientists from 2173 are astounded that twentieth-century society failed to grasp the nutritional merits of cream pies and hot fudge."[18] "Jeez," I thought. Could I be missing the nutritional merits of media, too?

Henry Jenkins, the media guru introduced in Chapter 2, figured out the answer to this question long ago. In addition to identifying the "new media literacies," he coined the term "participatory culture." This, he says, is an environment where people not only *consume* media but also *create* and *distribute* it. Currently, we live in a participatory culture. It offers wonderful opportunities to make and share content. Never in the history of humankind have ordinary individuals had this kind of power in their hands. It has transformed the definition of literacy, and to miss out on its benefits would be a shame.

"If you look at the definition of media literacy," explains Erin Reilly, "it's not just about being able to critically inquire about the media. . . . It's also about how we can create and participate and act within the media that we engage with. Media literacy is about relationships. That's where media has gone today. It's moved from individual expression and consumption to social engagement and community involvement."[19]

To better understand what Reilly is talking about, it helps to look at the phenomenon of *fandom*. Fandom is a subculture of passionate fans who bond over their favorite books, TV shows, movies, bands, or any other form of pop culture ("Potterheads," fans of the Harry Potter book series, are a good example). In a participatory culture, fans don't have to wait for their next book club meeting to share their passions. They can express and share their enthusiasm with thousands, sometimes millions, of other fans in myriad ways online.

Many kids today enthusiastically embrace the opportunities a participatory culture offers. For instance, peek into the world of *The Guardian Herd*. This is a series of fantasy novels for youth, written by Jennifer Lynn Alvarez, that star magic flying horses, or Pegasi. These books have spawned numerous vibrant online communities, where examples of individual expression and social engagement are off the Richter scale.

"It started pretty quickly after *Starfire*," Alvarez told me. *Starfire* is the first book in the series. "Kids immediately wanted to respond creatively to the story, so I was pretty quickly receiving fan art. Kids would email me pictures of the characters."[20] Alvarez, who has her own children ranging from ages thirteen to twenty, says the average age of her fans is probably around eleven. These young readers send her drawings of their own original characters. "Using the constructs of the story, the type of herds that I created, and the type of naming that I used for my Pegasi, they make up their own characters, decide which herd they were in, and then give them a Pegasus name based off the series."

Alvarez's fans go to impressive lengths in creating their Pegasi. "One kid made all of my characters out of Legos, I've seen clay, and one child made my main character out of mosaic tiles," she told me. Along with these handmade creations, her fans create art digitally, too, using websites like Doll Maker. "It's a fantasy tool maker where you can make fairies," says Alvarez. "You can make unicorns, you can make Pegasi, you can make different characters."

Many of Alvarez's fans share their creations on a site called DeviantArt. com, otherwise known as DA. It's the world's largest online social network for artists and art enthusiasts. Her fans have posted thousands of images on DA, and many include vivid descriptions of the characters they've created. "The great thing is they get immediate feedback on their work," Alvarez told me. "I think kids can actually get better faster when they get feedback, instead of just doing stuff alone in their room and not showing it to anyone."

In addition to art, Alvarez's books have inspired a wealth of "fanfiction," when fans of a piece of fiction create their own story based on the original and share it with other fans. Many of Alvarez's fans share their work on Wattpad, a free app that lets budding authors publicly share their fiction writing in a blog-like format, and read and comment on other people's work. Per *The Guardian*, Wattpad has been "discovered" by teenage girls, who have turned it into a "global sensation" in young adult literature.[21] "What I love about fan fiction is that kids get to explore their own alternate endings, write about side characters, and make up back stories," says Alvarez. "Jumping off an existing world is easier for young writers than making up their own from scratch. But through this process, they learn worldbuilding and the writer's technique of asking, 'What if?'"

You can also find an active community of *Guardian Herd* fans on Fandom, a wiki-hosting site (think Wikipedia), where users share their passions and encyclopedic knowledge of books, television shows, and movies. According to Alvarez, fans also share their book-inspired work on Instagram, YouTube, Vimeo, Snapchat, and other sites. An active fan community even posts to the message board on her website. "It's not even a year old, and I've gotten almost forty or fifty thousand views on that," she says.

It's important to note that some of the social networks mentioned here require kids to be at least thirteen years of age to use them. Alvarez always encourages her fans to get their parents' permission before going online. But not being old enough to join social networks doesn't stop some of her youngest fans from emailing their creations to her.

Engagement with her readers, and her readers with one another, "has exploded with digital media," says Alvarez. "Kids are becoming authors, illustrators—and they're connecting with other fans to share their work. Many even have their own fan groups. Others read their stories and beg them to write more."

One of Alvarez's fans who boasts her own following is thirteen-year-old Lilly from Oregon. Alvarez sent me a link to one of Lilly's videos on

YouTube—a well-made work called "How to Make a Guardian Herd Pegasus" (I'm married to a guy who has eight Emmys for cinematography, so I don't compliment media lightly). I also went to Wattpad to read some of Lilly's fanfiction and found it so well written that what Alvarez told me next was no surprise. "She has become inspired to be an author . . . she met another fan online. Both girls are about the same age, and they just wrote a book together, their first book."

"I wish I'd had this when I was a kid," says Alvarez. "I feel like it's opened the door for our society. For kids to create art, to find their own tribe, their own fandom. Plus, it's encouraging creativity."

The passion and creativity inspired by Alvarez's books reminded me of a story Reilly told me about her son's friend, who is similarly passionate about the Netflix series *Stranger Things*. "This boy even dressed up as the character Lucas for Halloween," said Reilly. When he discovered that no one had created a fan Snapchat following for the series, he started one himself.

"This boy is sharing his passion, gathering information about something he loves. There's a lot of learning skills going on there," says Reilly, "all driven by passion."[22]

Listening to Alvarez and Reilly describe how the web offers boundless opportunities for youth to express creativity and passion, I couldn't help but wonder at the headlines that dominate the same web where this creativity and passion is thriving. Every day we read about teens depressed or ruined by their smartphones. It's as though we're stuck in our own episode of *Stranger Things*, where there are two parallel universes: one where everything appears grand, and another where everything appears hellish. Stranger things, indeed.

PRODUCING VS. CONSUMING

If you learn one lesson from this book, please let it be this: *Technology is just a tool*. A hammer can be useful in making a beautiful structure; it can be used to destroy one, too. He who wields the tool holds the power of creation or destruction in his hands.

Think of that the next time you look at your kids' devices and wince. Try to remember they could be using them to make wonderful videos, write elaborate fanfiction, and draw magical pegasi. Encourage and help your children to partake in the benefits of the "participatory culture" that Jenkins writes of: "A participatory culture is a culture with relatively low barriers to artistic expression and civic engagement, strong support for creating and sharing one's creations, and some type of informal mentorship whereby what is known by the most experienced is passed along to novices. A participatory culture is also one in which members believe their contributions matter, and feel some degree of social connection with one another (at the least they care what other people think about what they have created).²³

While many kids intuitively avail themselves of a participatory culture's benefits, many more need nudging. So show them how they can participate online. Inspire them with stories of others who are contributing to a vibrant web of ideas, resources, and knowledge. This is what we do during our final year of Cyber Civics. One of the awesome online resources we study and where they can see, to borrow Jenkins's words, that "their contributions matter," is Wikipedia.

THE WONDERS OF WIKIPEDIA

Wikipedia is the quintessential example of a participatory culture at work. Anyone, anywhere, who is connected to the internet can contribute to Wikipedia, making this free online resource "as good as a source of accurate information as Britannica, the venerable standard-bearer of facts."²⁴ Wikipedia embodies the argument James Surowiecki makes in *The Wisdom of Crowds*, that "groups are remarkably intelligent, and are often smarter than the smartest people in them."²⁵

The nice thing about Wikipedia is that *anyone* who knows *something* about *anything* can be an editor. This year, while the Winter Olympics were underway, I told my students that I was probably one of the few people in the world who knew *something* about two relatively new Olympic sports—ski cross and boardercross. Years ago, I worked in sports marketing with Jim "Too Tall" Essick (in case you are wondering, he is tall). Our small firm, Recreational Sports Marketing, produced sporting events for corporate sponsors, including ski races that Essick thought we could make more exciting by pitting four racers against one another on the course at the same time, like motocross. Since my job was to take his ideas, put them on paper, and try to convince brands to sponsor them, that's what I did. I flew to New

York and pitched his idea to a handful of companies. They all turned me down. But years later, one of the companies I'd pitched produced Essick's concept themselves, exchanging skis for snowboards and calling it "board-ercross." A few years after that, it became an Olympic sport, with "ski cross" following shortly thereafter.

Essick read all about it on Wikipedia, and I felt badly about giving away his idea. "How often does someone have the opportunity of thinking up the idea for an Olympic sport?" he asked. "It would be nice to get credit somewhere."

I decided to give him the credit he deserves by becoming a Wikipedia editor and writing the short history that appears on the ski cross page today.[26]

My students were surprised to hear that anyone, even their teacher, can author content on Wikipedia—and that I know anything about snowboarding. I hope I inspired them to try doing both!

SHIFT YOUR PERSPECTIVE

Today my classes at Journey School are large, sixty kids per grade, so it takes longer to know each student as well as I'd like. Sometimes I peg kids all wrong, as I did with Mark. A lanky boy with shaggy blond hair, he talked endlessly about YouTube, so I assumed he was binge-watching something ridiculous, or worse, like watching the horribly offensive "Jeffy" videos that are all the rage with many ten- to twelve-year-olds. When I took the time to *ask* what he was watching, he told me he'd discovered some videos on how to make a computer from spare parts. Which he did.

Because incidents like this one are happening more often at Journey School, the school's perspective toward media has slowly shifted. For grades K–5, the school still asks for elimination of electronic media during the school week, from Sunday evening to Friday after school, so students can use that precious time to hone the social and behavioral skills they'll need when they do go online. However, for its middle school students, the school encourages media "production" over "consumption." Here's how the media policy reads today:

In recognition of the maturing capacities and needs of the twelve- to fourteen-year-olds, we encourage and will support parents to

dialogue with their children in grades six to eight about the appropriate use of media and technology. . . . We suggest that your child should
participate in media, not simply consume media. We recommend limited one-way media from Sunday evening through Thursday night
(watching a movie). However, rather than simply consuming media,
we encourage participatory media throughout the week (creating a
movie). There is a vast difference between creating a short video that
captures your friend's multiple attempts to surf (and final success),
than simply watching a movie.[27]

Shelley Glaze-Kelley, Journey School's educational director whom you
met in Chapter 1, says the school has made a dramatic turnaround. "Our
kids have gone from binge-watching YouTube to becoming interested in
coding, blogging, filming, and art production," she says. "Over a five-year
span, the culture has changed from a mostly consuming media culture to a
much more productive one."[28]

I encourage you to make this shift, too—encourage media participation
vs. consumption—within your own families and communities. When you
do, stand back and prepare to be amazed. Because that's when *really* good
things start happening online.

CYBER CIVICS MOMENTS
Detecting Crap

Teach your children how to detect the misinformation they are sure to
encounter online by teaching them the acronym C.R.A.P. and its meaning. If
C.R.A.P. offends your sensibilities, add another A—C.R.A.A.P.—and
explain that it stands for "accuracy." Your kids can put the C.R.A.P. test to
work:

1. Search for fake news. A great way to do this is to sit down with your
   children and scroll through your Facebook feed, or any social network
   you might use to get and share news. Together, look for news stories.
   Keep your eyes open for those with catchy headlines that include
   words and phrases like "shocking," "amazing," or "wait 'til you see

this!" Click on one of the stories you find, and apply the test by finding answers to these questions (some "Googling" required):

- Is the website/story current?
- Does the website/story seem reliable?
- Who is the author? What are the author's credentials?
- Is the information presented accurate?
- What is purpose of the website/article? Do you detect a point of view?

2. If you don't use Facebook, peruse other social media sites that share news. Many kids get their news from Snapchat, through a feature called "Discover." If your children use Snapchat, ask them to show you some of the featured stories on Discover. Most are produced by reputable organizations like The Food Network, *Seventeen*, the *New York Times*, and *National Geographic*. See if you can help your children detect misinformation on their own apps.

3. Explain to your children that, today, anyone with a connected device can publish anything online. Tell them that many people use social media to get their news and sometimes even find fake stories there more believable than real news. (A Yale University study found that fake news stories that are repeated, through likes or sharing on social media, are perceived as more accurate than real stories.[29]) Both Google and Facebook have started cracking down on this phenomenon. Tell your children that Facebook users can report fake stories. Show them how to do so by referring to the steps I outlined earlier in this chapter.

Are You a Consumer or a Producer?

This is a different spin on the "Weigh In" activity in Chapter 4. This time, when your children assess their digital diets, they won't be looking at *how much* time they spend with media, but whether they spent that time consuming or producing.

1. Ask your children to track their media use for twenty-four hours on a typical, nonschool day (you can do it, too!). Have them write down all

the digital media they use, from the time they wake up to the moment they fall asleep.

2. At the end of the twenty-four hours, have your children sort their media use into two categories: *media consumed* and *media produced*. Next, have them total the time spent in each category. This is harder than it sounds, as some media use straddles both categories. Here are some general examples: If they took and posted pictures, that's producing; if they binge-watched YouTube videos, that's consuming. However, if they used YouTube to make and post a video, or commented on another person's video, that's producing.

3. It helps kids to visualize consumption vs. production, so encourage them to convert their data into a pie chart, a great math skill. Here is an example from one of my students:

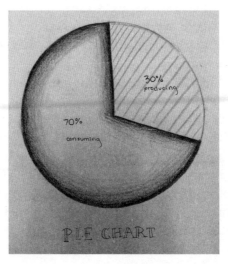

4. Look at your lists and pie charts and talk. Ask your children questions: Did you spend more time producing or consuming? What did you produce? What skills did you learn or use as producers? In what ways can you produce more and consume less in the future? (Remember, we all need a little consumption now and then, too!). This will help your family shift your media conversations away from "time spent online" and toward "positive use of time spent online." Good luck!

Chapter 8

Digital Leadership

•

So, it seems that we are faced with a remarkable irony: in an age of increasing artificiality, children first need to sink their hands deeply into what is
real; that in an age of light-speed communication, it is crucial that children
take the time to develop their own inner voice; that in an age of incredibly
powerful machines we must first teach our children how to use the incredible powers that lie deep within themselves.
—LOWELL MONKE, "THE HUMAN TOUCH"[1]

Every year I tell my students that while our time together will offer
plenty of opportunity for class discussion, the rule is: *When I'm talking,
they're listening.* It was hard for Luis, a wiry boy with unbridled energy,
to obey this simple rule. He was much more interested in chatting with his
classmates than in listening to me. Frankly, nothing I had to say seemed to
engage Luis. He was always anxious for Cyber Civics to end, so he could
head to his favorite activity, recess. I had nearly given up hope of ever connecting with him. But that changed the day of our "app" lesson.

A couple of months into each year, I challenge sixth graders to apply the
principles of good citizenship—*honesty, compassion, respect, responsibility,*
and *courage*—to online communities they might either join or invent. Their
task is to create—on paper—a website or app where at least one of these
principles would be a central tenet.

Luis was all-in. An avid mountain biker, he decided to "invent" an app
called *Hurt Alert* that would make it easy for bikers, hikers, and others to
show compassion for one another when they were out on a trail. Here's how
it would work: Imagine you were mountain biking alone, and you got hurt.
The app would automatically notify nearby riders, hikers, runners, or others
who were also using the app, letting them know you needed help. If you
were setting out for a ride or a hike, you could log in to *Hurt Alert*, and the

app would let others know to keep an eye out for you or that you were available to help them if needed. Luis was so excited about his idea that this normally unengaged student followed me around the room for the entirety of the class, pen and paper in hand, explaining every feature of his app in excruciating detail. He even gave up a good portion of his coveted recess time to finish telling me about *Hurt Alert*.

To be fair, since I'm an avid mountain biker, too, I may have egged Luis on with my own enthusiasm. "What a great idea," I thought the next day, as I headed out on a solo mountain bike ride. I was thinking about Luis and his app when, mid-turn, I hit some loose dirt, lost traction, and fell. I wasn't hurt, but did find myself in an awkward position and temporarily unable to twist my shoe out of the pedal it was clipped into. As I lay there, trying to dislodge myself, I thought about how particularly handy it would have been to have Luis's app on my phone.

The next time I saw Luis, I told him what happened and how I had wished for his app. His face lit up. Then he turned serious and admonished me, "Ms. Graber, it isn't wise for you to ride alone. I'd better get that app made right away."

IT SHOULDN'T BE THAT HARD TO DO GOOD

Whether or not Luis takes the next step—learning how to make an app—remains to be seen. But the point is that, via this simple activity, Luis and his classmates got to imagine how they might use their powerful devices in positive and world-improving ways. This seems important as we watch so many apps and websites add socially beneficial features as an afterthought, or only in response to public outcry. Let me present a few examples:

- A 2017 report that pegged Instagram as the worst social media network for mental health and well-being recommended that the app, and other apps, "identify users who could be suffering from mental health problems by their posts and other data and provide them with discreet information about where they can find help."[2] Shortly thereafter, Instagram added "three new safety and kindness features," including one that lets users flag others who may need help.[3] Now, if notified, Instagram will send those users a message of support, and provide options for where to turn for help.

- After being widely criticized for failing to address cyberbullying on its site, Twitter began placing online bullies in "time out" in early 2017. Today, bullies "will have the reach of their tweets temporarily restricted. During this time, abusers' tweets will only be shown to their followers."[4]
- Through a campaign called "Stop, Speak, Support," the UK's Prince William convinced both Facebook and Snapchat to initiate a trial program that would support cyberbullying victims and implement safety guidelines for internet users. According to a news report, "For the first time ever the world's social media firms are adapting their platforms to provide direct access to support when bullying strikes."[5] Prince William stated he hopes this program "can become a global blueprint."[6]

While these are wonderful developments, they beg the question: What took so damn long?

Features to protect users and combat online cruelty should not be add-ons—they should be prerequisites. They should be the civic responsibility of every app maker. They should be as ubiquitous as seat belts for cars.

For these reasons, I challenge students to imagine the functionalities they would build into the apps/sites/services they might develop one day. Here are some ideas they've offered:

- Algorithms that detect and then automatically transform mean comments into kind ones.
- Software that sends bullies two warnings and then, upon a third transgression, immediately deletes their accounts. Additionally, if bullies try to open new accounts, even under different usernames, "software will detect and block them."
- An app that facilitates the delivery of food to the homeless (via drone, of course), every time a paying customer orders a meal.

In an age when the world's biggest and most influential social media network, Facebook, was born in a college dorm room, anything seems possible. The only obstacle standing between good ideas and reality is a few lines of code, and even that isn't much of a deterrent these days.

My students routinely ask me if they are going to learn to code during our Cyber Civics classes. "I'm sorry, but no," I told a towheaded sixth grader named Jake when he asked me this question one year. "But you should check out Codeacademy.com," I suggested.

Codeacademy is an online site that offers free coding classes in twelve different programming languages, including HTML, CSS, Javascript, and more. I had heard of young kids learning to code from this site, and had even tried a few lessons myself and found them pretty easy and fun. I recommend it to my students and usually never hear about it again.

Except for the afternoon I was helping an eighth-grade class with their end-of-the-year presentations. They were using various online presentation tools I'd shown them, when one of the girls ran into a technical glitch; she couldn't get her audio to play in sync with her presentation. Since I had no idea how to help her, she asked if she could go get technical assistance. "Sure," I said, and a few minutes later saw Jake walk into the room. In the time it took me to figure out that Jake was the "technical assistance" she was referring to, he had hacked into the site and was writing code that would allow his sister's audio to play.

"Jake, where did you learn how to do that?" I asked.

"On Codeacademy," he responded, reminding me that I had recommended it to him.

"I visited Codeacademy for one hour every night before I went to bed. My mom timed me," he said. "I had to do two of the languages twice through, but now I'm fairly proficient in both," and with a quick smile he slipped out of the room and returned to his sixth-grade class.

WHEN KIDS MAKE GOOD APPS

Early one morning, I received a phone call from Lucy Cadova. She was responding to my request for information about FaceUp.com, an antibullying app that connects threatened or harassed students with the adult staff members of a school. According to the app's impressive website, a group of friends came up with the idea for FaceUp because they found high school life to be "anything but rainbows and unicorns."[7]

Cadova was calling from Brno, a city located in the southeastern region of the Czech Republic (I'd seen a California address on FaceUp's website, so this surprised me). She immediately apologized for her English (which, aside from a slight accent, was nearly perfect) and said she'd "been studying English longer" than anyone else on FaceUp's small staff, who were mostly still in high school; Cadova told me she had just turned eighteen. Thus, it fell on her to return calls to the U.S., which she did after school.

FaceUp was not the group's first venture. They had already launched a website where students anonymously report bullying. Per Cadova, 20 percent of the schools in the Czech Republic use it.

That success encouraged the friends to think bigger. As Cadova told me, "There's no time to stop when you want to help someone."

Although each of the kids on the FaceUp team has experienced bullying firsthand, the app—the brainchild of Jan Slama—was designed primarily with bystanders in mind. Cadova told me that kids often stand by and watch bullying happen because they have no idea how to help without exposing themselves to bullying. "FaceUp enables anyone to speak up for a friend, for someone you don't know that much, or even for yourself without the risk of being exposed," she explained.

What an interesting twist on anonymity, I thought. Usually, anonymous apps like Ask.fm, Whisper, After School, and others earn an automatic bad rap simply for being anonymous. Everyone figures that, because kids can hide their true identities, they use the apps primarily to bully. FaceUp turns this notion upside down, with the premise that kids who need help or want to help others may want to remain anonymous, too.

Cadova said that FaceUp, a free app for schools, has three main features. First are "reports," an "easy, anonymous way to speak up and seek help for yourself or someone else." The next feature, "messaging," is a real-time chat that lets kids anonymously seek help from a teacher, counselor, or administrator. "Sometimes it's not easy to talk about problems face-to-face," Cadova explained. Finally, there's an SOS button for emergency situations. "Like a fight in school, or something that needs immediate action," she told me.

When I asked how the team was marketing the app, she giggled. "It's hard to call it marketing—we are just a group of kids." But these kids had just returned from Silicon Valley, where they met with mentors, teachers, and representatives from schools considering use of the app. Two schools in the San Francisco area had already signed up. Cadova told me that in the past two weeks she'd probably talked to over forty U.S. schools, "but with school and spring break, I really need to catch up," she said.

FaceUp is one of the many apps created by young entrepreneurs hoping to make the world a better place. Here are a few more:

- After watching her mother struggle to get her grandfather, who suffered from dementia, to remember to take his medication, thirteen-year-old Ellie Tilford and five of her middle school classmates created Pharm Alarm. In addition to reminding users to take their meds, this app sends a prerecorded message to three emergency contacts if the user forgets. If the contacts don't respond in a set amount of time, the user's doctor is notified.
- Sixteen-year-old Natalie Hampton created the Sit With Us app to help kids find someone to sit with in the school lunchroom. Using her app, kids can communicate privately to set up safe tables, where they can eat in others' company and don't have to suffer the humiliation of eating alone.
- Teenage girls in India used the MIT App Inventor, a free tool for making apps, to create Paani, an app that helps women and children stay safe while collecting water at the community tap in Mumbai's Dharavi slum. The app creates an online queue and alerts households when it's their turn to collect water, helping them avoid the wait in long, sometimes unsafe, lines.

Discovering these amazing, kid-created apps made me wonder what would happen if all kids had the opportunity or were encouraged to use their creativity, ingenuity, empathy, and kindness online. What if we spent less time focusing on the terrible ways kids use tech, or the horrible things that tech does to them, and refocused our energies on helping kids become positive creators online, rather than passive consumers? What if we celebrated kids when they lived up to this vision? Thank goodness, someone does.

CELEBRATING THE GOOD

Matt Soeth is a tall, affable guy who hails from California. This former high-school teacher is the founder, along with teacher Kim Karr, of #ICAN-HELP, an organization that aims "to educate and empower students to use social media positively."[8]

"So much of the conversation out there is on the negative things happening to kids," Soeth told me. "Every news story, every report, every warning, every moral panic and fear, is all about how we need to protect kids and that they can't take care of themselves. Our reality at school is that, with the right training and guidance, kids do some really amazing stuff."[9]

Soeth and Karr decided to highlight that stuff by launching #Digital-4Good, an event that celebrates "student voice and digital leadership in social media." He told me that this one-day event, staged at Twitter's national headquarters in 2017, honors remarkable kids who use their devices in positive ways. Each one is nominated by peers and selected by a panel of educators and industry representatives.

When I asked Soeth to recall last year's most memorable honoree, he thought of a thirteen-year-old girl named Maeve. "She was our youngest winner," he said. "She suffered from multiple food allergies and loved to bake. So she started researching recipes, and then making some of her own, and then posting them to a website, until it sort of took off." According to Soeth, others with similar dietary restrictions gravitated to her site, called *Baker Delights: Gluten and Dairy Free Desserts Made from Scratch*, and now "she really has quite a following."

At the #Digital4Good event, all winners present their projects. "Maeve was so nervous," Soeth told me. That's understandable, because not only did she have to address approximately a hundred people at Twitter, but the event was also livestreamed to thousands more. According to Soeth, "But Maeve got up on stage and asked, 'Just because I have an allergy doesn't mean I can't eat food that tastes good, does it?' It was very adorable—you should watch her video."[10]

I did watch her video, and in the corner of the screen, capturing Maeve's presentation on her phone, was her mother—Liz Repking of Cyber Safety Consulting.

Surprised that Repking hadn't shamelessly bragged about her daughter when we spoke a few weeks earlier, I called to ask about Maeve's project. "Well, that all started years ago," Repking said, "when I told Maeve that I wanted her to start journaling over the summer. She just looked at me like I was crazy."[11]

That's when Maeve's dad stepped in to help her set up a blog, where she could share her love of baking. Although he initially taught Maeve how to set up a website—"they spent hours together working on it," says Repking—today Maeve manages the site herself, and uploads all her own recipes, photos, and more. "She'll go in her room and spend lots of time tweaking things," Repking told me. "But her passion is the baking. Technology is simply the means to share that passion."

"What we have discovered is this: Kids are capable of really good things, but what they're looking for is an adult who will support them, who will guide them, and really push them," Soeth informed me.[12]

After that, watch them fly.

IF YOU WANT YOUR KIDS TO FLY, GIVE THEM WINGS

Most parents looking for digital parenting help aren't regaled with stories about kids doing awesome stuff online. I wasn't. I remember attending my first "online safety" presentation almost ten years ago. The speaker, who was the owner of a local computer repair company, had a reputation for giving presentations that were engaging and informative. I went to one in my neighborhood, pen and paper in hand, and found myself surrounded by nearly two hundred other anxious parents. For two hours we sat at the edges of our seats as he recounted one horror story after another about cyberbullying, predators, pornography, and so forth. It was terrifying!

I drove home that night with the notes I'd scribbled shoved down into my pocket. They included a long list of "bad apps" he told us to go home and "immediately delete from our kids' devices." I wondered what the success rate was of parents who did so. How long before those curious kids went right back to the cookie jar their parents had hidden in a new location?

That was a long time ago, and one might presume we've come a long way since. Wrong. Just last week, Peter Kelley, who works with me, got a call from a local community group seeking a presentation for middle school girls and their parents. He was prepared to lead them through one of our digital reputation activities when he received a second phone call from the organizer, who wanted to confirm he was going to "scare the hell out of the girls." Kelley politely explained, "That's not what we do," because, in our experience, teaching kids through fear is counterproductive. Fear elicits a physiological reaction in humans known as the "fight or flight response." Though kids probably won't "fight" you during a presentation, mentally they *will* take "flight," meaning they'll respond to the terrifying things you tell them by not listening. So if you want kids to learn something, scaring the hell out of them doesn't work.

Kelley lost the gig. The woman on the other end of the line thanked him and hired another, scarier guy for the job.

"Here's the problem," says NAMLE's Michele Ciulla Lipkin. "We spend most of our time worried about the negative stuff online, and we spend hardly any time celebrating and empowering the good stuff. Why is it with technology that all we ever do is think about the worst-case scenario? Why do we do that to our kids? Why do we do that to ourselves? And why does the media only cover that?"[13]

In addition to her full-time job with NAMLE, Ciulla Lipkin regularly visits schools to deliver her "Parenting in the Digital Age" presentation. She starts her talks by assessing parents' feelings about tech and has found, as have I, parental angst to be at an all-time high. "I'm amazed at the struggles parents are still having," she said. "I've had parents moved to tears because all they do is fight with their kids about media. Then when I talk to the kids, I can't believe how nervous they are about digital life, all because their parents are petrified. It *really* doesn't have to be this hard."

Ciulla Lipkin believes the reason parenting in the digital age feels this hard is because it's so new. "There's *always* been a disconnect between adults and teens," she says, "but now the changes in society are happening so fast, we are really struggling to figure out how to parent in a new world."

As three-time Pulitzer winner Thomas Friedman puts it in his newest book, *Thank You for Being Late: An Optimist's Guide to Thriving in the Age of Accelerations*, "the rate of technological change is now accelerating so fast that it has risen above the average rate at which most people can absorb all these changes."[14] As a result, most people can't keep up. Friedman's solution to this conundrum is "dynamic stability," which he likens to riding a bicycle. Like riding a bike, you cannot stand still. You must keep pedaling.

Since I've never met a bicycle metaphor I didn't like, let me take Friedman's a bit further and apply it to my favorite kind of bike, a mountain bike. On a steep downhill, forward momentum is your best friend. The worst thing you can do is take it too slowly. The faster you ride, even pushing yourself to a pace that feels uncomfortable, the more successfully you'll navigate the terrain.

Digital parenting is the same. You have to move forward, even if it feels uncomfortable to open a Snapchat account or to try *Minecraft*. And you've got to look beyond the depressing research, to see what your own children are really doing, or could be doing, online.

As Ciulla Lipkin put it, "For every study you read about kids being addicted to social media, you will find another one saying that they are empowered by social media. So that's the hard part. There's a lot of stuff we just don't know."

Let's look at what we *do* know. According to Ciulla Lipkin, "We know we spend a lot of time with media, and we know that media is really important to us. We know, without a shadow of a doubt, that media impacts us. We know that can be positive or that can be negative. We know there is a risk with media use, and we know there's opportunity. We also know parents are really worried and overwhelmed."

"And that," she says, "is all we *really* know."[15]

GO WITH WHAT YOU KNOW

The main objective of this book has been to equip you with tools to help your children build a healthy relationship with technology. While you don't need any technical skills for this job, you do need to draw upon what you already know about being a parent.

"The biggest thing that parents undervalue is their life experience as human beings," said Soeth. "They've all been in relationships. They've had good friends; they've had bad friends. They've had people who've been fake and people who are real coming in and out of their lives for however long they've been on this earth. But I think there's a wall that goes up when technology is involved. Parents think, 'I don't get tech; therefore I can't help you.'"[16]

Soeth believes parents perceive a distinct difference between online life and offline life. "But for young people, there's no online and offline," he said. "It's *all* life." And kids today need their parents' help to navigate their lives.

Ciulla Lipkin concurs, "So often I see parents give their power away to technology. They forget that most of the issues that arise with kids and technology or social media are not technology issues—they're social issues."

Let me provide a few examples:

- A parent says, "I tell my kids they are not allowed to watch [fill in the blank]. Then they go over to Timmy's house, and they're watching it there, and I know they are lying to me!" Ciulla Lipkin's response is, "Okay, that's not a technology issue—that's a lying issue. How would you respond if they were lying to you about something else?"

- A parent says, "My daughter is upset about something that happened on Snapchat, and I can't help her." Ciulla Lipkin responds, "Of course you can. Didn't you ever experience teenage drama?"
- Here's one of my favorites: A parent says, "My nine-year-old daughter really wants a Snapchat account, and I don't know what to say to her." My response: "That's easy. Say 'N-O.' It's a tried-and-true response that has stood the test of time. When your nine-year-old dissolves into tears and says, 'But you don't understand!' you say, 'Yes, I do! When I was fourteen, I really wanted to drive a car, but the rules were that you had to be sixteen. I waited, and I survived. So will you."

See how easy that is? Draw upon your own hard-earned wisdom, gleaned from years on this earth, to help your children navigate new terrain. Empathize with them and have conversations. Did your teenage son just break up with his first girlfriend? Chances are he is experiencing the additional heartbreak of seeing posts and pictures that show how much fun she's having without him—or worse, with someone else. Talk to him about it. Does your daughter spend more time playing video games than reading books? Maybe she's learning something via the game that she's not learning elsewhere. Or maybe she's experiencing a lot of stress at school, and gaming is providing a respite. Or perhaps she finds it easier to connect with peers via her game than she does in real life. Talk to her about it. Dig deep into your own memories to remember when you got dumped by a girlfriend/boyfriend, or watched a TV show that taught you something new, or found it easier to talk to peers on the phone rather than face-to-face. You *can* do this.

Remember, you are not in this alone. Parents everywhere are struggling with these same issues. Talk to them, too.

"I think parents have to open up a dialogue about these issues in their communities and find support," says Ciulla Lipkin. "Parents and schools have to work together, because we no longer live in a world where we can separate home and school. Administrators must support teachers getting professional development, because teachers have to understand these issues, too. We all have to ask if we are having these conversations in our communities."

FORWARD!

When the time draws near for me to say goodbye to another crop of students I've been lucky enough to shepherd through three years of Cyber Civics lessons, I cross my fingers and pray I've adequately prepared them for whatever the technological future brings. Who knows what lies ahead? Flying, driverless Uber rides that deliver pizza? An internet searchable with the blink of an eye? Thin, plastic membranes you can stick on your body that turn into tiny computer displays? (That last one is already a thing.)

I figure the best way to prepare students for an uncertain technological future is to inspire them with stories of how other young people have used the technology at their disposal in positive and productive ways. I used to find my best stories by drawing upon other cultures. For example, I'd tell them about the Arab Spring, the wave of pro-democracy protests and uprisings that took place in the Middle East and North Africa in 2010 and 2011. Students there used social media to orchestrate the rapid and relatively peaceful disintegration of authoritarian regimes. Facebook provided a place where they could organize, meet, and share ideas. They even used Facebook to orchestrate what many consider Egypt's first organized protest, which resulted in an eighteen-day, near countrywide stand against Egyptian president Mubarak. President Obama lauded technology's role in the uprising, which resulted in Mubarak leaving office, and praised young Egyptians who used "their own creativity and talent, and technology to call for a government that represented their hopes and not their fears."[17]

Today, I don't have to reach beyond U.S. shores to find an inspiring story to share. I've begun telling my students how Marjory Stoneman Douglas High School students in Parkland, Florida, used their tools to spur significant social and cultural change.

When a mass shooting on their high school campus on Valentine's Day 2018 left seventeen students and teachers dead, distraught students decided they wanted to advocate for new gun-control laws, so they picked up their devices and got to work. At first, they used their phones to capture, in real time and in graphic detail, the horrific scene during the shooting and their reactions to it, and then shared those online. Next, students posted their thoughts to Facebook and Instagram, which led to on-air appearances and passionate speeches that went viral. Soon, even more students took to social media, especially Twitter, subtweeting and retweeting with zeal. The

#NeverAgain movement was born and along with it an army of civically engaged youth. Using the social media savvy they are often derided for using, students commandeered the gun-control conversation and demanded immediate action from lawmakers. In the time it would have taken the average adult to compose a press release, these kids brought more awareness to this issue than all the politicians in Washington combined.

Don Tapscott, author of *Grown Up Digital*, told the *New York Times* that he believes today's teenagers are better communicators than any previous generation. "They didn't grow up being the passive recipients of somebody else's broadcast. . . . They grew up being interactors and communicators."[18] In the same article, clinical psychologist Wendy Mogel, author of *Voice Lessons for Parents: What to Say, How to Say It, and When to Listen*, had this to say about today's youth: "They're courageous, energetic, optimistic, and really smart."[19]

I agree. We entirely underestimate young people when we write them off as unengaged, apathetic, or depressed. Worse, defining an entire generation by the headlines we read about them displays our ignorance about the complex—and yes, sometimes depressing—world they have no choice but to grow up in. A world that, whether we like it or not, is inextricably entwined with technology. Lest we forget, it's our generation that made connected devices a part of theirs. We thrust gadgets into their little palms with virtually no guidance, no role models, and sometimes even years before they were cognitively prepared to use them well. Even so, many young people are doing pretty darn well *despite* being left to their own devices. How many more would do even better, I wonder, with a little help from us?

BEING HUMAN IN THE DIGITAL AGE

One late May weekend, during a Cyber Civics workshop at Journey School, a visiting teacher asked our eighth graders, "What was the most important digital skill you learned?" None of the students answered right away, which had me kind of worried. After what seemed an eternity, Seb, a thoughtful young man with dark brown eyes, responded, "We didn't learn digital skills." I could see the teacher was as surprised by his answer as I was. To my relief, he continued, "We learned life skills." He could tell the teacher still didn't understand. "Basically," he said, "we learned how to be human, online and off."

In this age of algorithms and bots, learning how to be human is more challenging than ever. Text messages are curt, Siri doesn't expect a *thank you*, and autoresponders can't detect when the sender needs a kind word or a hug. To raise kids who will wield technology with empathy, understanding, thoughtfulness, compassion—and all the other age-old human capacities that make life worth living—we must sow the seeds of each of these qualities offline, when kids are young. That way, as they get older and smarter, they'll have these essential human qualities to draw upon and use where they are really needed, in the online world. Perhaps they'll also remember to put down their devices now and then and collect the rewards of offline life, like real hugs, genuine smiles, and hearty high fives. I hope this book can help you help your children do just that.

Wrapping up this chapter, I wanted to find an easy-to-remember phrase, a simple motto, or a snappy synopsis to summarize what it means to be human in a digital world—something you could tell your kids, that they'd get right away. Since I'd started to worry about my caffeine intake a couple of chapters ago, I'd switched to drinking Kombucha—a "healthy" alternative that still delivers a moderate dose of caffeine—and in a moment of boredom read the label on the back of the bottle in front of me. Lo and behold, there under "Words of Enlightenment" was the short maxim I'd hoped for. Coincidentally, I knew who had authored the words, too: Conrad Anker. Anker is a climbing buddy of my husband. Not the "let's hit the climbing gym" kind of climbing buddy, but rather the "we're going on an expedition, and with any luck we'll return in two months with all our fingers and toes intact" sort of buddy. Over the years, they've survived some big mountain, high-altitude suffer-fests together—from first ascents in Antarctica's Queen Maud Land, to filming a retracing of Sir Ernest Shackleton's epic journey across South Georgia Island. Anker's illustrious climbing career has catapulted him to international recognition, so I imagine his experiences have provided plenty of opportunity to ponder life's big questions. Dangling on a rope several thousand feet off the deck tends to give one clarity.

So here, courtesy of Anker, is the perfect maxim to remind your kids— and you—how to be human in a digital age. Simply:

"Be Good. Be Kind. Be Happy."

Epilogue

•

If you've read through this book and completed all the "Cyber Civics Moments" with your children, your work is finished! You understand the importance of laying a strong foundation of social and emotional skills, and you know how to help your children build a sturdy structure with four strong pillars that will withstand any digital storms that may blow their way. You'll encourage them to engage with online communities in positive and productive ways, and you understand this all takes a ton of time and effort. Is it worth it?

I used to wonder that myself and decided the best way to find out was to check in with my first crop of Cyber Civics students, starting way back in 2010, my daughter Piper's class. Essentially my guinea pigs, these kids enthusiastically participated in any activity I challenged them with, as we figured out together which ones worked best. Did it have an impact on their actual digital lives, I wondered, now that they are in college or working?

I asked my assistant, Anna Dieckmeyer, to find out. At nineteen, she is the same age as my former students, so I figured they'd be more forthright with her. I gave her one directive: Find out what their relationship is with their digital tools. I also told her that we could assign each student a pseudonym, as I've done with all the other kids in this book. Interestingly, they all agreed to the use of their real names. I took that as a good sign.

Anna's firsthand account follows:

When Diana asked me to interview her former students about their current "relationship with their digital tools," I first stopped to consider my own. Personally, I never really thought about the internet, social media, and technology as *tools*—I mean, sure I use these things all the time, like anybody else. But like most people I know, I tend to directly associate them with the bad consequences that occur with misuse. Plus, technology has always been this large, invasive *thing*. Something that you can't ignore—that you need— no matter how badly you wish the opposite. I guess I'm trying to say that I never viewed the internet as a beneficial innovation, weird as that might sound coming from someone of my generation. That changed with these interviews. Here's what I learned:

Garrett Wallace

The first person I interviewed was Garrett Wallace, a freshman at Saddleback College. Though he admitted, speaking rather laconically, that he couldn't recall specific lessons, I discovered that his social media use is unique. For instance, most people our age have public Instagram profiles alongside a separate, private "Finsta," where they can share things (often NSFW, "not safe for work") for only close friends to see. Garrett explained, "I stayed away from that. My main account is private, for no other reason than I just want to know who's looking at my stuff." And he describes his posts as "pretty family friendly. . . . I don't cuss or post videos of me and my friends doing bad things." He stays smart and cautious, eliminating any chance of damage to his reputation. This, to me, sounds a lot like what Cyber Civics teaches.

Quinn Shaw

Next, I interviewed Quinn Shaw, a charismatic freshman at Sonoma State University, who's dual majoring in English and psychology and minoring in gerontology. I've known Quinn about as long as I've known Piper, Diana's daughter, so I was already aware that she uses social media limitedly. When I asked if she believes that Cyber Civics helped her with her digital life, she said, "I wasn't necessarily ever *unprepared*—you know, it was never like I was gonna be sending nudes in the first place." She laughed. "But in the sense of understanding that your digital footprint doesn't go away, [those classes] solidified that I shouldn't do anything like that."

Quinn remembers having class discussions and playing games surrounding real-life examples of social media activities gone wrong. It makes sense that she would remember those things, as any kind of hands-on or interactive activity is key in earning the interest of children and teens. I also asked Quinn if she thought her use of social media is unique, and she responded with a good example: "Some of the time I'm talking to my friends and say, 'Oh, I wanna disable my Instagram,' and they're like, 'Why would you ever, ever, ever do that?' And I'll just say it's because you kinda get caught up in it, and it's annoying, and they're like, 'What?' So while I think part of this is obviously due to who I am, I think this is more typical of kids who have taken classes about this."

Personally, while I've experienced the urge to take a break from apps like Instagram and Snapchat, too, I've never brought myself to follow through with it. But as I talked to Quinn and the others, I began to realize how much more at ease they were with the thought of life without social media, perhaps because they had learned its pros and cons early on.

Elias Burlison

Elias Burlison, a bright mechanical engineering major and computer science minor in Sacramento State University's honors program, had a lot to say about social media. Like Quinn, he believes in limited use of Instagram and similar apps, and worries about a decline in face-to-face social interaction: "I know a lot of people our age don't really think this, but I see it [social media] replacing basic interactions with other people. You know, instead of meeting someone for lunch, you end up calling them, or texting them, or FaceTiming them, and it's a problem."

He continued, "I think you shouldn't limit yourself to just digital interaction. You should have more than that. Obviously, I still have all that stuff, but if I had the option, I would opt not to use it."

I'd like to believe there are a lot more people like Elias and Quinn in my age group, and that we're more social in the "real" world than the media portrays. But in reality, it seems that our ranks are growing thin, which makes this kind of education even more critical.

Elias also pointed out, "[Kids] don't really have anybody telling them what's publicly/socially acceptable to put online. That's something we talked about. I am the oldest of four, so I shared everything I learned with my siblings."

He went on to explain, "We learned how to use [social media] to our advantage, versus posting stuff that would affect us in a negative way later on. Diana was really keen on explaining everything, too, which I think is awesome, especially when you're a little kid, and someone's telling you to do something. Usually you don't listen unless you understand."

Sophia Fazli

At this point in the interviews, I noticed that the impact of one's digital reputation stuck with this first wave of students, including Sophia Fazli, an easygoing fashion merchandise major. "It definitely forced me to be more aware," she told me. For her, the lessons have carried over into her use of social media today. "I'm just careful about what I post," she says.

The consequences of oversharing personal information and controversial content affected her indirectly when a friend in a sorority got caught posting an inappropriate photo on a private account. Sophia explained, "[It's risky] even if you're being private—like she got a warning, and it was a big deal. She had to go in and meet with all the heads of her sorority."

Sophia also talked about the importance of posting family-friendly content, and how allowing her family to view her posts keeps her away from any situations like the one her friend experienced.

Nicholas Rocha

Nicholas Rocha, an outgoing freshman at Saddleback College, who plans to transfer to UC Santa Cruz to continue pursuing a degree in marine biology, immediately remembered learning how to make safe and memorable passwords: "The whole class was separated into different groups, and we had to think of creative passwords using the rules. It stressed the importance of keeping passwords different for important things—so using a different password for your email, or like your Facebook or stuff like that."

Nicholas remembered that social media was just starting to become a big thing when he took the class, especially Instagram: "It was just the start of it all when we took Cyber Civics. We learned that it was gonna be used more in the future for jobs, college, and so forth, and that people were going to use it to judge you in a professional sense. In high school, a lot of my friends didn't take the class, of course. They didn't think about that."

Here's what Nicholas discovered recently while applying for two different jobs:

They asked me, "Hey, can you come in tomorrow, and can we go over your social media accounts and see what's going on there? 'Cause we wanna make sure there's nothing too inappropriate."

Luckily, Nicholas had nothing to worry about. He already understood that there are a lot of things you shouldn't post online.

MY CONCLUSION

After conversing with everyone, I discovered two big differences between these students and others of my generation. First, they understand how to use the internet efficiently and in positive ways, and are more aware of the kinds of mistakes that could harm their digital reputations. Second, unlike many others of our generation, none seem to be slaves to their devices.

In the words of Elias Burlison, "I think eventually this will be integrated into some sort of public curriculum, because how could it not? Especially when every kid who's capable of wiggling their fingers has an iPad in their hands. It's a huge part of society now. One way or another, education about it is going to find its way in."

Acknowledgments

●

If it takes a village to raise a child, it certainly takes a bustling metropolis to help a first-time author turn an idea into a book. I am grateful to so many for their help and encouragement.

First and foremost, thank you to my family. For longer than I hate to admit, they've been staring at the back of my head as I sat staring at my screen. Thanks to my daughters, Elizabeth and Piper, for graciously allowing me to probe them about the intricacies of their digital lives. My deepest gratitude, however, is reserved for my husband, Michael. He's been my biggest cheerleader, encouraging me through four years of grad school that I assured him would fit easily in to an already-busy mom's schedule, and then another eight years of work, study, and travel as I fell further into the digital literacy rabbit hole. Having the unwavering support of one's spouse is truly one of life's most precious gifts.

This book would not have been possible without the help of the many experts I interviewed. Some of these names you may not know, but you should. Each works diligently to make the online world safer and saner. Thank you Alan Katzman, Brad Shear, Brittany OIer, Chip Donohue, Cynthia Lieberman, David Greenfield, David Kleeman, Erin Reilly, Gabe Zichermann, Jack McArtney, Jason Ohler, Jennifer Lynn Alvarez, Jim Essick, Joani Siani, Kelly Mendoza, Liz Repking, Lucy Cadova, Matt Soeth, Michele Borba, Michelle Ciulla Lipkin, Michelle Drouin, Michele Whiteaker, Ouri Azoulay, Pamela Hurst-Della Pietra, Pamela Rutledge, Patti Connolly, Peter Kelley, Richard Guerry, Ross Ellis, Sameer Hinduja, Shaheer Faltas, Shauna Leff, Shelley Glaze-Kelley, and Sue Scheff.

I never would have written this book without the encouragement of author Sue Scheff, who convinced me I could do it. My gratitude to her also for introducing me to my agent, the indefatigable Jacqueline Flynn of Joelle Delbourgo Associates. Surviving Jacquie's rigorous proposal-writing tutelage made actual book-writing seem almost easy! Thanks also to my editor Tim Burgard at HarperCollins Leadership for patiently guiding me from first draft to finished copy, to Amanda Bauch, Jeff Farr, and Leigh Grossman for applying their editing magic to my words, and to Hiram Centeno and Sicily Axton for their marketing acumen. Gratitude also to my hard-working colleague Peter Kelley and husband Michael for editing my first drafts.

My journey from idea to book began with the incredible education I received at Fielding Graduate University while pursuing a masters in "media psychology and social change." While every professor I studied under was amazing, a special thanks to Dr. Pamela Rutledge for sharing her deep well of knowledge and practical advice, and most of all, for inspiring me with her unwavering optimism about the positive potential of new technologies.

Out of the Fielding experience I gained a precious group of brainy and passionate friends: Cynthia Lieberman, Tina Hoover, Carla Casilli, Lisa Snow Macdonald, Lara Hoefs, and Cynthia Vinney. I am grateful for many years of bi-monthly breakfasts pondering humanity and technology. Thanks most of all to Cynthia Lieberman. Eight years ago, armed only with new M.A.'s and a mutual passion, we launched Cyberwise (aka, "No Grownup Left Behind") determined to share our knowledge of digital media with parents and teachers. Thank you for going on that journey with me!

Thanks to all the friends who have provided encouragement over the years, especially Patti Connolly and Shelley Glaze-Kelley who convinced to "lean in"!

Writing a book about raising kids inevitably reminds one of their own childhood. I am blessed to have experienced a wonderful—if somewhat raucous—upbringing surrounded by four independent and outspoken siblings who still make dinnertime conversations interesting. Thanks to my parents, Elizabeth and Donald Schulz, for making our childhood home full of love and laughter, and keeping it that way today.

I'm particularly grateful to the warm community of Journey School. Thanks to Shaheer Faltas, the school's former administrator, who took a chance on Cyber Civics and encouraged me to make it available to others. For that I will be eternally grateful. Thanks also to Gavin Keller, my daughter's 6th grade teacher and Journey's current administrator, for graciously inviting me into his classroom to deliver the very first lessons.

A heartfelt thank you to the students of Mr. Keller's class, especially those who agreed to be interviewed for this book by my bright assistant Anna Dieckmeyer. Thank you, Elias Burlison, Garrett Wallace, Nicholas Rocha, Quinn Shaw, and Sophia Fazli.

Last, but certainly not least, my deepest gratitude to every child I've had the privilege of sharing Cyber Civics with, those I've taught directly and those who have received the lessons from their own teachers. I am especially grateful to the many teachers and schools delivering Cyber Civics—or any kind of digital literacy lessons—in their own communities. Thank you for the part you play in raising kind, good, and happy humans in a digital world.

Endnotes

●

Introduction

1. Shriver, Lionel. *We Need to Talk About Kevin: A Novel* (New York: Harper Perennial, 2006), p. 177.
2. Unless otherwise noted, all student names are pseudonyms.
3. Third, Amanda, et al., "Young and Online: Children's Perspectives on Life in the Digital Age," *The State of the World's Children 2017 Companion Report* (Sydney: Western Sydney University, 2017): 6. DOI: 10.4225/35/5a1b885f6d4db.
4. Lenhart, Amanda, "Teens, Technology, and Friendships," Pew Research Center (August 6, 2015), p. 6. Retrieved on October 27, 2017 from http://www.pewinternet.org/2015/08/06/chapter-4-social-media-and-friendships.
5. Ibid., p. 5
6. Common Sense Media, "Social Media, Social Life: How Teens View Their Digital Lives," *A Common Sense Research Study* (Summer 2012), p. 22.
7. Reich, S. M., Subrahmanyam, K., and Espinoza, G., "Friending, IMing, and Hanging Out Face-to-Face: Overlap in Adolescents' Online and Offline Social Networks," *Developmental Psychology* 48(2), 2012, pp. 356–368; Coyne, S. M., Padilla-Walker, L. M., Day, R. D., Harper, J., and Stockdale, L. A., "Friend Request From Dear Old Dad: Associations Between Parent-Child Social Networking and Adolescent Outcomes," *Cyberpsychology Behavior and Social Networking* 17(1), January 2014, pp. 8–13.
8. Middaugh, Ellen, Lynn Schoefield Clark, and Parissa J. Ballard, "Digital Media, Participatory Politics, and Positive Youth Development," *Pediatrics* 140 (Supplement 2), November 2017, S127–S131; DOI: 10.1542/peds.2016-1758Q: S129.
9. Schaffer, Russell, "Kaplan Test Prep Survey: College Admissions Officers Say Social Media Increasingly Affects Applicants' Chances." Kaplan Test Prep (February 10, 2017). Retrieved on December 1, 2017 from http://press.kaptest.com/press-releases/kaplan-test-prep-survey-college-admissions-officers-say-social-media-increasingly-affects-applicants-chances.
10. Wanshel, Elyse, "Teen Makes 'Sit With Us' App That Helps Students Find Lunch Buddies," *Huffington Post* (November 16, 2016). Retrieved on

December 2, 2017 from https://www.huffingtonpost.com/entry/teen
-creates-app-sit-with-us-open-welcoming-tables-lunch-bullying_us_
57c5802ee4b09cd22d926463.

11. Theocharis, Y. and Quintelier, E. "Stimulating Citizenship or Expanding
Entertainment? The Effect of Facebook on Adolescent Participation," *New
Media and Society* 18(5), 2016, pp. 817–836.

12. Third, A., Bellerose, D., Dawkins, U., Keltie, E., and Pihl, K., "Children's
Rights in the Digital Age," *Children Around the World* (2nd edition) (Mel-
bourne: Young and Well Cooperative Research Centre, 2014), p. 36.

13. Common Sense Media, "The Common Sense Media Census: Media Use by
Tweens and Teens," 2015, Retrieved on October 10, 2017 from https://www
.commonsensemedia.org/sites/default/files/uploads/research/census_
executivesummary.pdf.

14. Kelly Mendoza (senior director of education programs for Common Sense
Media), in discussion with author, April 23, 2018. Used with permission.

15. Anderson, Monica, "How Having Smartphones (Or Not) Shapes the Way
Teens Communicate." Pew Research Center (August 20, 2015). Retrieved
on December 2, 2017 from http://www.pewresearch.org/fact-tank
/2015/08/20/how-having-smartphones-or-not-shapes-the-way-teens
-communicate/; Lenhart, Amanda. "Teens, Technology, and Friendships,"
Pew Research Center (August 6, 2016). Retrieved on January 23, 2018 from
http://www.pewinternet.org/2015/08/06/teens-technology-and
-friendships/.

16. Jack McArtney (former director of messaging at Verizon), in discussion
with author, November 20, 2017. Used with permission.

17. Dokoupil, Tony. "Is the Internet Making Us Crazy? What the New Research
Says," *Newsweek* (July 9, 2012). Retrieved on December 2, 2017 from http://
www.newsweek.com/internet-making-us-crazy-what-new-research-says
-65593.

18. Twenge, Jean M. PhD. *iGen: Why Today's Super-Connected Kids Are Growing Up Less Rebellious, More Tolerant, Less Happy—and Completely Unprepared for Adulthood* (New York: Atria Books, 2017), p. 5.

19. Twenge, Jean. "Have Smartphones Ruined a Generation?" *The Atlantic*
(September 2017). Retrieved November 28, 2017 from https://www
.theatlantic.com/magazine/archive/2017/09/has-the-smartphone
-destroyed-a-generation/534198/.

20. Ibid.

21. Felt, Laurel, and Robb, M. B., "Technology Addiction: Concern, Controversy, and Finding Balance," Research Brief (San Francisco: Common
Sense Media, 2016), p. 25.

22. Jamieson, Sophie. "Children Ignore Age Limits By Opening Social Media Accounts," *The Telegraph* (February 9, 2016). Retrieved on December 12, 2017 from http://www.telegraph.co.uk/news/health/children/12147629 /Children-ignore-age-limits-by-opening-social-media-accounts.html.

23. Capistrano Unified School District website. Retrieved on December 1, 2017 from http://capousd.ca.schoolloop.com.

24. "U.S. News Best High School Rankings," *U.S. News & World Report* (2017). Retrieved on December 2, 2017 from https://www.usnews.com/education /best-high-schools/rankings-overview.

25. Oppenheimer, Todd, "Schooling the Imagination," *The Atlantic* (September 1999). https://www.theatlantic.com/magazine/archive/1999/09/schooling -imagination/309180/.

26. Jenkin, Matthew. "Tablets Out, Imagination In: The Schools That Shun Technology," *The Guardian* (December 2, 2016). Retrieved on December 2, 2017 from https://www.theguardian.com/teacher-network/2015/dec/02 /schools-that-ban-tablets-traditional-education-silicon-valley-london.

27. "The Incredible Growth of the Internet Since 2000," Solarwinds Pingdom (October 22, 2010). Retrieved on December 10, 2017 from http://royal .pingdom.com/2010/10/22/incredible-growth-of-the-internet-since-2000/.

28. Rideout, V. J., Foehr, U. G., and Roberts, D. F., "Generation M2: Media in the Lives of 8–18 Year Olds," Kaiser Family Foundation (January 10, 2010). Retrieved on December 1, 2017 from https://www.kff.org/other/event /generation-m2-media-in-the-lives-of/.

29. Shaheer Faltas (former Journey School administrator), in discussion with author, November 6, 2017. Used with permission.

30. Graber, Diana, and Mendoza, Kelly, "New Media Literacy Education (NMLE): A Developmental Approach," *Journal of Media Literacy Education* 4(1), 2012. Retrieved on December 22, 2017 from http://digitalcommons.uri .edu/jmle/vol4/iss1/8/.

31. Faltas, discussion.

32. Lieu, Eric, "Why Ordinary People Need to Understand Power," TED Ideas Worth Spreading (September 2013). Retrieved on November 27, 2017 from https://www.ted.com/talks/eric_liu_why_ordinary_people_need_to_ understand_power.

33. Ibid.

34. Media Smarts Website. Retrieved on December 28, 2017 from http:// mediasmarts.ca/digital-media-literacy-fundamentals/digital-literacy -fundamentals.

35. Williams, Lauren, "Digital Literacy Yields Test Gains, Better Behavior," *District Administration* (August 2015). Retrieved on December 3, 2017 from

https://www.districtadministration.com/article/digital-literacy-yields -test-gains-better-behavior.

36. "Plato, The Phaedrus—A Dialogue Between Socrates and Phaedrus Written Down by a Pupil of Socrates, Plato, in Approximately 370 B.C." Digital Humanities (n.d.). Retrieved on December 2, 2017 from http://www.units .miamioh.edu/technologyandhumanities/plato.htm.

37. Bell, Vaushan. "Don't Touch That Dial!" *Slate* (February 15, 2010). Retrieved on December 15, 2017 from http://www.slate.com/articles/health_and_ science/science/2010/02/dont_touch_that_dial.html.

38. "Teaching Good Citizenship's Five Themes," *Education World* (n.d.) Retrieved on November 2, 2017 from http://www.educationworld.com/a_ curr/curr008.shtml.

Chapter 1

1. Aiken, Mary, *The Cyber Effect: A Pioneering Cyberpsychologist Explains How Human Behaviour Changes Online* (New York: Spiegel & Grau, 2016), pp. 113–114.

2. Rideout, V. "The Common Sense Census: Media Use by Kids Zero to Eight," Common Sense Media (2017), p. 3. Retrieved on December 5, 2017 from https://www.commonsensemedia.org/sites/default/files/uploads /research/csm_zerotoeight_fullreport_release_2.pdf.

3. Kabali, Hilda K., Irigoyen, Matilde M., Nunez-Davis, Rosemary, Budacki, Jennifer G., Mohanty, Sweta H., Leister, Kristin P., and Bonner, Robert L., "Exposure and Use of Mobile Media Devices by Young Children," *Pediatrics* 136.6 (November, 2015), peds.2015-2151; DOI: 10.1542/peds.2015-2151. Retrieved on December 6, 2017 from http://pediatrics.aappublications.org /content/early/2015/10/28/peds.2015-2151.

4. Wilson, Jacque, "Your Smartphone Is a Pain in the Neck." CNN (November 20, 2014). Retrieved on November 27, 2017 from http://www.cnn.com /2014/11/20/health/texting-spine-neck-study/index.html.

5. Kabali, H. et al., "Exposure and Use of Mobile Media Devices by Young Children," *Pediatrics* 136.6 (2015): 1044–50.

6. Hirsh-Pasek et al., "Putting Education in 'Educational' Apps: Lessons From the Science of Learning," *Association for Psychological Science*, Vol. 16(1), 2015, pp. 3–34. DOI: 10.1177/1529100615569721.

7. Shuler, C., "iLearn II: An Analysis of the Education Category of the iTunes App Store." The Joan Ganz Cooney Center at Sesame Workshop (January 2012), p. 3. Retrieved on December 30, 2017 from http://www.joanganz cooneycenter.org/wp-content/uploads/2012/01/ilearnii.pdf.

8. Courage, Mary, "Chapter 1- Screen Media and the Youngest Viewers: Implications for Attention and Learning." *Cognitive Development in Digital Contexts* (2017), pp. 3–28. Retrieved on December 22, 2017 from http://www.sciencedirect.com/science/article/pii/B9780128094815000018.

9. Kardefelt-Winther, Daniel, "How Does the Time Children Spend Using Digital Technology Impact Their Mental Well-Being, Social Relationships, and Physical Activity? An Evidence Focused Literature Review," UNICEF (December 2017), p. 25. Retrieved on December 11, 2017 from https://www.unicef-irc.org/publications/pdf/Children-digital-technology-wellbeing.pdf.

10. Dr. Pamela Hurst-Della Pietra (founder and president of Children and Screens: Institute of Digital Media and Child Development), in discussion with author, December 13, 2017. Used with permission.

11. United Nations Children's Fund, "The State of the World's Children 2017: Children in a Digital World." UNICEF (December 2017), p. 3. Retrieved on December 14, 2017 from https://www.unicef.org/publications/index_101992.html.

12. Lerner, Claire, and Barr, Rachel. "Screen Sense: Setting the Record Straight," Zero to Three (2014), p. 1. Retrieved on December 22, 2017 from https://www.zerotothree.org/resources/1200-screen-sense-full-white-paper.

13. Campaign for a Commercial-Free Childhood, Alliance for Childhood, and Teachers Resisting Unhealthy Children's Entertainment, "Facing the Screen Dilemma: Young Children, Technology and Early Education," Campaign for a Commercial-Free Childhood (October, 2012), p. 6. Retrieved on December 11, 2017 from http://www.allianceforchildhood.org/sites/allianceforchildhood.org/files/file/FacingtheScreenDilemma.pdf.

14. Louv, R., *Last Child in the Woods: Saving our Children from Nature-Deficit Disorder* (expanded and revised ed.) (New York: Algonquin Press, 2008), p. 48.

15. Institute of Medicine, *From Neurons to Neighborhoods: The Science of Early Childhood Development* (Washington, D.C.: The National Academies Press, 2004), p. 190.

16. Begley, S., "Your Child's Brain," *Newsweek,* 127.8 (1996), pp. 55–61.

17. Aiken, Mary, *The Cyber Effect*, p. 91.

18. Radesky, Jenny S., et al., "Patterns of Mobile Device Use by Caregivers and Children During Meals in Fast Food Restaurants," *Pediatrics* 133(4), April 2014; DOI: 10.1542/peds.2013-3703: e843–e849.

19. Adamson, L., and Frick, J. "The Still Face: A History of a Shared Experimental Paradigm," *Infancy* 4(4), 2003, pp. 451–473, DOI: 10.1207/S15327078IN0404_01.

20. Fulwiler, Michael. "The Research: The Still Face Experiment," The Gottman Institute (n.d.), Retrieved on December 6, 2017 from https://www.gottman.com/blog/the-research-the-still-face-experiment/.

21. Aiken, Mary, *The Cyber Effect*, pp. 113–114.

22. Hurst-Della Pietra, discussion.

23. Kardaras, Nicholas, *Glow Kids: How Screen Addiction is Hijacking Our Kids and How to Break the Trance* (New York: St. Martin's Press, 2016), p. 65.

24. Christakis, D. A., Zimmerman, F. J., Digiuseppe, D. L., and McCarty, C. A., "Early Television Exposure and Subsequently Attentional Problems in Children," *Pediatrics* 113 (2014), pp. 708–713.

25. Lillard, A. S. & Peterson, J., "The Immediate Impact of Different Types of Television on Young Children's Executive Function," *Pediatrics* 128(4), 2011, pp. 644–649.

26. Anderson, Daniel R., and Subrahmanyam, Kaveri, on behalf of the Cognitive Impacts of Digital Media Workgroup, "Digital Screen Media and Cognitive Development," *Pediatrics* 140 (Supplement 2) (November, 2017), S57–S61; DOI: 10.1542/peds.2016-1758C.

27. DeLoache, J. S., Chiong, C., Vanderborght, M., Sherman, K., Islam, N., Troseth, G. L., and O'Doherty, K., "Do Babies Learn from Baby Media?" *Psychological Science* 21 (2010), pp. 1570–1574. *DOI:* 10.1177/0956797610384145.

28. Barr, R., and Hayne, H., "Developmental Changes in Imitation from Television During Infancy," *Child Development* 70 (1999), pp. 1067–1081. DOI:10.1111/1467-8624.00079.

29. Lerner, Claire, and Barr, Rachel, "Screen Sense: Setting the Record Straight," Zero to Three (2014), p. 2. Retrieved on December 15, 2017 from https://www.zerotothree.org/resources/1200-screen-sense-full-white-paper.

30. Myers, L. J., LeWitt, R. B., Gallo, R. E., and Maselli, N. M., "Baby FaceTime: Can Toddlers Learn From Online Video Chat?" *Developmental Science* 20 (July 2017). DOI:10.1111/desc.12430.

31. Ibid., p. 1.

32. "Building the Brain's Air Traffic Control System: How Early Experiences Shape Development of the Executive Function," Center on the Developing Child at Harvard University, Working Paper, No. 11 (2011), p. 1. Retrieved on December 22, 2017 from https://developingchild.harvard.edu/resources/building-the-brains-air-traffic-control-system-how-early-experiences-shape-the-development-of-executive-function/.

33. Anderson and Subrahmanyam, "Digital Screen Media and Cognitive Development," pp. S57–S61.

34. Diamond, A., "Executive Functions," *Annual Review of Psychology* 64 (2013), pp. 135–168.

35. "National Survey of Children's Health," Centers for Disease Control and Prevention (September 6, 2017). Retrieved on December 6, 2017 from https://www.cdc.gov/nchs/slaits/nsch.htm.

36. Alderman, Lesley. "Does Technology Cause ADHD?" *Everyday Health* (August 31, 2010). Retrieved on December 15, 2017 from https://www .everydayhealth.com/adhd-awareness/does-technology-cause-adhd.aspx.

37. Kardaras, Nicholas, *Glow Kids*, p. 125.

38. Shelley Glaze-Kelley (Journey School educational director), personal interview with author, November 15, 2017. Used with permission.

39. Glaze-Kelley, discussion.

40. Hurst-Della Pietra, discussion.

41. David Kleeman (vice president of global trends for Dubit), in discussion with author, February 20, 2018. Used with permission.

42. Kleeman, discussion.

43. "Technology and Interactive Media as Tools in Early Childhood Programs Serving Children from Birth Through Age 8, a Joint Position Statement." National Association for the Education of Young Children and the Fred Rogers Center for Early Learning and Children's Media at Saint Vincent College (January 2012). Retrieved November 30, 2017 from https://www .naeyc.org/sites/default/files/globally-shared/downloads/PDFs/resources /topics/PS_technology_WEB.pdf.

44. Dr. Chip Donohue (director of the technology in Early Childhood (TEC) Center at the Erikson Institute), email communication with author, December 5, 2017. Used with permission.

45. "Key Messages of the NAEYC/Fred Rogers Center Position Statement on Technology and Interactive Media in Early Childhood Programs," National Association for the Education of Young Children and the Fred Rogers Center for Early Learning and Children's Media at Saint Vincent College (2012). Retrieved on December 14, 2017 from https://www.naeyc .org/sites/default/files/globally-shared/downloads/PDFs/resources /topics/12_KeyMessages_Technology.pdf.

46. American Academy of Pediatrics, "New Recommendations for Children's Electronic Media Use," *ScienceDaily* 21 (October 2016). Retrieved on November 29, 2017 from www.sciencedaily.com/releases/2016/10 /161021121843.htm.

47. Donohue, email communication.

48. Paciga, K. A. and Donohue, C., "Technology and Interactive Media for Young Children: A Whole Child Approach Connecting the Vision of Fred Rogers with Research and Practice," Fred Rogers Center for Early Learning and Children's Media at Saint Vincent College (2017), p. 10. Retrieved November 30, 2017 from http://teccenter.erikson.edu/wp-content /uploads/2017/06/FRC-Report-2-1.pdf.

49. Donohue, email communication.

50. Davis, J., "Face Time: Class Acts," *Grok* (October, 2000), p. 26–36.

51. Newton, E., and Jenvey, V., "Play & Theory of Mind: Associations with Social Competence in Young Children," *Early Child Development and Care* 181.6 (2011), pp. 761–73.

52. "General Guidelines for Parents," Children and Screens: Institute of Digital Media and Child Development (n.d.). Retrieved on December 15, 2017 from https://www.childrenandscreens.com/wp-content/uploads/2017/10 /general-guidelines-for-parents.pdf.

53. Donohue, email communication.

54. Patti Connolly (school development specialist), in discussion with author, December 20, 2017. Used with permission.

55. Connolly, discussion.

56. Maheshwari, Sapna, "On YouTube Kids, Startling Videos Slip Past Filters," *New York Times* (November 4, 2017). Retrieved on December 22, 2017 from https://www.nytimes.com/2017/11/04/business/media/youtube-kids -paw-patrol.html.

Chapter 2

1. Rogers, Fred, *You Are Special: Words of Wisdom from America's Most Beloved Neighbor* (New York: Penguin Books, 1994), p. 89.

2. Molnar, Michele, "Half of K–12 Students to Have Access to 1-to-1 Computing by 2015–16." *Edweek Market Brief* (February 24, 2015). Retrieved on December 2, 2017 from https://marketbrief.edweek.org/marketplace-k-12 /half_of_k-12_students_to_have_access_to_1-to-1_computing_by_ 2015-16_1/.

3. Sarigianopoulos, Rena, "Is Technology in Schools Making Our Kids Smarter?" KARE 11 (November 1, 2017). Retrieved on December 2, 2017 from http://www.kare11.com/news/is-technology-in-schools-making-our -kids-smarter/488159029.

4. Ibid.

5. Richtel, Matt, "A Silicon Valley School that Doesn't Compute," *The New York Times* (October 22, 2014). Retrieved on December 3, 2017 from http:// www.nytimes.com/2011/10/23/technology/at-waldorf-school-in-silicon -valley-technology-can-wait.html.

6. Jenkins, H., with Purushotma, R., Clinton, K., Weigel, M., and Robinson, A. J., "Confronting the Challenges of Participatory Culture: Media Education for the 21st Century," *The John D. and Catherine T. MacArthur Foundation Reports on Digital Media and Learning* (2006). Retrieved December 12, 2017 from http://www.newmedialiteracies.org/wp-content/uploads/pdfs /NMLWhitePaper.pdf.

7. Reilly, Erin, Jenkins, Henry, Felt, Laurel J., and Vartabedian, Vanessa, "Shall We Play?" USC Annenberg Innovation Lab (Fall 2012). Retrieved on December 23, 2017 from https://www.slideshare.net/ebreilly1/play-doc -01-15613677?from_search=3.

8. Erin Reilly (CEO and founder of Reilly Works), in discussion with author, December 11, 2017. Used with permission.

9. Reilly, Erin, Jenkins, Henry, Felt, Laurel J., and Vartabedian, Vanessa, "Shall We Play?"

10. Lewis, Paul, "'Our Minds Can Be Hijacked': The Tech Insiders Who Fear a Smartphone Dystopia," *The Guardian* (October 6, 2017). Retrieved on April 20, 2018 from https://www.theguardian.com/technology/2017/oct/05 /smartphone-addiction-silicon-valley-dystopia.

11. Bernard, Zoe, & Tweedie, Steven, "The Father of Virtual Reality Sounds Off on the Changing Culture of Silicon Valley, the Impending #MeToo Backlash, and Why He Left Google for Microsoft," *Business Insider* (December 16, 2017). Retrieved on December 24, 2017 from http://www .businessinsider.com/jaron-lanier-interview-on-silicon-valley-culture -metoo-backlash-ai-and-the-future-2017-12.

12. Alter, Adam, *Irresistible: The Rise of Addictive Technology and the Business of Keeping Us Hooked* (New York: Penguin Press, 2017), p. 2.

13. In preface to the paperback edition of Kardaras, Nicholas, *Glow Kids: How Screen Addiction Is Hijacking Our Kids and How to Break the Trance* (New York: St. Martin's Press, 2016), pp. xx–xxi.

14. Faltas, discussion.

15. Kardaras, Nicholas, *Glow Kids*, p. 127.

16. Reilly, discussion.

17. Samuel, Alexandra, "Parents: Reject Technology Shame," *The Atlantic* (November 4, 2015). Retrieved on December 23, 2017 from https://www .theatlantic.com/technology/archive/2015/11/why-parents-shouldnt -feel-technology-shame/414163/.

18. Connolly, discussion.

19. Reilly, discussion.

20. Prensky, Marc, *Teaching Digital Natives: Partnering for Real Learning* (Thousand Oaks, CA: Corwin, 2010), p. 12.

21. Davis, K., Katz, S., James, C., and Santo, R., "Fostering Cross-Generational Dialogues about the Ethics of Online Life," *Journal of Media Literacy Education* 2(2), November 9, 2010, p. 126.

22. Crain, W., *Theories of Development: Concepts and Applications* (5th ed.) (Upper Saddle River, NJ: Pearson Prentice Hall, 2005), p. 118.

23. Donovan, Jay. "The Average Age for a Child Getting Their First Smartphone is Now 10.3 Years," *TechCrunch* (May 19, 2016). Retrieved on

December 31, 2017 from https://techcrunch.com/2016/05/19/the-average
-age-for-a-child-getting-their-first-smartphone-is-now-10-3-years/.

24. Blake, B., and Pope, T., "Developmental Psychology: Incorporating Piaget's
and Vygotsky's Theories in Classrooms," *Journal of Cross-Disciplinary Perspectives in Education* 1(1), May, 2008, pp. 59–67.

25. Nucci, Larry, "Moral Development and Moral Education: An Overview,"
Domain Based Moral Education Lab at the Graduate School of Education,
University of California, Berkeley. Retrieved on December 26, 2017 from
https://www.moraledk12.org/about-mde.

26. Crain, W., *Theories of Development*, p. 155.

27. Mercogliano, Chris, and Debus, Kim, "An Interview with Joseph Chilton
Pearce," *Journal of Family Life Magazine* 5(1), 1999. Retrieved on December
27, 2017 from https://iamheart.org/the_heart/articles_joseph_chilton_
pearce.shtml.

28. Harding, Eleanor, "Six in Ten Parents Say They Would Let Their Children
Lie About Their Age Online to Access Social Media Sites," *Daily Mail* (January 23, 2017). Retrieved on January 18, 2018 from http://www.dailymail
.co.uk/news/article-4150204/Many-parents-let-children-lie-age-online
.html#ixzz4WmrvHLyo.

29. Gates, Melinda, "Melinda Gates: I Spent My Career in Technology. I
Wasn't Prepared for its Effect on My Kids," *The Washington Post* (August
24, 2017). Retrieved on January 1, 2018 from https://www.washingtonpost
.com/news/parenting/wp/2017/08/24/melinda-gates-i-spent-my-career
-in-technology-i-wasnt-prepared-for-its-effect-on-my-kids/?utm_term
=.673f3502f09c.

30. Borba, Michele, "To Raise Kids with More Empathy, We Need To Do
Everything Wrong," *Time* (September 19, 2016). Retrieved on December 31,
2017 from http://time.com/4495016/parenting-empathy/.

31. Konrath, S. H., O'Brien, E. H., and Hsing, C., "Changes in Dispositional
Empathy in American College Students Over Time: A Meta-Analysis," *Personality and Social Psychology Review* 15(2), 2011, pp. 180–198. http://doi
.org/10.1177/1088868310377395.

32. Konrath, S., "The Empathy Paradox: Increasing Disconnection in the Age
of Increasing Connection," In Rocci Luppicini (ed.) *Handbook of Research
on Technoself: Identity in a Technological Society* (IGI Global, 2012), pp.
204–228.

33. Michele Borba (educational psychologist and author), in discussion with
author, January 10, 2018. Used with permission.

34. Swanbro, Diane. "Empathy: College Students Don't Have as Much as They
Used To," *Michigan News, University of Michigan* (May 27, 2010). Retrieved

on December 31, 2017 from http://ns.umich.edu/new/releases/7724
-empathy-college-students-don-t-have-as-much-as-they-used-to.

35. Ibid.

36. Borba, discussion.

37. Borba, discussion.

38. Wolpert, Stuart, "In Our Digital World, Are Young People Losing the Ability To Read Emotions?", *UCLA Newsroom* (August 21, 2014). Retrieved on December 29, 2017 from http://newsroom.ucla.edu/releases/in-our-digital-world-are-young-people-losing-the-ability-to-read-emotions.

39. Pink, Daniel H., *A Whole New Mind: Why Right Brainers Will Rule the Future* (New York: Riverhead Books, 2006), p. 115.

40. Rutledge, Pamela, "The Psychological Power of Storytelling," *Psychology Today* (January 16, 2011). Retrieved on January 3, 2017 from https://www.psychologytoday.com/blog/positively-media/201101/the-psychological-power-storytelling.

41. Glaze-Kelley, discussion.

42. Brittany Oler (co-founder of Kids Email), in discussion with author, January 5, 2018. Used with permission.

43. Oler, discussion.

Chapter 3

1. "Socrates Quotes," BrainyQuote.com. Xplore Inc, 2018. Retrieved on April 19, 2018. https://www.brainyquote.com/quotes/socrates_385050.

2. Natanson, Hannah, "Harvard Rescinds Acceptances for At Least Ten Students for Obscene Memes," *The Harvard Crimson* (June 5, 2017). Retrieved on November 21, 2017 from http://www.thecrimson.com/article/2017/6/5/2021-offers-rescinded-memes/.

3. "Kaplan Test Prep Survey Finds Colleges and Applicants Agree: Social Media is Fair Game in the Admissions Process," Kaplan Test Prep (April 17, 2018). Retrieved on April 21, 2018 from http://press.kaptest.com/press-releases/kaplan-test-prep-survey-finds-colleges-applicants-agree-social-media-fair-game-admissions-process.

4. Ibid.

5. Ibid.

6. Wallace, Kelly, "Surprise! Social Media Can Help, Not Hurt, Your College Prospects," CNN (February 10, 2017). Retrieved on December 5, 2017 from http://www.cnn.com/2017/02/10/health/college-admissions-social-media-parents/index.html.

7. Ibid.

8. Alan Katzman (founder and CEO of Social Assurity), email communication with author, December 1, 2017. Used with permission.

9. Katzman, email communication.

10. Katzman, email communication.

11. Katzman, email communication.

12. Katzman, email communication.

13. Katzman, email communication.

14. Katzman, email communication.

15. Career Builder, "Number of Employers Using Social Media to Screen Candidates at All-Time High, Finds Latest CareerBuilder Study," *Cision PR Newswire* (June 15, 2017). Retrieved on December 16, 2017 from https://www.prnewswire.com/news-releases/number-of-employers-using-social-media-to-screen-candidates-at-all-time-high-finds-latest-careerbuilder-study-300474228.html.

16. Brooks, Chad, "Keep It Clean: Social Media Screening Gain in Popularity," *Business News Daily* (June 16, 2017). Retrieved on December 27, 2017 from https://www.businessnewsdaily.com/2377-social-media-hiring.html.

17. Singer, Natasha, "They Loved Your G.P.A. Then They Saw Your Tweets," *The New York Times* (November 9, 2017). Retrieved on December 28, 2017 from http://www.nytimes.com/2013/11/10/business/they-loved-your-gpa-then-they-saw-your-tweets.html.

18. Bradley Shear (founder and general counsel of Digital Armour), discussion with author, December 29, 2017. Used with permission.

19. Shear, discussion.

20. "Digital Birth: Welcome to the Online World," *Business Wire* (October 6, 2010). Retrieved on December 16, 2017 from https://www.businesswire.com/news/home/20101006006722/en/Digital-Birth-Online-World.

21. Rose, Megan, "The Average Parent Shares Almost 1,500 Images of Their Child Online Before Their 5th Birthday," *ParentZone*, n.d. Retrieved on December 16, 2017 from https://parentzone.org.uk/article/average-parent-shares-almost-1500-images-their-child-online-their-5th-birthday.

22. Bennett, Rosemary, "Parents Post 1,500 Pictures of Children on Social Media Before Fifth Birthday," *The Times* (September 6, 2016). Retrieved on December 16, 2017 from https://www.thetimes.co.uk/article/parents-post-1-500-pictures-of-children-on-social-media-before-fifth-birthday-wb7vmmg55.

23. Rose, Megan, "The Average Parent Shares Almost 1,500 Images of Their Child Online Before Their 5th Birthday."

24. Sue Scheff (author and digital reputation expert), discussion with author, November 15, 2017. Used with permission.

25. American Academy of Child and Adolescent Psychiatry, "The Teen Brain: Behavior, Problem Solving and Decision Making," *Facts for Families*, no. 95 (September 2016). Retrieved on December 29, 2017 from https://www .aacap.org/App_Themes/AACAP/docs/facts_for_families/95_the_teen_ brain_behavior_problem_solving_and_decision_making.pdf.

26. Jacobs, Tom, "Humblebragging Just Makes You Look Like a Fraud," *Pacific Standard* (October 18, 2017). Retrieved on December 29, 2017 from https:// psmag.com/news/your-humblebrag-raises-a-red-flag.

27. Sezer, Ovul, Gino, Francesca, and Norton, Michael I., "Humblebragging: A Distinct—and Ineffective—Self-Presentation Strategy," *Harvard Business School Working Paper*, No. 15-080 (April 2015).

28. Richard Guerry (founder and executive director of The Institute for Responsible Online and Cellphone Communication), in discussion with author, January 4, 2018. Used with permission.

29. Guerry, discussion.

Chapter 4

1. Kamenetz, Anya, *The Art of Screen Time* (New York: PublicAffairs, 2018), p. 10.

2. Anderson, Monica and Jiang, Jingjing, "Teens, Social Media & Technology 2018," Pew Research Center (May 31, 2018). Retrieved July 10, 2018 from http://assets.pewresearch.org/wp-content/uploads/sites/14/2018/05 /31102617/PI_2018.05.31_TeensTech_FINAL.pdf; Lenhart, Amanda, "Teens, Social Media & Technology Overview 2015," Pew Research Center (April 9, 2015). Retrieved February 17, 2018 from http://www.pewinternet .org/2015/04/09/teens-social-media-technology-2015/.

3. Anderson, Monica and Jiang, Jingjing, "Teens, Social Media & Technology 2018."

4. Geng, Y., Su, L., and Cao, F., "A Research on Emotion and Personality Characteristics in Junior 1 High School Students with Internet Addiction Disorders," *Chinese Mental Health Journal* 23 (2006), pp. 457–470; Williams, Rachel, "China Recognizes Internet Addiction as New Disease," *The Guardian* (November 11, 2008). Retrieved on April 4, 2018 from https:// www.theguardian.com/news/blog/2008/nov/11/china-internet.

5. Common Sense Media, "Technology Addiction: Concern, Controversy, and Finding Balance," 2016, https://www.commonsensemedia.org/sites

/default/files/uploads/research/csm_2016_te chnology_addiction_
research_brief_o.pdf.

6. Joni Siani (media and communications professor, filmmaker, and author),
   in discussion with author, February 19, 2018. Used with permission.

7. Siani, Joni, *Celling Your Soul*, Createspace Independent Publisher (2013).

8. Siani, discussion.

9. American Psychiatric Association, "Diagnostic and Statistical Manual of
   Mental Disorders" (5th ed.) (Washington, D.C.: American Psychiatric Publishing, 2013).

10. Dr. David Greenfield, 2015 presentation at Digital Citizenship Summit; and
    in discussion with author.

11. Greenfield, discussion.

12. Kardaras, Nicholas, "It's Digital Heroin: How Screens Turn Kids into Psy-
    chotic Junkies," *New York Post* (September 27, 2016), Retrieved on Decem-
    ber 1, 2017 from http://nypost.com/2016/08/27/
    its-digital-heroin- how-screens-turn-kids-into-psychotic-junkies/.

13. Sherman, Lauren E., et al., "The Power of the Like in Adolescence," *Psycho-
    logical Science* 27(7), May 31, 2016, pp. 1027–1035. http://journals.sagepub
    .com/doi/abs/10.1177/0956797616645673#articleCitationDownload
    Container.

14. Jensen, Frances E. and Ellis Nutt, Amy, *The Teenage Brain: A Neuroscientist's
    Survival Guide to Raising Adolescents and Young Adults* (Toronto: Harper-
    Collins, 2015).

15. Chambers, R. A., Taylor, J. R., and Potenza, M. N., "Developmental Neuro-
    circuitry of Motivation in Adolescence: A Critical Period of Addiction Vul-
    nerability," *American Journal of Psychiatry* 160 (2003), pp. 1041–1052. https://
    www.ncbi.nlm.nih.gov/pmc/articles/PMC2919168/.

16. Bergland, Christopher. "Why Is the Teen Brain so Vulnerable?" *Psychology
    Today* (December 19, 2013). https://www.psychologytoday.com/blog/the
    -athletes-way/201312/why-is-the-teen-brain-so-vulnerable.

17. Stanford Persuasive Tech Lab website. Accessed on February 17, 2018 from
    http://captology.stanford.edu/about/what-is-captology.html.

18. MacKay, Jory. "Here's Why You Can't (or Won't) Delete Distracting
    Apps from Your Phone." *The Startup on Medium* (February 13, 2018).
    Retrieved on February 17, 2018 from https://medium.com/swlh/heres
    -why-you-can-t-or-won-t-delete-distracting-apps-from-your-phone
    -ae1c50445f1e.

19. Fogg, B. J., *Persuasive Technology: Using Computers to Change What We
    Think and Do* (Boston: Morgan Kaufman Publishers, 2013), pp. 8–9.

20. Ouri Azoulay (former CEO of PureSight), in discussion with author, July 7,
    2017. Used with permission.

21. Gabe Zichermann (entrepreneur, behavioral designer, public speaker, and author), in discussion with author, March 19, 2018. Used with permission.

22. Zichermann, discussion.

23. Shafer, Scott, "Design Ethicist Tristan Harris on How to Fight Back Against Your Smartphone," KQED News (August 22, 2017). Retrieved on April 2, 2018 from https://www.kqed.org/forum/2010101861248.

24. Ibid.

25. Smith, Craig, "140 Amazing Snapchat Statistics and Facts (February 2018)," *DMR* (March 31, 2018). Retrieved on March 31, 2018 from https://expande dramblings.com/index.php/snapchat-statistics/.

26. Gelles, David. "Tech Backlash Grows as Investors Press Apple to Act on Children's Use," *The New York Times* (January 8, 2018). Retrieved on April 2, 2018 from https://www.nytimes.com/2018/01/08/technology/apple -tech-children-jana-calstrs.html.

27. Gibbs, Samuel, "Apple's Tim Cook: 'I Don't Want My Nephew on a Social Network,'" *The Guardian* (January 19, 2018). Retrieved on March 30, 2018 from https://www.theguardian.com/technology/2018/jan/19/tim-cook -i-dont-want-my-nephew-on-a-social-network.

28. Allen, Mike, "Sean Parker Unloads on Facebook: 'God Only Knows What It's Doing to Our Children's Brains,'" Axios (November 9, 2017). Retrieved on March 30, 2018 from https://www.axios.com/sean-parker-unloads-on -facebook-god-only-knows-what-its-doing-to-our-childrens-brains -1513306792-f855e7b4-4e99-4d60-8d51-2775559c2671.html.

29. Kang, Cecilia, "Turn Off Messenger Kids, Health Experts Plead to Facebook," *The New York Times* (January 30, 2018). Retrieved on April 2, 2018 from https://www.nytimes.com/2018/01/30/technology/messenger -kids-facebook-letter.html.

30. Wait Until 8th website. Retrieved on April 30, 2018 from https://www .waituntil8th.org/take-the-pledge/.

31. Center for Humane Technology website. Retrieved on April 30, 2018 from http://humanetech.com.

32. Ibid.

33. Zichermann, discussion.

34. American Academy of Pediatrics. "New Recommendations for Children's Electronic Media Use," *Science Daily* 21 (October 2016). Retrieved on November 29, 2017 from www.sciencedaily.com/releases/2016 /10/161021121843.htm.

35. "The Common Sense Census: Plugged-In Parents of Tweens and Teens," Common Sense Media (2016). Retrieved on December 10, 2017 from https://www.commonsensemedia.org/sites/default/files/uploads/research /common- sense-parent-census_executivesummary_for-web.pdf.

36. Ibid.

37. Siani, discussion.

38. Michele Whiteaker (writer and certified interpretive guide), in discussion and in email communication with author, April 23, 2018. Used with permission.

39. Hill, Taylor, "Graffiti Artist Defaces 10 National Parks—and Instagrams It," *Take Part* (October 22, 2014). Retrieved on May 13, 2017 from http://www.takepart.com/article/2014/10/22/one-person-decided- make-art -national-parks-and-post-it-all-over-social-media; Ortiz, Eric, "Ex-Scout Leaders Who Knocked Over Ancient Rock Get Probation," NBC News (March 19, 2014). Retrieved on May 12, 2017 from https://www.nbcnews .com/news/us-news/ex-scouts-leaders-who-knocked-over-ancient-rock -get-probation-n56596.

40. Mazza, Ed. "Hiker Plunges to His Death While Taking a Selfie at a Water-fall," *Huffington Post* (May 31, 2017). Retrieved on May 15, 2017 from http://www.huffingtonpost.com/entry/selfie-waterfall-death_us_592e5a36e4 boco608e8c7e8b.

41. Louv, Richard, *Last Child in the Woods: Saving Our Children from Nature-Deficit Disorder* (Chapel Hill: Algonquin Books, 2005). Print.

42. Siani, discussion.

Chapter 5

1. Instagram Terms of Use.

2. Suler, John, "The Online Disinhibition Effect," *CyberPsychology & Behavior* 7(3), June 2004, 321–326.

3. Olsen, Jan M., "Swedish Man Convicted Over 'Online Rape' of Teens Groomed into Performing Webcam Sex Acts," *Independent* (December 1, 2017). Retrieved on December 27, 2017 from http://www.independent .co.uk/news/world/europe/online-rape-conviction-bjorn-samstrom -grooming-webcams-sex-acts-victims-uk-us-canada-uppsala-court -a8086261.html.

4. Londberg, Max, "A 14-Year Old Girl Sexted on Her Crush. She May Have to Register as a Sex Offender," *Kansas City Star* (December 23, 2017). Retrieved on December 27, 2017 from http://www.kansascity.com/news /nation-world/article191405954.html#storylink=cpy.

5. Fucci, Robert, "Sutton Teen's Suicide Raises Awareness of Cyberbullying," *Millbury-Sutton Chronicle* (December 27, 2017). Retrieved on December 27, 2017 from http://www.millburysutton.com/articles/sutton-teens-suicide -raises-awareness-of-cyberbullying/.

6. Myers, Russell, "Reports of Children Being Groomed on the Internet Have Increased Five Fold in Four Years," *Mirror* (December 12, 2017). Retrieved on December 27, 2017 from http://www.mirror.co.uk/news/uk-news /reports-children-being-groomed-internet-11681027.

7. Scheff, Sue, "Top Health Concerns for Parents: Bullying, Cyberbullying and Internet Safety," *Huffington Post* (December 22, 2017). Retrieved on December 27, 2017 from https://www.huffingtonpost.com/entry/top -health-concern-for-parents-bullying-cyberbullying_us_5a3d7681e4b0d fode8b06522.

8. Erikson, Erik H., *Identity and the Life Cycle* (New York: International Universities Press, 1959), p. 119.

9. Dr. Pamela Rutledge (professor of media psychology at Fielding Graduate University and director of the Media Psychology Research Center), in discussion with author, December 6, 2017. Used with permission.

10. Rutledge, discussion.

11. Rutledge, discussion.

12. Lenhart, Amanda, "Social Media and Friendships," chapter 4 in *Teens Technology and Friendships*. Pew Internet (August 4, 2018). Retrieved on January 27, 2018 from http://www.pewinternet.org/2015/08/06/chapter-4-social -media-and-friendships/.

13. "Digital Friendships: The Role of Technology in Young People's Relationships," UK Safer Internet Center (February 6, 2018). Retrieved on February 26, 2018 from https://www.saferinternet.org.uk/digital -friendships.

14. Kardefelt-Winther, Daniel, "How Does the Time Children Spend Using Digital Technology Impact Their Mental Well-Being, Social Relationships and Physical Activity? An Evidence-Focused Literature Review," *Innocenti Discussion Papers* no. 2017-02 (2017), UNICEF Office of Research, Innocenti, Florence.

15. Shapiro, Lauren, and Margolin, Gayla, "Growing Up Wired: Social Networking Sites and Adolescent Psychosocial Development," *Clinical Child and Family Psychology Review* 17(1), 2014, pp. 1–18.

16. Teppers, Eveline, et al., "Loneliness and Facebook Motives in Adolescents: A Longitudinal Inquiry into Directionality of Effect," *Journal of Adolescence* 37(5), July 2014, pp. 691–699.

17. McKenna, Katelyn Y. A., Green, Amie S., and Gleason, Marci E. J., "Relationship Formation on the Internet: What's The Big Attraction?" *Journal of Social Issues* 58(1), 2002, pp. 9–31.6.

18. Best, P., Manktelow, R., and Taylor, B., "Online Communication, Social Media and Adolescent Well-Being: A Systematic Narrative Review." *Children and Youth Services Review* 41 (June 1, 2014), pp. 27–36.

19. Weale, Sally, "Digital Media Can Enhance Family Life, Says LSE Study," *The Guardian* (February 5, 2018). Retrieved on February 9, 2018 from https://www.theguardian.com/media/2018/feb/06/digital-media -can-enhance-family-life-says-lse-study.

20. "The State of the World's Children 2017: Children in a Digital World," UNICEF (December 2017), p. 64.

21. Rutledge, discussion.

22. Irvine, Martha, "Survey: Nearly Every American Kid Plays Video Games," ABC News (February 13, 2018). Retrieved on February 19, 2018 from https://abcnews.go.com/Technology/story?id=5817835&page=1.

23. Lenhart, Amanda, "Teens, Technology and Friendships," Pew Research Center (August 6, 2015). Retrieved on February 28, 2018 from http://www .pewinternet.org/2015/08/06/teens-technology-and-friendships/.

24. Ibid.

25. Kleeman, discussion.

26. Granic, Isabela, Lobel, Adam, and Engels, Rutger C. M. E., "The Benefits of Playing Video Games," *American Psychologist* 69(1), January 2014, pp. 66–78. DOI: 10.1037/a0034857.

27. Forde, Killian, and Kenny, Catherine, "Online Gaming and Youth Cultural Perceptions," *Slideshare*. Retrieved on March 1, 2018 from https:// www.slideshare.net/KillianForde1/onlinegamingandyouthcultural perceptions.

28. Fox, Maggie, "World Health Organization Adds Gaming Disorder to Disease Classifications," NBC News (June 18, 2018). Retrieved on July 10, 2018 from https://www.nbcnews.com/health/health-news/who-adds -gaming-disorder-disease-classifications-n884291.

29. "Grand Theft Auto V." *Common Sense Media* website. Retrieved on April 16, 2018 from https://www.commonsensemedia.org/game-reviews/grand -theft-auto-v.

30. Weinberger, A. H., Gbedemah, M., Martinez, A. M., Nash, D., Galea, S., and Goodwin, R. D., "Trends in Depression Prevalence in the USA from 2005 to 2015: Widening Disparities in Vulnerable Groups." *Psychological Medicine* 1 (2017). DOI: 10.1017/S0033291717002781.

31. Twenge, Jean M., *iGen*, pp. 77–78.

32. Wong, C., Merchant, R., and Moreno, M., "Using Social Media to Engage Adolescents and Young Adults with Their Health," *Healthc* 2(4) (Amst), December 2014, pp. 220–224. DOI: 10.1016/j.hjdsi.2014.10.005.

33. Davis, K., Weinstein, E., and Gardner, H., "In Defense of Complexity: Beware of Simplistic Narratives about Teens and Technology," *Medium* (August 13, 2017). Retrieved on February 14, 2018 from https://medium

.com/@kedavis/in-defense-of-complexity-beware-of-simplistic-narratives
-about-teens-and-technology-f9a7cb59176.

34. Rutledge, discussion.

35. Twenge, J. M., Martin, G. N., and Campbell, W. K., "Decreases in Psychological Well-Being Among American Adolescents After 2012 and Links to
Screen Time During the Rise of Smartphone Technology," *Emotion* (January 22, 2018). Advance online publication. http://dx.doi.org/10.1037
/emo0000403.

36. Przybylski, Andrew K. and Weinstein, Netta, "A Large-Scale Test of the
Goldilocks Hypothesis: Quantifying the Relations Between Digital-Screen
Use and the Mental Well-Being of Adolescents," *Psychological Science* 28(2),
2017, pp. 204–215. DOI: 10.1177/0956797616678438.

37. Madden, Mary, Lenhart, Amanda, Cortesi, Sandra, Gasser, Urs, Duggan,
Maeve, Smith, Aaron, and Beaton, Meredith, "Teens, Social Media and Privacy," Pew Research Center (May 21, 2013). Retrieved on January 27, 2018
from http://www.pewinternet.org/2013/05/21/teens-social-media-and
-privacy/.

38. Dunbar, R. I. M., "Coevolution of Neocortical Size, Group Size and Language in Humans," *Behavioral and Brain Sciences* 16 (1993), pp. 681–735.

39. Konnikova, Maria, "The Limits of Friendship," *New Yorker* (October 7,
2014). Retrieved on February 9, 2018 from https://www.newyorker.com
/science/maria-konnikova/social-media-affect-math-dunbar-number
-friendships.

40. Koons, Stephanie, "Penn State Researchers Study Nuances of Social Media
'Likes,'" *Penn State News* (June 23, 2016). Retrieved on February 9, 2018
from http://news.psu.edu/story/415749/2016/06/23/research/penn
-state-researchers-study-nuances-social-media-%E2%80%98likes%
E2%80%99.

41. Yau, Joanna C., and Reich, Stephanie M., "It's Just a Lot of Work: Self-Presentation Norms and Practices on Facebook and Instagram," *Journal of
Research on Adolescence* (February 12, 2018), DOI 10.1111/jora.12376 [epub
ahead of print].

42. "Digital Friendships: The Role of Technology in Young People's Relationships," UK Safer Internet Center (February 6, 2018). Retrieved on February
26, 2018 from https://www.saferinternet.org.uk/digital-friendships.

43. Koons, Stephanie, "Penn State Researchers Study Nuances of Social Media
'Likes.'"

44. "Life in 'Likes': Children's Commissioner Report Into Social Media Use
Among 8–12 Year Olds." *Children's Commissioner* (2017). Retrieved on February 10, 2018 from https://www.childrenscommissioner.gov.uk/wp

-content/uploads/2018/01/Childrens-Commissioner-for-England-Life-in
-Likes-3.pdf.

45. "Status of Mind: Social Media and Young People's Mental Health and Wellbeing," Royal Society for Public Health (2017). Retrieved on October 19, 2017 from https://www.rsph.org.uk/our-work/policy/social-media-and -young-people-s-mental-health-and-wellbeing.html.

46. Ibid.

47. "Life in 'Likes.'"

48. Liz Repking (founder and CEO of Cyber Safety Consulting), in discussion with author, February 16, 2018. Used with permission.

49. Peter Kelley (outreach director of Cyber Civics), in discussion with author, October 21, 2017. Used with permission.

50. Kelley, discussion.

51. Mobile Guard Media, "California Laws Pertaining to Sexting in the State of California," Retrieved on January 27, 2018 from http://mobilemediaguard .com/states/sexting_laws_california.html.

52. Madigan S., Ly A., Rash C. L., Van Ouytsel, J., and Temple, J. R., "Prevalence of Multiple Forms of Sexting Behavior Among Youth: A Systematic Review and Meta-analysis." *JAMA Pediatrics* (February 26, 2018). Published online. DOI: 10.1001/jamapediatrics.2017.5314.

53. Dr. Michele Drouin (developmental psychologist and professor of psychology at Purdue University Fort Wayne), in discussion with author, January 23, 2018. Used with permission.

54. Drouin, discussion.

55. Hayworth, Bret, "Storm Lake Students Charged in Connection with Sexting of Nude Photos," *Sioux City Journal* (February 13, 2018). Retrieved on February 14, 2018 from http://siouxcityjournal.com/news/local/crime -and-courts/storm-lake-students-charged-in-connection-with-sexting-of -nude/article_32d83afo-35a8-52fa-be30-48b5181f9d97.html.

56. Shropshire, Terry, "High School Teen Faces 10 Years in Prison for Sexting Female Classmate," *Michigan Chronicle* (February 28, 2017). Retrieved on February 14, 2018 from https://michronicleonline.com/2017/02/28/high -school-teen-faces-10-years-in-prison-for-sexting-female-classmate/.

57. Duncan, Jericka, "20 Students Suspended in Long Island Sexting Scandal," CBS Evening News (November 11, 2015). Retrieved on January 14, 2018 from https://www.cbsnews.com/news/20-students-suspended-in -long-island-sexting-scandal/.

58. Rosenberg, Eli, "One in Four Teens Are Sexting, A New Study Shows. Relax, Researchers Say, It's Mostly Normal," *Washington Post* (February 27, 2018). Retrieved on February 28, 2018 from https://www.washingtonpost .com/news/the-switch/wp/2018/02/27/a-new-study-shows-one-in

-four-teens-are-sexting-relax-experts-say-its-mostly-normal/?utm_term=.77847d5900fa.

59. Patchin, Justin, "You Received a 'Sext,' Now What? Advice for Teens," Cyberbullying Research Center Blog (February 22, 2011). Retrieved on November 9, 2017 from https://cyberbullying.org/you-received-a-sext-now-what-advice-for-teens.

60. Dr. Sameer Hinduja (co-director of the Cyberbullying Research Center and professor of criminology and criminal justice), email communication with author, February 28, 2018. Used with permission.

61. Lenhart, Amanda, et al., "Teens, Kindness and Cruelty on Social Network Sites," Pew Research Center (November 9, 2011), Retrieved on April 17, 2018 from http://www.pewinternet.org/2011/11/09/teens-kindness-and-cruelty-on-social-network-sites/.

62. Myers, Gene, "Family of 12-Year-Old Who Committed Suicide After Cyberbullying to Sue School District," *USA Today* (August 2, 2017). Retrieved March 1, 2018 from https://www.usatoday.com/story/news/nation-now/2017/08/02/mallory-grossmans-parents-say-school-district-didnt-do-enough-save-their-daughter/532165001/.

63. Eltagouri, Marwa, "A 10-year-old's Schoolyard Fight Was Posted on Social Media. She Hanged Herself Two Weeks Later," *Washington Post* (December 1, 2017). Retrieved on March 1, 2018 from https://www.washingtonpost.com/news/education/wp/2017/12/01/a-10-year-olds-schoolyard-fight-was-posted-on-social-media-she-hanged-herself-two-weeks-later/?utm_term=.28540c25356e.

64. Almasy, Steve, Segal, Kim, and Couwels, John, "Sheriff: Taunting Post Leads to Arrests in Rebecca Sedwick Bullying Death," CNN (October 16, 2013). Retrieved on March 1, 2018 from https://www.cnn.com/2013/10/15/justice/rebecca-sedwick-bullying-death-arrests/index.html.

65. Ross Ellis (founder and CEO of STOMP Out Bullying™), in discussion with author, February 19, 2018. Used with permission.

66. Hinduja, email communication.

67. Smith, Craig, "22 Musical.ly Statistics and Facts | By the Numbers," *DMR Business Statistics | Fun Gadgets* (December 10, 2017). Retrieved on December 27, 2017 from https://expandedramblings.com/index.php/musically-statistics/.

68. Herrman, John, "Who's Too Young for an App? Musical.ly Tests the Limits," *Gulf News* (September 23, 2016). Retrieved on December 27, 2017 from http://gulfnews.com/business/sme/who-s-too-young-for-an-app-musical-ly-tests-the-limits-1.1909779.

69. McPherson, Emily, "Predator Posing as Teen Star JoJo Siwa Asks Victorian Girl for Nude Videos," 9News (December 21, 2017). Retrieved on

January 31, 2018 from https://www.9news.com.au/national/2017/12
/21/10/34/sexual-predator-posing-as-us-teen-star-targets-nine-year
-old-victorian-girl.

70. Hinduja, email communication.

71. Lenhart, Amanda, et al., "Teens, Kindness, and Cruelty on Social Network
Sites."

72. Ibid.

73. Hinduja, email communication.

74. Ellis, discussion.

75. Van Evra, Jennifer, "Sarah Silverman's Response to a Twitter Troll is a Master Class in Compassion," CBC (January 3, 2018). Retrieved on March 10, 2018 from http://www.cbc.ca/radio/q/blog/sarah-silverman-s-response
-to-a-twitter-troll-is-a-master-class-in-compassion-1.4471337.

Chapter 6

1. Taplin, Jonathan, *Move Fast and Break Things: How Facebook, Google, and Amazon Cornered Culture and Undermined Democracy* (New York:Little, Brown and Company, 2017), p. 150.

2. Shear and Social Media Law & Tech Blog. Retrieved on February 15, 2018 from http://www.shearsocialmedia.com/2017/06/june-30th-national
-student-data-deletion-day-k-12-schools.html.

3. Bradley Shear (founder and general counsel of Digital Armour), discussion with author, March 8, 2018. Used with permission.

4. Herold, Benjamin, "Maryland Dad Wants June 30 to Be 'National Student Data Deletion' Day," *Education Week* (June 30, 2017). Retrieved on February 28, 2018 from http://blogs.edweek.org/edweek/DigitalEducation
/2017/06/dad_wants_june_30_student_data_deletion_day.html.

5. Strauss, Valerie, "How the SAT and PSAT Collect Personal Data on Students—And What the College Board Does With It," *Washington Post* (March 30, 2017). Retrieved on March 12, 2018 from https://www.washingtonpost
.com/news/answer-sheet/wp/2017/03/30/how-the-sat-and-psat-collect
-personal-data-on-students-and-what-the-college-board-does-with-it
/?utm_term=.fc872303d185.

6. Herold, Benjamin, "Google Acknowledges Data Mining Student Users Outside Apps for Education," *Education Week* (February 17, 2016). Retrieved on February 15, 2018 from http://blogs.edweek.org/edweek
/DigitalEducation/2016/02/google_acknowledges_data_mining_
GAFE_users.html.

7. Maheshwari, Sapna, "YouTube is Improperly Collecting Children's Data, Consumer Group Says," *New York Times* (April 9, 2018). Retrieved on April 15, 2018 from https://www.nytimes.com/2018/04/09/business/media /youtube-kids-ftc-complaint.html?mtrref=www.google.com.

8. Shear, discussion.

9. Hart Research Associates, "Parents, Privacy & Technology Use," Family Online Safety Institute (November 17, 2015).

10. Shauna Leff (vice president of marketing and communications of PRIVO), discussion with author, March 18, 2018. Used with permission.

11. "Snap Inc. Terms of Service." Retrieved on July 10, 2018 from https://www .snap.com/en-US/terms/.

12. Ibid.

13. Ibid.

14. "Your Brain on Tech: Technology and Teachable Moments," *NBC Today Show* (March 22, 2018). Retrieved on July 10, 2018 from https://www.today .com/video/the-average-teen-spends-more-time-online-than-they-do -sleeping-1192061507944.

15. Meyer, Robinson, "The Cambridge Analytica Scandal, in 3 Paragraphs," *The Atlantic* (March 20, 2018). Retrieved on March 22, 2018 from https://www .theatlantic.com/technology/archive/2018/03/the-cambridge-analytica -scandal-in-three-paragraphs/556046/.

16. Leff, discussion.

17. Sunstein, Cass R., *Republic.com* (Princeton, NJ: Princeton University Press, 2002), p. 8.

18. Pariser, Eli, "Beware Online Filter Bubbles," TED Ideas Worth Spreading video (March 2011). Retrieved on March 19, 2018 from https://www.ted .com/talks/eli_pariser_beware_online_filter_bubbles.

19. Ibid.

20. Ibid.

21. Ibid.

22. "New Survey: Snapchat and Instagram Are Most Popular Social Media Platforms Among American Teens," *Science Daily* (April 21, 2017). Retrieved on March 19, 2018 from https://www.sciencedaily.com/releases /2017/04/170421113306.htm.

23. "See the Moments You Care About," Instagram Terms of Service (March 15, 2016). Retrieved on March 21, 2018 from http://blog.instagram.com /post/141107034797/160315-news.

24. Delaney, Kevin, "Filter Bubbles are a Serious Problem with News, Says Gates," *Quartz* (February 21, 2017). Retrieved on March 21, 2018 from https://qz.com /913114/bill-gates-says-filter-bubbles-are-a-serious-problem-with-news/.

25. "Teen Privacy and Safety Online: Knowledge, Attitudes, and Practices," Youth + Tech + Health, Digital Trust Foundation, and Vodaphone (2015). Retrieved on March 25, 2018 from http://yth.org/wp-content/uploads /Teen-Privacy-and-Safety-Online-Knowledge-Attitudes-and-Practices.pdf.

26. Puchko, Kristy, "15 Things You Should Know About *Self-Portrait with Thorn Necklace and Hummingbird*," *Mental Floss* (June 1, 2015). Retrieved on March 28, 2018 from http://mentalfloss.com/article/64204/15-facts-about -frida-kahlos-self-portrait-thorn-necklace-and-hummingbird.

27. "The Bright Side: Social Media, Selfies, and Gaming," *Better Worldians*, Podcast #144 (February 12, 2018). Retrieved on March 29, 2018 from https://www.betterworldians.org/Dr-Pamela-Rutledge-The-Bright -Side-Social-media-selfies—gaming.

28. Rutledge, discussion.

29. Steinmetz, Katy, "Top 10 Everything of 2012," *Time* (December 4, 2012). Retrieved on March 29, 2018 from http://newsfeed.time.com/2012/12/04 /top-10-news-lists/slide/selfie/.

Chapter 7

1. Anderson, Janna, and Rainie, Lee, "The Future of Truth and Misinformation Online," Pew Research Center Internet & Technology (October 19, 2017). Retrieved on April 2, 2018 from http://www.pewinternet.org /2017/10/19/the-future-of-truth-and-misinformation-online/.

2. Reilly, discussion.

3. Michelle Ciulla Lipkin (executive director of the National Association for Media Literacy in Education), discussion with author, April 2, 2018.

4. "Word of the Year Is…" English Oxford Living Dictionaries website. Retrieved on April 2, 2018 from https://en.oxforddictionaries.com/word -of-the-year/word-of-the-year-2016.

5. Ciulla Lipkin, discussion.

6. Shearer, Elisa, and Gottfried, Jeffrey, "News Use Across Social Media Platforms," Pew Research Center (September 7, 2017). Retrieved on March 18, 2018 from http://www.journalism.org/2017/09/07/news-use-across-social -media-platforms-2017/.

7. Silverman, Craig, and Alexander, Lawrence, "How Teens in the Balkans are Duping Trump Supporters with Fake News," BuzzFeed News (November 3, 2016). Retrieved on March 18, 2018 from https://www.buzzfeed.com /craigsilverman/how-macedonia-became-a-global-hub-for-pro-trump -misinfo?utm_term=.gbq7XBV3q#.uyy9QlZ87.

8. Silverman, Craig, "This Analysis Shows How Viral Fake Election News Stories Outperformed Real News on Facebook," BuzzFeed News (November 16, 2016). Retrieved on April 3, 2018 from https://www.buzzfeed.com/craigsilverman/viral-fake-election-news-outperformed-real-news-on-facebook?utm_term=.pjMR7evdj#.mvY7AdMaq.

9. Stevan, Alex, "Pence: 'Michelle Obama Is the Most Vulgar First Lady We've Ever Had,' Newslo (October 14, 2016). Retrieved on March 18, 2018 from http://www.newslo.com/pence-michelle-obama-vulgar-first-lady-weve-ever/.

10. "Evaluating Information: The Cornerstone of Civic Online Reasoning," Stanford History Education Group (November 22, 2016). Retrieved on April 3, 2018 from https://stacks.stanford.edu/file/druid:fv751yt5934/SHEG%20Evaluating%20Information%20Online.pdf.

11. Rheingold, Howard, *Smart Mobs: The Next Social Revolution* (Cambridge, MA: Basic Books, 2002), p. 194.

12. Rheingold, Howard, *Net Smart: How to Thrive Online* (Cambridge, MA: The MIT Press, 2012), p. 16.

13. Ibid.

14. Zeal, Cillian, "Shock Revelation: Obama Admin Actively Sabotaged Gun Background Check System," *Conservative Tribune* (March 16, 2018). Retrieved on July 10, 2018 from https://www.westernjournal.com/ct/obama-admin-gun-background/.

15. "Media Bias/Fact Check" website. Retrived on July 10, 2018 from https://mediabiasfactcheck.com/about/.

16. "Media Bias/Fact Check" website. Retrieved on July 10, 2018 from https://mediabiasfactcheck.com/conservative-tribune/.

17. Gibbs, Samuel, "Apple's Tim Cook: 'I Don't Want my Nephew on a Social Network.'"; *The Guardian,* January 19, 2018. Retrieved on April 5, 2018 from https://www.theguardian.com/technology/2018/jan/19/tim-cook-i-dont-want-my-nephew-on-a-social-network; Gates, Melinda, "Melinda Gates: I Spent My Career in Technology. I Wasn't Prepared For Its Effect On My Kids." *Washington Post,* August 24, 2017. Retrieved on April 5, 2018 from https://www.washingtonpost.com/news/parenting/wp/2017/08/24/melinda-gates-i-spent-my-career-in-technology-i-wasnt-prepared-for-its-effect-on-my-kids/?utm_term=.8993865fdobe.

18. Johnson, Stephen, *Everything Bad is Good For You* (New York: Penguin Group, 2005), p. xvi.

19. Reilly, discussion.

20. Jennifer Lynn Alvarez (author of *The Guardian Herd* series), in discussion with author, April 15, 2018. Used with permission.

21. Kirci, Hazal, "The Tales Teens Tell: What Wattpad Did for Girls," *The Guardian* (August 16, 2014). Retrieved on April 6, 2018 from https://www.theguardian.com/technology/2014/aug/16/teen-writing-reading-wattpad-young-adults.

22. Reilly, discussion.

23. Jenkins, et al., "Confronting the Challenges of Participatory Culture Media Education for the 21st Century," The John D. and Catherine T. MacArthur Foundation (2009), p. 3.

24. Terdiman, Daniel, "Study: Wikipedia as Accurate as Britannica," CNET (December 16, 2005). Retrieved on April 18, 2018 from https://www.cnet.com/news/study-wikipedia-as-accurate-as-britannica/.

25. Surowiecki, James, *The Wisdom of Crowds* (New York: Anchor Books, 2005), p. xiii.

26. "Ski Cross" on Wikipedia. Retrieved on July 10, 2018 from https://en.wikipedia.org/wiki/Ski_cross.

27. "Media and Technology at Journey School," Journey School website. Retrieved on May 3, 2018 from http://www.journeyschool.net/media-technology-at-journey-school/.

28. Glaze-Kelley, discussion.

29. Pennycook, Gordon, Cannon, Tyrone, and Rand, David G., "Implausibility and Illusory Truth: Prior Exposure Increases Perceived Accuracy of Fake News but Has No Effect on Entirely Implausible Statements," *Journal of Experimental Psychology* (forthcoming). Retrieved on March 16, 2018 from https://ssrn.com/abstract=2958246 or http://dx.doi.org/10.2139/ssrn.2958246.

Chapter 8

1. Monke, Lowell, "The Human Touch," *Education Next* 4(4), Fall 2004. Retrieved on April 11, 2018 from http://educationnext.org/thehuman touch/.

2. "Status of Mind: Social Media and Young People's Mental Health and Well-being," Royal Society for Public Health (May 2017). Retrieved on December 3, 2017 from https://www.rsph.org.uk/uploads/assets/uploaded/62be270a-a55f-4719-ad668c2ec7a74c2a.pdf.

3. Lanquist, Lindsey, "Instagram Launches 3 New Safety Features—Here's How to Use Them," *Self* (September 26, 2017). Retrieved on November 3, 2017 from https://www.self.com/story/new-instagram-features.

4. Perez, Sarah, "Twitter Starts Putting Abusers in 'Time Out,'" *TechCrunch* (February 16, 2017). Retrieved on April 11, 2018 from https://beta .techcrunch.com/2017/02/16/twitter-starts-putting-abusers-in-time-out /?_ga=2.37566819.23505104.1523456549-1685009490.1486857013.

5. Oldfield, Edward, "Facebook and Snapchat Trial New Features to Tackle Online Bullying in Campaign Headed by Prince William," *DevonLive* (November 16, 2017). Retrieved on November 3, 2017 from http://www .devonlive.com/news/devon-news/facebook-snapchat-trial-new -features-785837.

6. Ibid.

7. Lucy Cadova (member of Faceup.com team), in discussion with author, April 6, 2018. Used with permission.

8. Matt Soeth (founder of #ICANHELP), in discussion with author, April 4, 2018. Used with permission.

9. Soeth, discussion.

10. Maeve Repking video. Retrieved on July 10, 2018 from https://www .icanhelpdeletenegativity.org/maeve.

11. Liz Repking (founder and CEO of Cyber Safety Consulting), in discussion with author, April 8, 2018. Used with permission.

12. Soeth, discussion.

13. Ciulla Lipkin, discussion.

14. Freidman, Thomas L., *Thank You for Being Late: An Optimists Guide to Thriving in the Age of Accelerations* (New York: Farrar, Straus and Giroux, 2016), p. 31.

15. Ciulla Lipkin, discussion.

16. Soeth, discussion.

17. "Remarks by the President on Egypt," The White House (February 11, 2011). Retrieved on April 12, 2018 from https://obamawhitehouse.archives .gov/the-press-office/2011/02/11/remarks-president-egypt.

18. Parker-Pope, Tara, "Are Today's Teenagers Smarter and Better Than We Think?" *New York Times* (March 30, 2018). Retrieved on April 12, 2018 from https://mobile.nytimes.com/2018/03/30/well/family/teenagers-generation -stoneman-douglas-parkland-.html?smid=fb-nytimes&smtyp=cur.

19. Ibid.

Index

●